BEHAVIOUR PROBLEMS IN
HANDICAPPED CHILDREN

HUMAN HORIZONS SERIES

BEHAVIOUR PROBLEMS IN HANDICAPPED CHILDREN

The Beech Tree House Approach

Malcolm C. Jones

A CONDOR BOOK
SOUVENIR PRESS (E & A) LTD

First published 1983 by
Souvenir Press (Educational & Academic) Ltd,
43, Great Russell Street, London WC1B 3PA
and simultaneously in Canada

ISBN 0 285 64988 4 Casebound
ISBN 0 285 64993 0 Paperback

Printed in Great Britain by
The Anchor Press, Tiptree

ACKNOWLEDGEMENTS

I was helped by many people to complete this book and I am grateful to them all. My deepest gratitude, however, is reserved for Kathleen Devereux whose strong friendship enabled her to tell me that my first attempt was 'quite unreadable'! Her help, as I unscrambled that unpromising start, was always enthusiastic, practical and generously given.

Despite all the advice and help I received the book remains very much a creature of my own making, and on reading through it I am reminded that, after the first public lecture I gave, I had to ring the organisers to ask if I could have at least one more chance to talk in the future. I justified this request on the ground that I knew I could do better because I was by then aware of some of the pitfalls. I confess to feeling very much the same way about this book and I wish I could have another go at it. For example, I know that stylistically it could be far, far better. I hope therefore that the reader's interest in the type of children with whom we work will carry them through the more prosaic passages.

I must offer special thanks to the Spastics Society who trusted Beech Tree House staff and myself to work with a group of very difficult children and who, over the years, have provided the buildings and the finance for the venture. We are all particularly indebted to Leslie Gardner, the Society's Principal Clinical Psychologist, who has both advised us and championed our effort over the years. There have been occasions when head office staff have raised their eyebrows at our untraditional methods of organisation – but we have been given our heads and the response from the children, their parents and other professionals appears to confirm that we have developed an effective model.

Some of my colleagues at Beech Tree House must be singled out for thanks for specific help they have given in preparing this book. Virginia Mallett produced the plans, Keith Ripley the line drawings of the equipment and Joyce Hutley typed the manuscripts until I discovered the magic of the word processor which was kindly made available to me by Peter Deakin of the Neath Professional Workshop. Nina Story, who has been Acting Head of Beech Tree House for the last year, must be thanked for fielding many problems which, but for her, would have encroached upon the free time I used to write this book. My daughter Rebecca must also be thanked for preparing the diagrams in the appendix and for doing virtually all of the lettering – a dreadful task. Janet Boddington has also played an important part by interviewing all the children's families. I hope we will be able to report on her findings in more detail at a later date.

Finally, I am grateful to Messrs. A.D. Peters & Co. Ltd. for giving me permission to quote a short passage, in Chapter 4, from *Medicines: A Guide for Everybody* by Peter Parish, published by Penguin Books.

To all of these and to the many unnamed colleagues, children and parents who have helped directly or indirectly I give my thanks.

Malcolm C. Jones

CONTENTS

INTRODUCTION

At the start of this decade there were more than 2,800 children in long stay hospitals. For most of them the picture was bleak. Fortunately things are changing and many long stay hospitals are now refusing to admit children solely because they have educational or social problems which are difficult for local authorities to cater for in their schools and children's homes. The new policy states that, as far as possible, handicapped children should be educated in ordinary schools in the community and that the small number for whom this is not appropriate should be educated in schools which meet their special needs.

Despite this new and enlightened philosophy, it is proving difficult to provide suitable services for one particular group of children, many of whom consequently remain in hospitals. The children concerned are mentally handicapped, many severely so, with physical handicaps and severe behaviour problems. Because such children have usually been catered for in a custodial rather than educational manner, often with the help of drugs to dampen down behaviour, there is only limited educational expertise upon which to draw and few documented accounts of good teaching and residential practice.

In the past, nurses were frustrated in their attempts to help these young people because they were understaffed, starved of funds and were working in ill-equipped, unsuitable environments. The many attacks upon them for the service they provided were therefore ill-judged and should rather have been directed at those responsible for the situation.

The recent change in policy has thrust the responsibility for this difficult group of children into the hands of local education and social service departments. A few are making valiant efforts to open suitable units, but many more are leaving the initiative to the charities or the private sector. The latter trend is disturbing. While there are no doubt some very good private schools for multiply handicapped children with behaviour problems, we have, in the course of our work, visited a number which are inadequate and we fervently hope that this largely defenceless group of children will not need a latter-day Dickens to shock our leaders into providing them with well run schools. For the present, while the private sector takes up the slack, we urge that a strong and well manned inspectorate be established to ensure good standards in privately run schools. It seems worth noting, by way of illustrating this point, that between January 1977 and the writing of this introduction in March 1983, no inspector of special schools has formally set foot in Beech Tree House.

The Spastics Society, in supporting the Beech Tree House venture, took the lead in educating multiply handicapped children with severe behaviour problems. One of the consequences has been a flood of visitors, countless requests for information and a steady demand for staff to give talks and run courses. There has been considerable publicity for our work in professional journals and the media generally, and the controversial television film *Silent Minority* favourably contrasted Beech Tree House with long stay hospitals. Perhaps the most significant accolade came in the Disablement Debate in July 1981, when on three occasions Beech Tree House was mentioned by name as a model unit. In Mr Jack Ashley's words, 'We cannot be content to write off so many children by leaving them in institutions when the Spastics Society has shown so admirably what can be done if they are placed in stimulating and supporting homes like its Beech Tree House.' The most significant aspect of the all-party interest has been the £250,000 matching funds made available to help us establish a second unit for children in the north of England. This project will initially concentrate on releasing children from long stay hospitals.

The culmination of all this interest is the present book which offers a report on our work. My goal has been to set out certain key aspects of our approach in the hope that parents and professionals who have children like ours will find some ideas that are helpful to them.

It is our contention that many of the problems encountered in teaching multiply handicapped children with behaviour problems arise from two main factors: **buildings** in which they are educated and the way in which **staff are managed**. There are chapters on both these topics. Certain **teaching strategies** seem to be particularly effective with our children; I have therefore included a chapter on behaviour modification and two on detailed **case studies** which exemplify our approach. We have developed a number of **electronic devices** which have streamlined our efforts. These, and the simple **data collecting** techniques we use, have a chapter each. A further chapter is devoted to the role played by **parents:** we see them as being the key to helping children to transfer new skills back to their home.

The photograph on the cover is of Peter who came to us from a subnormality hospital at the age of eleven. Both his parents are dead and he had a history of running away. Tracey, the residential therapist pictured with him, was working on a programme to control this behaviour when the photograph was taken. Our analysis of the problem suggested that Peter, who had no spoken, symbol or signed means of communication, was very interested in what went on in the world beyond his ward or the confines of Beech Tree House. This idea was supported by staff at Peter's hospital who reported that when he ran away he was usually found by the gardener's shed or digging with a spade. They felt that he often noted the location of such tools while out on supervised walks and ran off to them when an opportunity presented itself.

Because it seemed reasonable to us that Peter should explore and make use of his more general environment, he was taught as part of his communication training programme to use his picture board to ask if he could 'Go' and 'Look'. Figure A shows the contents of one of his boards. He is holding this particular one in the picture. In his training Peter learns that if he points to 'Go' and 'Look' he can usually do just that – but from time to time his request is refused. Peter initially found not being allowed to go extremely difficult to tolerate and would often have violent tantrums when this happened. If he tried to run away Tracey could restrain him with reins. Tantrums were dealt with by immediately returning him to Beech Tree House. As a result he learned that trantruming was completely ineffective in getting his way, and he has now virtually dropped this strategy from his repertoire. Moreover, he has learned that many good things can be obtained rapidly if he uses his communication board.

The six main goals for children who come to the unit are listed below:

SIX GOAL AREAS

Communication
Problem Behaviour
Attending Skills
Continence
Self-help Skills
Transfer Determined Skills

Like Peter, the majority of children educated in Beech Tree House have a **Communication** problem when they arrive. These

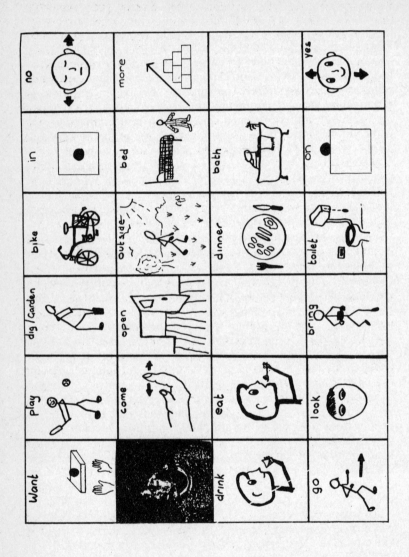

Figure A.   Peter's Picture Board.

are not always as severe as Peter's, but disorders of this type are so common (28 out of 29 children educated in Beech Tree House have had problems in this area) that we suspect communication difficulties and behaviour disorders may be linked in some way. Possibly some children are violent because they are frustrated by being unable to understand the verbal demands made upon them and by their own inability to make their needs known to others. More severely mentally handicapped children may have developed some of their apparently inexplicable behaviour patterns as rudimentary forms of communication. For example, face slapping may get adult attention which is absent when the child is passive and good. Whatever the reasons might be, it is our impression that all the children we have educated in the unit have become less explosive once they have started to share a communication system with the staff.

Peter had a variety of **behaviour problems** which included: screaming; head butting of people; stuffing his cheeks with paper and rubbish; massive temper tantrums in which he smashed everything around him; ritualistic play in which he lined up objects, and a number of less important but irritating behaviour patterns. Most of these have been tackled successfully, some by simply stopping them regardless of Peter's anger (stuffing his mouth); some by ignoring the behaviour (screaming); some by use of time out (head butting); and some by rewarding desirable alternatives (constructive play as opposed to stereotyped patterns).

Peter also had to learn how to learn. When he arrived it was virtually impossible to engage him in any new task for more than a few seconds; he could however, concentrate for long periods on established stereotyped patterns of behaviour. He was in urgent need of **attention** training to appropriate tasks. Many children who join us need to learn this fundamental skill if they are to benefit from the teaching we offer and continue to learn once they have left. We use a variety of strategies. In Peter's case he started his training in our distraction low room and received consumable rewards for short periods of attending to task. As he progressed he graduated to token rewards and was taught in the general teaching area.

Approximately one third of our pupils show double **delayed continence** when they arrive. This can be particularly distressing when teenage children are involved – they seem to 'produce' so much when they perform at the wrong time and place. Peter responded well to a programme of frequent toileting in which he was rewarded with sandwiches for going in the right place!

Although we have a classroom and train children to perform

well in classroom environments, we put considerably more emphasis upon teaching **self-help skills.** It is for this reason that teachers are fully integrated into the residential therapist's (care staff) rota. Peter is learning to prepare and serve breakfast and he is taught the requisite skills three mornings per week by teachers who commence duty at eight o'clock. Likewise, one evening per week Peter is taught bathing and bedtime skills by the teacher whose turn it is to do the Monday night sleeping-in duty. Residential therapist continue this training during the remainder of the week. We are convinced that there is too much time spent by teachers on the relatively trivial, table-top skills which are pursued in many classrooms for the mentally handicapped. Teachers could be much more profitably employed using their skills to teach mentally handicapped children to cope with life rather than with form boards and bead threading.

When children leave Beech Tree House it is usually vital for them to have acquired a number of specific skills to ensure that their change to a new school and their return home go smoothly. For example, a **transfer determined skill** for one cerebral palsied boy was to be able to get up and down stairs safely. This was essential if he was to return home because his mother had recently become handicapped herself. We are uncertain what transfer determined goals will be set for Peter. He has only been with us for one year and is making such good progress that it is difficult to predict what school will best serve his needs when his two years' education in Beech Tree House is completed. No doubt he will spend a term or two in our classroom where he will learn to meet one transfer determined goal – to behave when seated at a desk in a classroom in a way which will not offend his teacher.

So far I have not referred to a Beech Tree House **curriculum.** We recognise how important it is to state one clearly and admit that we have found it difficult to formulate. This is not only because of the wide divergence of age, intelligence, skills and needs of our children but also because we regard the six goal areas discussed earlier as forming the key curriculum components for each child. The two year limit focuses our minds wonderfully upon teaching to these essential targets. Therefore our approach is pragmatic, direct and without frills. Nevertheless our children are offered a rich variety of activities covering all areas of the traditional curriculum. We depart from usual school practice by pursuing aesthetic, physical and social aspects of the curriculum during evenings and weekends. These activities complement the pursuit of the six goals upon which we concentrate during the teaching day.

1   ESTABLISHING BEECH TREE HOUSE

Meldreth Manor School and the Problems posed by Difficult Children

In 1967 the Spastics Society opened Meldreth Manor School, a purpose built establishment designed and staffed to educate one hundred and twenty severely mentally handicapped cerebral palsied children. During the early years it was essential to be selective about the children who were admitted; 'difficult' children were not offered places and the occasional one or two who were not identified at assessment were excluded during the 'trial period'. At the time, four years before the 1970 Education Act (Handicapped Children) was implemented, this appeared to be a very reasonable policy. The majority of severely mentally handicapped children, if they attended any education establishment at all, went either to training centres in hospitals or to those administered by the Ministry of Health. Because the Spastics Society was pioneering new territory by offering education in a school setting, it was important that they should demonstrate that multiply handicapped children could make significant progress in an educational environment; difficult and disruptive children would have put the entire project at risk. At that early date it was recognised that children with severe behaviour problems would need separate and specialised provision – even if they were additionally handicapped by cerebral palsy and low intelligence. They were therefore not admitted.

The Spastics Society was aware that many of the children who were turned away would be admitted to long stay subnormality hospitals and that the main treatment for most of them would be drug therapy to control their difficult behaviour. They were also aware that a significant proportion would be excluded from whatever formal education was offered in the hospitals because their behaviour would be considered too disruptive. Such luckless children would remain all day on generally understaffed wards (Maureen Oswin had vividly described the conditions in which they lived). With hindsight it is all too easy to be critical of the school policy which turned children away to face such bleak futures, but what must be remembered is that by taking the steps described in this book the Spastics Society was probably the first organisation in Britain to open a successful small school specifically adapted and staffed to educate multiply handicapped children with severe behaviour problems.

My association with Meldreth Manor School, where the Beech Tree House project was born, dates from 1973 when I was appointed as senior clinical psychologist. The post was not a new one but changes had been made in the job description, so that instead of spending my time assessing the children's progress, I was to be actively involved in developing training techniques.

The first major project appeared to be more a test of the psychologist's ability than the children's, for it was concerned with the education of the six children who had made least progress in the preceding two years. As a preliminary, approximately fifty children in the junior part of the school were evaluated by the staff who knew them well, in order to identify those needing the most attention. These were brought together as a special progress group. I was put in charge and was allowed to select one of the school's established junior teachers to run the class. This particular post was not generally considered to be an attractive one, but fortunately a very able young lady was persuaded to become the class teacher and the project got under way.

The Special Progress Group
Within a year some of the children had made remarkable progress and the project was generally agreed to be a success. In fact many of the techniques now used on a routine basis in Beech Tree House were piloted in that project classroom. We were particularly impressed by the speed with which children could be taught better working patterns, simply by praising them when they worked and by ignoring them when they were inattentive or disruptive. Very careful studies of the impact of this approach were possible because of the one-way screen facility in the classroom and the tiny short range radio which the teacher wore. The latter made it possible for me to control very precisely indeed the way the teacher interacted with the children. A number of the studies completed at that time are still used in training both new Beech Tree House staff and participants who attend courses organised by the Beech Tree House team.

We also learned another important lesson: that, despite a great deal of goodwill, it was very difficult to get every member of staff who worked with the 'progress group' children to follow programmes in a consistent manner. Perhaps this should not have been surprising; in those days each child at Meldreth Manor School divided his or her time between teachers, care staff, nurses, physiotherapists, speech therapists, classroom assistants, volunteers and ancillary staff, most of these being organised into separate departments, each with its own head. Despite a variety of formal and informal meetings, on occasions the service to the children became fragmented.

Programmes that we devised at that time were written in very straightforward language. This was especially true of toilet training programmes, where we not only described what should be done but supplied all the necessary equipment, We felt quite confident that programmes presented in this manner would run successfully without our minute-by-minute supervision, particularly since we ourselves had trained the care staff who were to be involved. Sadly this was not the case. Sometimes it appeared to us that our very success provoked certain key staff into undermining the programmes.

Perhaps this was the most important lesson we were to learn in those early days at Meldreth Manor School: that even a slight difference of opinion among staff makes it impossible to carry through detailed programmes. The training and professional background of staff, rather than the immediate needs of the child, seemed to determine which aspects of a programme should be emphasised, and it was therefore very difficult to set programme priorities. For example, a physiotherpaist might insist on completing an exercise routine before allowing a child to pay his half-hourly visit to the toilet. This decision could be taken, despite the parents' expressed wish that their child be taught to use the toilet as soon as possible, not through perverseness but because of the overriding importance of physiotherapy in the eyes of the therapist.

It must be stressed that the tendency for staff to fragment along departmental lines was not excessive at Meldreth; compared to most organisations catering for multiply handicapped children, the difficulties were minimal. The very serious problems that prevail in many subnormality hospitals are widely recognised – frequent interdepartmental misunderstandings being caused by minimal contact between the nursing and teaching staff who work with the same children. It was because some departments within Meldreth Manor School *did* work well together that the concept of 'multi-role' staff was pursued so enthusiastically once the Beech Tree House project got under way.

A Special Unit is proposed to educate Children with Difficult Behaviour

Almost every year prior to the Beech Tree House experiment, one or two children were excluded from Meldreth Manor School because their behaviour was too disruptive, too destructive or too dangerous to the other children. Although only a few were involved and the decision was never made lightly, it was always regretted. Nevertheless, this was the accepted practice until January 1977 when Beech Tree House opened.

The idea was conceived early in 1976 that Meldreth Manor School should provide a facility of some sort to help children with behaviour problems. Initially, a class of eight children was formed in the junior part of the school, in addition to the special progress group. Responsibility for planning the programmes was given to me as the psychologist, and I was fortunate to have another able young teacher to run the group and a full time classroom assistant. The classroom was modified by having a 'quiet area' and a 'protected area' installed. The 'quiet area' was the precursor of the Beech Tree House time-out rooms which are described in Chapter 2; the 'protected area' was a zone in which expensive and delicate equipment could be used by children who were not being disruptive. The remaining two-thirds of the classroom were used by all the children for general teaching activities.

The results were immediately encouraging. A number of children's behaviour problems reduced considerably and one particular girl, of whom we made detailed video recordings, was the subject of a paper at the Annual Conference of the British Psychological Society at Easter, 1976. However, despite such successes, it became increasingly clear that much greater progress would be possible if we could give the children consistent handling twenty-four hours a day, week after week. Clearly, if this was to be done, additional facilities and staff would be required. It was at this point that the Head of Meldreth Manor School, Mr Brown, made available to us two four-bedroomed, terraced staff houses and provided us with £1,566 to equip the unit. Even at 1976 prices this was a very limited amount of money, however welcome, to pay for furnishings and for doors to be knocked through between the buildings. Staff became proficient at sorting through second-hand furniture stores and bidding at auctions!

A number of us believe that this modest start to the work was important. There were problems, but despite these we demonstrated that expensive buildings are not essential for people to work successfully with difficult handicapped children. Our argument is that any authority in the country can afford to set aside and equip two large, semi-detached council houses to help children like ours. If this were done nationally, only the most severely disturbed handicapped children and teenagers would need the very special facilities that will be provided in our second generation Beech Tree House.

Senior Spastics Society staff endorsed the Beech Tree house idea and set certain limits to the venture: it was to be regarded as a research project with a five-year 'life'. I became head of the unit and was detailed to produce periodic reports on the progress of the work. At that time there was little evidence to suggest that multiply handicapped children with severe behaviour problems could be helped; the normal treatment was to place them in sub-normality hospitals where they received drug 'therapy' and, if they were not too disruptive, attended the hospital school.

Beech Tree House is Opened

Six children were admitted during the first year. The majority of these came from Meldreth Manor School – they were the ones who, before the opening of the new unit, would have been excluded. Six care staff were appointed in addition to myself but no teacher, since we felt that the 'table-top' type activitites prevalent in classrooms for the mentally handicapped at that time were possibly not priority skills for the Beech Tree House children. In any case, they would be able to attend the main school when classroom work was thought to be appropriate.

The first children educated in our 'budget' Beech Tree House were angels compared to those we worked with after the first eighteen months, and in due couse they were all able to return to the main school where the majority settled very successfully. Today we continue to take the occasional child from Meldreth Manor School, but pupils recruited since 1979 have been qualitatively different: we now actively seek children with severe behaviour problems and no longer restrict our intake to children with cerebral palsy, nor do we specify that they should be severely mentally handicapped. A small number of our children have been very normal in appearance; it was their problem behaviour which brought them to us. Until 1981, when a sixteen year-old girl on trial bit the end off the thumb of a member of staff, we had never turned a child down for having problems which were too severe for us to consider treating. We could probably have helped this young person too, if we had had more male members of staff, a stronger environment and fewer vulnerable young children.

Beech Tree House is Extended

By the end of 1977 senior Spastics Society staff agreed that the Beech Tree House children were making significant progress and that the project should be granted further support. The first year's experience had highlighted a number of changes and additions that were necessary to provide a better training environment, and it had also become clear that more staff were required to ensure that programmes ran twenty-four hours a day, both during the week and at weekends. These could only be provided by attracting more fees – children who attend a Spastics Society school are paid for by their local education authority. In order to provide the new facilities and to house three additional children, £35,000 was made available to build an extension to the unit. This was completed by Easter 1979.

In September 1977 a teacher was appointed to the staff. It had become clear that, if our children were to transfer successfully to a school-type setting, they would have to learn to cope with teacher behaviour! We divided the children into two teaching groups: the Playroom Teaching Group, which most children joined on arrival, where we tackled problems with communication, toileting, violent behaviour, inattention, stereotyped behaviour and certain fundamental self-help skills; and the Classroom Group to which most children graduated after a successful period in the Playroom Group, where they were taught how to cope with a classroom environment. The Classroom Group can to some extent be regarded as the Beech Tree House finishing school.

Philosophy and Practice

The guiding assumption behind the Beech Tree House work has been that the children have *learned* to produce the difficult behaviour which led to their admission. How this can happen will be discussed in detail in later chapters. If we are right in believing this, then it should be possible to train the children to abandon their unacceptable behaviour and to teach them alternative, acceptable habits. A technique known as behaviour modification is particularly suitable for this work and it is used extensively in Beech Tree House. This approach involves very careful observation and recording of behaviour; decisions about training are based upon data and progress can be charted precisely. Although we use behaviour modification in many cases, we are well aware that other techniques can be used and are likely to be far more successful where problem behaviour is not simply a learned response to a certain situation. There are a variety of counselling techniques which can help children who have severe emotional problems and we readily use these when the need arises. We know that all the rewards in the world cannot dispel the unhappiness of a child who is ill treated; only a change in environment and the affection offered there can help.

Our experience in data collecting has enabled us to develop a small number of straightforward techniques, in contrast to the first two or three years when we had a tendency to produce 'one off' strategies for each child. This involved considerable effort in training staff and in refining the techniques before we were satisfied that everyone knew what he or she should be doing. Use of the more limited range of techniques, which will be described in Chapter 8, has meant that staff can be trained rapidly and collect information reliably.

Data collecting has been enhanced by the work of the Spastics Society Electronic Aids Unit Engineer, Ken Ketteridge, who has developed a range of devices which have streamlined our efforts. Ken has also produced a number of gadgets which reward the children for performing correctly; these have ranged from sweet dispensers to toys which start automatically when a child urinates in the toilet. It is not an overstatement to say that, but for his contribution, we could not have achieved our results without considerably more staff. Chapter 3 will be devoted to describing the devices in Beech Tree House developed in the Electronic Aids Unit.

Myths spring up readily about any group of people who are different from the general population. One such myth concerns the strength of difficult mentally handicapped children, and most staff who work with these young people will be familiar with tales describing feats of near Herculean destructive strength. It may well be that one or two of these refer to individuals who were exceptionally strong, but in most cases the destruction was caused by children of normal strength who were *uninhibited* in what they did. Most of us treat our environment with great care and few of us test the strength of the average door by battering it down. We therefore believe we are surrounded by well made, strong and enduring structures. I, however, know otherwise. I worked as a part-time fireman for eight years and in the course of my duties I had to burst in and out of many doors and windows and even through walls. None presented me with any particular difficulty. I gained further support for the idea that our normal environment is fragile when I worked for some weeks helping to demolish houses. Not only was this great fun, it proved surprisingly easy to rip up toilet pedestals, drag sinks from walls and tear out pipe work. These experiences were useful when it came to specifying to the architect the strong, protected facilities that are necessary for a robust toilet training area, safe bedrooms and an enduring Beech Tree House. Without such precautions uninhibited newcomers to the unit would have had a field day.

2 ARCHITECTURE

Because I believe the environment is so important I have used this chapter to describe what we created on the Meldreth Manor School site. Many features of Beech Tree House have, in my opinion, been sufficiently tested to stand as models and I anticipate that they will reappear in their present form in our new unit. The reader's attention will be drawn to any problems we have experienced and to changes which we propose to make.

Photograph 1 in the plates section shows the front of the first Beech Tree House; Figures 1 and 2 are the plans of its ground and first floors. The readers will see that a great deal was squeezed into the building. This was reasonably acceptable when young children were pupils, but the economic recession of the early eighties led local authorities to keep children until they became too difficult for their own special schools to contain; consequently we found ourselves admitting progressively older and larger young people and the unit became somewhat cramped. On the basis of this experience we advise that a unit for young adults should be built on a more generous scale.

The initial impression gained by many visitors to the first Beech Tree House was one of homeliness. In part they were reacting to the scale of the building and in part to the absence of corridors in the two original houses. As they passed into the extension a few would remark that this was more like the buildings to which they were accustomed. Corridors are an acknowledged feature of institutions; they will be avoided as far as possible in our future planning. The homeliness of the original Beech Tree House is something that we hope to recapture in our new unit.

Locked Doors
One feature which surprised many visitors to Beech Tree House was that all doors could be locked. This had not always been the case and it was an expensive exercise to fit a standard lock to every door. We changed to a locked outer-door policy initially when we accepted children with long histories of running away from their homes, their schools, their hostels and their wards. Few of these children had any concept of danger and none had any road sense; they were obviously at great risk if they were away from the unit unsupervised. We decided that the most positive approach to these

children was to train them to give reliable evidence of the following skills: 'Return to unit', 'Stop when commanded', 'Ask to go and look', 'Walk sensibly on the pavement', and so on. Such training was conducted outside the unit in a controlled manner when staff were timetabled to do it, *not* as a response to a child's escape.

In contrast to our pragmatic locked door approach, it is probably worth describing typical practices in other institutions at that time, where policy dictated that all wards should be unlocked except for a few specially designated wards. In one hospital, nursing staff were employed on a full time basis to watch the unlocked doors and retrieve 'runners'. To us this still seems a flagrant misuse of staff who were always at a premium. We were told by the senior nursing officer at this hospital that, if agreement could have been reached to lock the doors, the members of staff allocated to guard them would have been withdrawn because they would no longer have been considered necessary! At another unit the union and the management had agreed that, if a particular girl evaded the 'door watcher' and the member of staff had to run more than twenty paces to retrieve her, she ceased to be their responsibility and Social Services should be informed! While such instances continue to crop up, I wonder what has happened to common sense. We at Beech Tree House hope that we shall never be obliged to comply with the same bureaucratic regulations which take little account of the special needs of certain children.

We found that it was also to the children's advantage to be able to lock our internal doors. During the day, when staff were most abundant, the children received tuition and care in very small groups or on an individual basis, so supervision was obviously relatively easy and the unit could be completely open within the building. During the early morning, the evening and the weekend, when fewer staff were available and small groups of children had to be formed to work and play together, it was reassuring for staff to know that the odd adventurous child could not slip away upstairs unnoticed. The door between the playroom and the entrance hall would therefore be locked. This approach ensured that staff could devote their full attention to working and playing with the children; it seemed infinitely preferable to having harassed staff leaving three or four children alone as they dashed out of the room to bring a child back downstairs for the twentieth time – a child who probably loved the diversion he caused and therefore repeated it again at the next opportunity. Once the means of escaping was removed such a child usually settled down and participated in the cookery lesson, or other activity, instead.

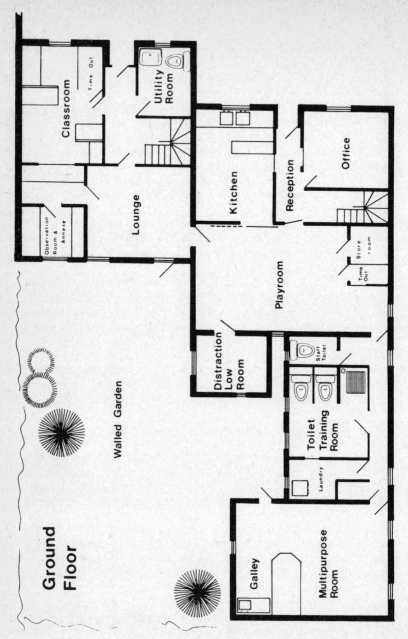

Figure 1.   Beech Tree House – Ground Floor Plan.

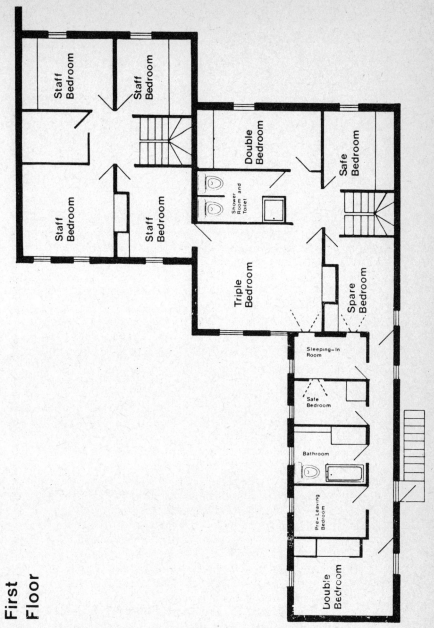

Figure 2.   Beech Tree House – First Floor Plan.

Most children are exceptionally difficult when they arrive at Beech Tree House. They have usually been excluded from every school in their local authority and probably from every private and voluntary establishment approached. Many have been receiving drugs in a vain attempt to control their behaviour. Because it is not our policy to use drugs for this purpose we often experience a difficult phase during each child's settling period. The following pages describe the special aspects of the Beech Tree House environment which enable us to cope with these reactions and eventually to implement training programmes designed to return the children as quickly as possible to more ordinary special schools.

The Kitchen
Virtually every book about handicapped children notes that their experience of the 'real' world is limited. This book is no exception. Unfortunately all too many of those who run residential homes and schools for the handicapped appear to have forgotten this fact, or else the Health and Safety regulations, which are rapidly encroaching on all potentially 'real' experiences, are being too slavishly followed.

At Beech Tree House we have found that there are two ways of ensuring that a child will not burn himself. The first is to cocoon him so thoroughly that he never encounters anything hot; the second is to teach him which things are likely to be hot and how they should be dealt with or avoided. Because we strive to teach our children to be as independent as possible, we have chosen the latter course. It is true that some children will probably receive the occasional scorching from a warm iron or a hot grill, but because such minor accidents happen in a supervised setting they can be minimised and treated straight away. In five years none of our children has had a serious accident in the kitchen and a number have left able to prepare simple meals; all of them have participated in a wide range of food preparing activities, with no doubts about which pieces of equipment should be treated with respect.

The Beech Tree House kitchen was designed to a child-sized scale; the work surfaces are low, as are the sink and cooker. The layout is shown in Figure 3. The serving bench, strategically positioned, protects the *one* child working at the cooker from any unwelcome attention from other children. Before it was built, staff either had to shut other children out of the kitchen or watch them constantly to prevent them from approaching the child working at the cooker or sink (see Photograph 2).

Wherever possible we designed Beech Tree House in a way

which minimised the time spent in purely supervisory duties. Virtually all Beech Tree House staff were employed to train children, so the equipment and environment had to facilitate this.

The serving bench had cupboards on both sides. Those facing the room contained the everyday crockery, enabling additional children to be involved in meal preparation. They could collect whatever they needed to lay the table without disturbing the child working at the cooker.

Cutlery was a particular hazard, especially sharp knives. It was our practice to store potentially dangerous equipment in a locked cupboard on the cooker side of the serving bench and all cleaning fluids were stored in the cleaners' lockable cupboard. Although knives were stored carefully, we did not expect capable children to cut up piles of sandwiches or prepare food with plastic or blunt table knives. Under supervision they used the correct tools for the job. Progressively less supervision was given as the children became more competent.

Kitchen

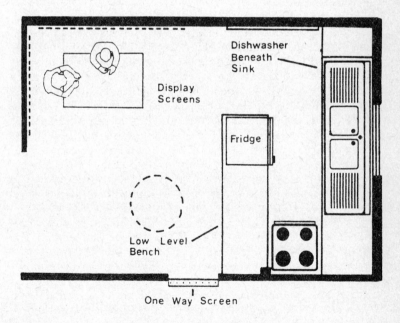

Figure 3.   Plan of Kitchen.

A number of the children had physical handicaps and needed adapted equipment if they were to participate in kitchen activities. We undertook such adaptations ourselves where we could, and purchased special equipment when this was not possible.

The lockable cupboard referred to above had other important uses for management and training. A number of children arrived with strong tendencies to 'steal' food. Usually this behaviour was merely irritating and of relatively minor importance; more obtrusive problems would take precedence in detailed training programmes. However, if such a child learned that no food was available even if he did manage to slip into the kitchen when it was unattended, then such forays tended to decrease in frequency. We are convinced that if cupboards are to be used to store things which should only be taken out under certain circumstances, then it is a good idea to fit them with standardised locks from the outset. Whatever is stored, it is certain that one day, a child will arrive who will have a passion for it. Until time has been found to bring such a passion under the child's control, the most satisfactory measure is to lock the cupboard. Much frustration and time wasting can be prevented by such selective locking. All cupboards can be left unlocked once all members of the group can be 'trusted'.

Considerable space has been devoted to describing the provision and use of locks because it appears to be an issue which arouses emotion. The 'locked wards' that created the present very sensitive climate were in many cases singularly unpleasant places, but it could be argued that this was due as much to starvation of resources, chronic shortages of staff, inadequate supervision and poor training as it was to the locks themselves. We maintain that in a well run unit locks can not only enhance the safety of the children but can also release staff to do the work for which they were trained.

The kitchen had a one-way screen through which observers could look from the entrance hall. This enabled teaching, cooking and dining sessions to be observed discreetly. As well as being a boon to data-collecting, such a screen separated visitors from the children and allowed parents to watch how their son or daughter coped when cooking or eating. Photograph 3 shows Malcolm's mother and father absorbed in watching him eating with a knife and fork.

Unobtrusive Observation
Our experience suggests that many parents need 'to see to believe'. Letters home describing improved self-help skills rarely seem to spur parents to work on those skills when the child returns

home for the holiday; chats between parents and staff seem equally ineffective. Perhaps parents doubt what is claimed. This should not be surprising because most children revert to old established patterns when not pressed to use newly acquired skills. It must be remembered that such 'pressing' is most effectively done by an enthusiastic adult who is familiar with the techniques that have been used to establish the new behaviour. The enthusiasm and skill of parents appears to be best fostered by their witnessing the child's new achievement and a one-way screen is an ideal way of doing this.

One-way screens are expensive. To avoid damage, those in Beech Tree House are protected with Macralon on the side facing the children. This double skin has the added advantage of reducing sound transmission so that the children are unaware of any discussion between observers.

To function effectively a one-way screen has to be darker on the observation side. This is achieved in Beech Tree House by the observation annexe being dimly lit and by drawing curtains in the laundry, sleeping-in room and entrance hall.

Insects

From time to time we have had children in the unit with quite revolting habits. Three of those resident during the Meldreth phase of the project picked up and ate whatever they found on the floor. None jibbed at eating dead flies! When children with such behaviour were in residence poisonous insect killing sprays could not be used, nor were sticky paper traps the answer because there were usually children in the group who would grab and pull them down. The uncontrolled flies posed hygiene problems in the kitchen, and the only satisfactory solution was to provide a trap which attracted the flies with ultra-violet light and then electrocuted them – such as can be seen in butcher's shops, for example.

The Kitchen Floor, Walls and Lights

The kitchen floor is colourful, slip resistant and curved up at the base of walls and cupboards. It is a well known industrial safety flooring – Taralay. Because a great deal of food and drink is spilt and thrown we have found it essential to do away with right-angled corners where the walls meet the floor; such inaccessible areas make cleaning difficult. Known throwers of meals start their training in the kitchen because clearing up is easy. This is important because if a child's disruptive acts significantly increase the work of the staff it is possible that they will react adversely towards the child. It is also for this reason that we provide a vacuum cleaner which sucks up spilt liquids. We assume that some children throw food because of the effect it had previously on parents, staff and other children. The measures we have taken to reduce the clearing up problems appear to defuse the situation as far as the staff are concerned. They are able to treat such episodes blandly or ignore them entirely if that is the treatment strategy. This reaction is possible because they know that tidying up will take only a matter of moments.

A small but useful feature is a circle of contrasting floor colour, two thirds of a metre across, positioned in the centre of the room. This is used in a programme developed to teach children to sweep the floor. In our experience children need a 'target' onto which to sweep the dust that they collect, and this could of course be painted on the floor. (See Photograph 2.)

To reduce damage to the walls of a unit for difficult children they should be finished with a plaster more robust than that commonly used for domestic purposes. This plaster should be painted with the hardest wearing, most chip-resistant and washable finish available. Unfortunately our kitchen has soft plaster and we periodically have to make good dents caused by ketchup bottles and furniture flung by untrained newcomers.

Lights, too, should be protected – fluorescent tubes must, at the very least, be fitted with commercially available diffuser covers. Recessed light fittings with plastic covers are our preferred alternative. These are attractive, give good light and to date have proved completely safe. The one disadvantage appears to be short bulb life. This is possibly the result of poor ventilation which causes high running temperatures. We think that this is an acceptable price to pay for the safety we enjoy.

The Multipurpose Room

By the time that the Spastics Society gave the go-ahead to our purpose-built extension it had become clear that there was a range of activities followed by staff and children which could not conveniently be sited in any of the available rooms. The staff needed somewhere to hold meetings; the children needed a carpeted room for physiotherapy; the visiting speech therapist required a quiet room to work with individual children; parents and staff had nowhere to relax and watch television; there was nowhere for staff to eat a meal when off duty other than with the children, and no room was suitable for entertaining or talking to visitors. When the plans were initially drawn up it became apparent that there was so little space that we would have to design one room to meet a multitude of needs. This consequently became known as the Multipurpose Room. Figure 4 shows the layout.

A significant feature is the floor-to-ceiling block of cupboards which separate the main two-thirds of the room from the galley. This room divider does more than provide cupboard space: it contains two blow-air heaters in its base, a permanently installed slide projector and a visual aids store.

We have found that unless equipment – particularly audio-visual equipment – is readily on hand it will rarely be used; it is for this reason that the slide projector is always ready for immediate use. The slides are projected through an optical glass panel in front of the cupboard on to a screen which is permanently fixed to the opposite wall. Slides are consequently used as a matter of course in staff training, to introduce visitors to the unit and to illustrate progress at case conferences. The screen can be written on with water based felt pens, thereby doubling as a 'whiteboard'. This is an exceptionally useful feature when it comes to teaching how to fill in data sheets and graph results: slides of unused schedules are projected and the instructor writes examples of information into the appropriate spaces. Similarly a slide of graph paper can be

Multi-purpose Room

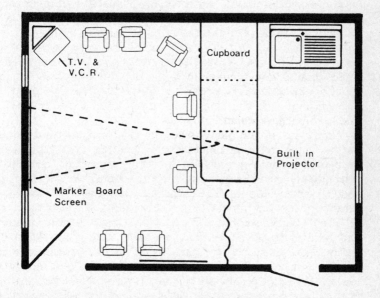

Figure 4. Plan of Multipurpose Room.

shown and a graph constructed. This approach is also used when staff are considering the often difficult problem of reallocating bedrooms to children when a new child arrives. A slide of the first floor of the unit is projected and various solutions are discussed.

Central Heating

Blow-air heaters, recessed into cupboards and walls, are a feature of Beech Tree House's central heating system. There are two built into the room divider. The reason for this system is as follows: during the winter of 1977–78, when the unit was first opened, a boy leant his face against a normal domestic water-filled radiator. He gave no indication of discomfort and the staff in the room were unaware of the danger and continued the game they were playing with the other children. After a few minutes, when it came to the boy's turn to join in, he was found to have a very serious burn on his face which required immediate hospital treatment. We had heard of children who had localised areas where they felt no pain but we did not know that someone with this condition was being educated in the unit. To guard against similar accidents in the future, we removed all radiators which were accessible to children and replaced them with blow-air type heaters. All pipe work was boxed in. At the same time, to ensure that children would not scald themselves, all hot water outlets, taps and showers had thermostatically controlled temperature regulators fitted to the hot water pipes supplying them.

Amenities

In the multipurpose room the small galley is used to prepare drinks for parents, staff and visitors and to serve pre-cooked staff meals from a heated food container. There are only very modest cooking facilities – it is not intended that staff should use this area for a good fry-up! Toasted sandwiches are the most advanced meals that they can prepare. However, if they are struggling with unwanted bulges produced by our somewhat fattening, 'institutionalised' menus, they can store their cottage cheese and yoghurt in the fridge provided in the galley. Staff eat their meals in the main body of the room.

A large colour television is provided for staff entertainment, staff training and for presenting video-recorded information to visitors, parents and participants at case conferences. Because children use the room, the television is mounted two metres above floor level on an arm which allows it to be manoeuvred to a comfortable viewing position. Although it is not out of reach of older children it is at least safe from being tipped off a table or flung across the room. Such a safety measure reduces the anxiety of staff working with children in the room. There is less need to fuss and the children have one less opportunity to manipulate the situation.

With the exception of the gallery area, the room is fully carpeted. This is not only for the comfort of the staff, it also makes it suitable for physiotherapy sessions. Additional mats and equipment are stored in the largest cupboard in the room divider. It is essential that such a multipurpose room has really ample storage, since a number of Beech Tree House staff live in cramped single rooms within the unit. The multipurpose room serves as their lounge and dining area, and it would be intolerable if the room's other functions encroached upon these aspects; it is most important that they have somewhere to relax as a group.

Timetabling use of the room does cause problems. For example, lectures to visitors on Thursdays tend to run on into the staff's first lunch break. When this happens staff are obliged to eat from plates balanced on their laps in the children's lounge. In the evening the member of staff on duty may disrupt colleagues' relaxation by doing the children's ironing or mending while watching television. Whenever such clashes cause difficulty the problem is referred to the Team Meeting for discussion. (See page 105).

The idea of the multipurpose room will be repeated in our new unit, but the new one will be larger. It is virtually impossible to gather all full- and part-time staff into our present room at the same time. The problem is particularly acute during the staff training week in which all staff participate. Although we have had two extractor fans installed, the atmosphere rapidly deteriorates into a 'fug' which is not conducive to efficient studying.

The Toilet Training Area
Most of our efforts to help children with delayed continence are based upon the work of Foxx and Azrin. Since this approach can lead to both the member of staff and the child spending a considerable proportion of each day, over an extended period of time, in the toilet training area, much thought went into the designing of this room. It had to be both a pleasant environment in which to work and an efficient place in which to undertake toilet training. Photograph 5 shows what we achieved.

In designing the toilet training area we had to bear in mind that in the early stages of any programme there would be copious quantities of soiled clothes to be dealt with. There would also be the need periodically to shower or at least wash the children. Figure 5 shows how the area has been laid out, but this plan is by no

Toilet Training Room

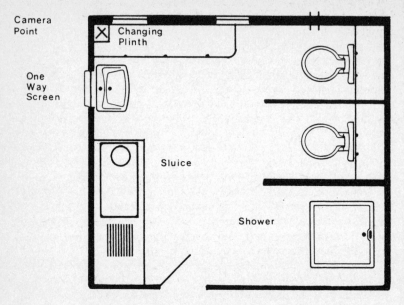

Figure 5. Plan of Toilet Training Area.

means ideal. In our new unit things will be done rather differently, and the problems we have encountered will be considered first.

From bitter experience we now realise that it is a mistake to have the sluice in the toilet training area. Children can be stimulated to the heights of creativity by a sluice with its handles controlling jets of water, its chains for flushing, its huge plug hole for stuffing things down, and so on. Equally tempting can be the presence of buckets of soaking underpants and of rubber gloves for dealing with soiled linen. Further problems are caused by the associated smells. Our original reason for including the sluice here was to avoid having to carry dirty linen from the toilet training area to the laundry. In our new unit the sluice will be in an adjoining room, and dirty items will be put into a bucket and popped through a locking hatch into the sluice room. This arrangement will ensure that the child will not be left alone while dirty items are disposed of and the problems mentioned above will be avoided.

The design of the shower has also created difficulties. Because our children tend to be so heavy-handed we were unable to instal a normal shower cabinet; our shower is built in. The non-slip waterproof flooring simple slopes down to the plug hole, which is of generous size so that faeces will not clog it. The shower tray is formed by the flooring being turned up the walls where it is overlapped by the tiles. All this is fine: the problem is that staff always end up with wet feet when they shower a child because the water splashes up from the floor. Another problem with the shower is the weakness of available flexible hoses which the children destroy rapidly. Hydraulic hose, as fitted to lorry breaking systems, is of the same diameter, is exceptionally strong and can be bought in bright colours. This has proved to be an effective alternative for connecting the shower head.

Ventilation in the toilet training area also proved difficult. We installed two large windows, thinking that these would be a good way of removing smells. They were, but the direction the smell travelled rather depended upon the direction of the wind. It could end up being wafted around the unit. The preferred alternative, which we had to instal later, is that of two heavy-duty extractor fans which draw tainted air out of the room. These are augmented by a battery of pleasantly scented aerosols.

Beneath the windows which, like all windows in the unit, are made of Makralon, is the plinth. This was designed to ease the cleaning and changing of any severely handicapped children who might come our way. Its surface is covered with polyurethane-treated cork tiles which are warm for children to lie on. Because we tend to admit mostly able-bodied children, the plinth is rarely used for its original purpose. However the top makes a useful table for filling in data sheets and a safe place for equipment. Beneath the plinth are cupboards, used to store spare clothes for each of the children involved in a toilet training programme. To ensure the smooth running of programmes, it is the responsibility of the toilet trainer to put a day's supply of spare clothes and all the other paraphernalia of toilet training into these cupboards first thing in the morning. It is considered pretty unforgivable for the trainer to have to distract a colleague from her work in order to supervise a wet child on the toilet while the trainer fetches spare pants from the bedroom. To guard against such interruptions the toilet trainers' check-list is positioned above the plinth.

Some of the older children we have taught in Beech Tree House have been strong and uninhibited in their behaviour. One or two of them have chosen pipework as a target for their destructive outbursts. It is for this reason that all cisterns and pipes are concealed behind strong false walls in our toilet training area and this precaution applies to all toilets and bathrooms in the unit. Keeping toilet lids and seats in place remains a problem: every fixing that we have ever used has been broken.

In the wall opposite the toilet pedestals is a small one-way screen. This enables parents and staff to watch a child's skills or an approach to training. It should be noted that it is not always necessary to provide optimal comfort on the viewing side of a screen. In the case of the one in the toilet training area viewers squeeze into our small laundry room to watch proceedings. The reader should therefore not be deterred from installing one-way screens simply because there will be no comfortable observation room to view from.

An additional observation facility permanently installed in the toilet training area is a wall mounted bracket, power supply and connection box for our remote-controlled closed circuit television system. The camera, zoom-lens and pan/tilt unit can be clipped into place in less than one minute. This arrangement therefore complies with our dictum that audio-visual aids must be quick and simple to set up. The television monitor and control unit are located in the observation room in house 16. Parents and staff can either watch a toilet training session live on the monitor or later by replaying a video recording.

Some severely handicapped children require special toilet pedestals. These we provide as the need arises. In the toilet training area we have installed one adult and one child-sized 'normal' toilet. Both have ordinary seats, and the two are separated by a robust screen. (See Photograph 4 which shows Dougal who, for fifteen years, had been described as doubly incontinent. He became entirely continent or urine within eleven months of entering Beech Tree House.) This is not to give privacy – only *one* child receives toilet training at a time – but to reduce to a minimum known distractions: for example many children find it particularly entertaining to bang adjoining toilet seats up and down. The screen prevents this. Children also find flushing the toilet repeatedly an attractive diversion, particularly if staff react adversely. We have found it valuable to eliminate the possibility of this behaviour in the early stages of a programme by inserting a small bolt into a threaded hole in the false wall behind the toilet. The head of the bolt protrudes beneath the flush handle which no longer works when the bolt is in place. A member of staff can screw the bolt in with her fingers and can thereby fool most 'flushers'.

We have been surprised at the number of schools catering for children of different heights which do not provide toilets of varying size. It is particularly important for unsteady children to have their feet securely on the floor when they are trying to open their bowels. Readers who think that this is a trivial point are invited to raise their feet next time they try to open their bowels and see how they get on.

Many children arrive in Beech Tree House unable to wash their hands and face. These important skills are taught both in class time and in residential time. The sink in the toilet training area is used to assess a child's ability in these areas and initial training is done there during class time.

The 'Safe' Bedrooms

Two of our six bedrooms have been adapted to provide as safe an environment as possible for the children who sleep in them. Safety is a two-way concept: the children using the bedrooms must themselves be protected as far as possible from the consequences of their sometimes excessive behaviour; equally the other children must be safe from such outbursts. This being the case, it should come as no surprise to the reader to learn that these bedrooms can

Safe Bedroom

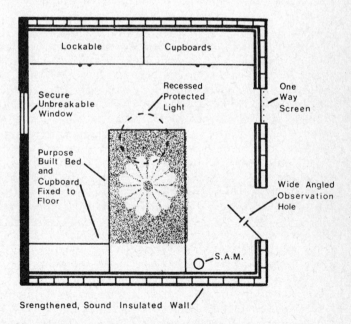

Figure 6. Plan of a Safe Bedroom.

be locked. Figure 6 shows a synthesis of the best features of the two safe bedrooms in Beech Tree House. This is the design which will be incorporated in our new unit. Photograph 7 shows a general view of a safe bedroom.

Certain features of the safe bedrooms result from incidents that occurred during the first five years at Beech Tree House. Children escaped; on one occasion a small girl opened a window which was secured by a supposedly burglar proof lock and jumped in pitch darkness to the concrete path below (her bedroom was on the first floor); a number of children banged their heads violently against hard and sharp objects; some children smeared their rooms with faeces – one particularly difficult child defecated, urinated and vomited in her room almost every night when she first arrived. Others systematically destroyed their environment by breaking windows, furniture and light fittings, and by ripping their bedding and pyjamas to shreds. A few have stripped off wallpaper and broken their way through plasterboard walls. Many have accompanied this behaviour with loud and protracted screaming and banging. Such children had to be safely contained while they were taught more appropriate behaviour.

Children who respond well to their training progress from a safe bedroom to a more normal bedroom. From here, depending on whether they will be returning home or moving to a residential school, they either graduate to a carpeted single room which they care for themselves or to a shared two or three-bedded dormitory-type room. In this way we try to ensure that the final night-time experience of our children is similar to that of their intended destination. The bedrooms shown on the first floor plan are equipped to allow progress of this type.

Safe bedrooms are lined to a height of two metres with a soft version of the floor covering used in the kitchen. At all points where the floor meets the walls, the fixed bed or the built-in cupboard, it is curved up to facilitate cleaning. All joints are 'welded'; the material is gaily coloured; patterned vinyl wallpaper extends from its top to the ceiling, and this is protected by Makralon fixed to the walls with countersuck screws; the join between the paper and the wall covering is protected by rounded hardwood strips which are screwed to the wall. Prior to this strip being added one young lady managed to rip the covering off the walls. Because all joins are now either welded or protected by hardwood strips it would appear to be impossible for any child to obtain the necessary grip to pull anything off.

In addition to its hygienic merits, the Taralay floor covering has the further advantage of cushioning the wall and floor and thereby reduces damage to children who practise self-injurious head banging.

Where a normal bedroom would have a partition wall made of plasterboard, a 'safe' bedroom has thick blockboard screwed to the studwork before the plasterboard is fitted. This exceptionally strong backing prevents children kicking holes in the plasterboard and thereby eventually splitting the wall covering.

All woodwork around the window and door is modified to provide a flush finish and the window itself has a sheet of perforated Makralon screwed over it. The window behind the Makralon is opened by turning a handle in the corridor outside the room. All built-in furniture has rounded edges and no handles, hinges, air vents, or the like, protrude. Again these measures reduce the possibility of severe self-injurious behaviour.

The light in the safe bedroom is controlled by a dimmer switch in the corridor. The light fitting is of the recessed variety and a sheet of perforated Makralon is screwed over it to give further protection. Dimmer switches are fitted to all bedroom lights in Beech Tree House. We have found that many handicapped children who do not have night time behaviour problems have prevailed upon their families to leave their light on all night. Our policy in such cases is to dim the light progressively over a series of nights so that the child eventually becomes accustomed to sleeping in the dark. Lights that dim are also useful for night staff who periodically need to check children without waking them.

In certain bedrooms a second set of light switches is provided. If the corridor switches are set in the 'on' position the internal switches can be used to control the lights. This allows a child who is soon to return home or transfer to a hostel to learn to cope with the lights unaided. One switch is located near the top of the bed so that the child can turn off the reading lamp after looking at a book or playing with a toy. This facility is not available in the safe bedrooms.

The safe bedroom bed, which is described in detail in Chapter 3, was a joint design of Stephen Thorpe, the Spastics Society's architect, Ken Ketteridge, and myself. It is a fixture, as is the other simple furniture in the room. In essence it is a box on which is fixed a shallow tray containing the mattress. We believe that such robust, fixed equipment is essential if initial training programmes are not to be affected by worries about beds being used as battering rams or splintered furniture being used for self-injurious acts. This latter possibility was highlighted by a girl who, one evening, broke a piece of wood from a veneered chipboard bedside cabinet and proceeded to gouge with great effect at a mole on her stomach. To guard against such incidents in the future, all edges of beds and other furniture are finished with rounded-off hard wood; all wooden surfaces are painted with polyurethane gloss varnish to protect the wood and to ease cleaning; the mattresses are foam with a strong waterproof cover. Fitted sheets, smother-proof pillows and colourful washable and fire-proof duvets are supplied.

A fitted locking wardrobe with drawers in the base is provided in each safe bedroom. The wardrobe doors have removable handles so that continual tugging, which might finally remove the doors, can be prevented. It would, of course, be possible to store children's clothes elsewhere, were it not that we hope to teach each child to develop progressively more appropriate behaviour within their safe bedroom. Thus a child's clothes and toys must be in the room so that the child can learn to tidy them away at night, get dressed in the morning, and so on. Eventually the wardrobe doors remain unlocked and a rug is provided, together with curtains, pictures for the wall and toys. When children can cope with these they move out.

Photograph 8 shows a girl who initially exhibited dreadful night-time behaviour, receiving reward tokens for having kept her room clean. The reader will see, from the general view of the safe bedroom in which the token transaction was photographed, that the room is quite attractive, and this has been the general opinion of visitors and parents. Nevertheless the room can appear some-what stark when a child is at the start of training and the room is cleared of all breakable and potentially dangerous objects.

Each safe bedroom has a small one-way screen fitted either in the door or the wall; one has a second such screen in the ceiling which enables observations to be made with a television camera located in the loft.

Staff are alerted that a child has got out of bed, back into bed, wet the bed or is making more than a predetermined level of noise by electronic devices made by Ken Ketteridge. These are described in Chapter 3.

The Classrooms
There are three formal teaching areas in Beech Tree House: the 'Classroom', the 'Distraction Low Room' and the 'Playroom'. Each is described below. Only the first one resembles a typical special school classroom.

The Classroom
The classroom, shown in Figure 7, was established to familiarise

pupils with much that they would be likely to meet in a typical special school. However, a number of features are unusual and peculiar to the Beech Tree House classroom, and I shall concentrate on these rather than on aspects common to ordinary special schools. Included among these 'normal things' are wall displays, books on open racks, work upon the wall, exercise books, reading schemes, work cards, personal work boxes, individual desks, collective play time, and so on. The special features have been included to ensure that the children remain safe in what is a relaxed and relatively low-staffed environment. Such precautions were necessary because a number of children who were happy to learn and work at domestic and self-help activities reacted badly to sitting in class to do table-top tasks. I include among these such good old teaching standbys as completing form boards, pairing similar pictures, sequencing picture story cards, threading beads, sorting by shape or texture, and so on. Although we sympathised with the children's reactions, it was necessary for those who were moving on to 'normal' special education to learn willingly to accept such tasks; unless they could do this many critics would claim that the Beech Tree House train-

Classroom

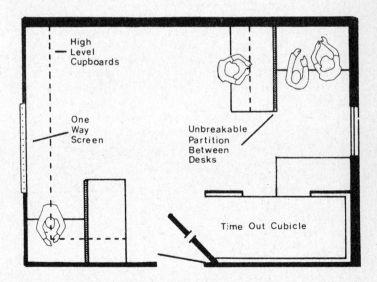

Figure 7. Plan of the Classroom.

ing was valueless. Since children were likely to be evaluated on in-class performance rather than 'life' skills we created our own 'finishing school' in the classroom.

From time to time 'classroom group' children do produce disruptive behaviour, particularly when they first join the group. In order to protect children from hurled equipment and in part to ensure immediate poetic justice as the equipment bounces back in the general direction of the thrower, I designed two built-in desks with Makralon screens set in very sturdy frames. These are shown in Diagram 1. A child seated at a special desk is not boxed in (see Photograph 6); he can see everything that is going on in the classroom and only has to push his chair back to participate fully.

The very solid fixed desks are also suitable for children who show their displeasure by tipping over their tables; before they were installed, many tables flew across the room. As such children become familiar with the work and atmosphere and adapt to the standards of the classroom, so they graduate to free standing desks in the main body of the room.

The classroom group has its own time-out cubicle as part of the

Classroom Desk

Diagram 1. Special fixed classroom desk with Makralon screen.

classroom itself. We have thought very carefully about the ethics, use and effectiveness of time-out procedures and the design of the cubicles we use. Our ethical position can, for the moment, be summed up by stating that we are prepared to use this somewhat draconian training method so long as we have data to show that it is working for the child concerned and when we have exhausted alternative strategies. This issue is discussed in detail in Chapter 7.

The design of the time-out cubicle shown in Diagram 2 has taken into account three factors: the safety of the children, the effectiveness of the cubicle to serve the programme requirements and the convenience of the cubicle when actually in use. It must be emphasised that children are not put into time-out to frighten them. The idea is that they should learn that acting-out, violent, attention-seeking behaviour will no longer be rewarded by adult and pupil attention – that, in fact, the result of any such behaviour is no attention at all!

Time-out cubicles should never resemble dark cells. It is true that ours are stimulation-low, but they have a large Makralon window through which light streams, located high enough to prevent most children from looking out. The cubicles are lined with the same slightly soft, colourful material used in the safe bedrooms. As stated before, this has a cushioning effect and is

Time Out Cubicle

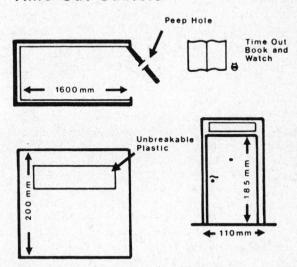

Diagram 2. Specifications of Time Out Cubicle.

easily cleaned if a child vomits, urinates or defecates.

It is vital for staff to be able to observe what a child is doing throughout his period in time-out because occasionally he may seize this opportunity to self-mutilate. If this happens, the time-out procedure is terminated and an alternative training strategy sought. We can observe through the Makralon window but prefer to use the anti-burglar, wide-angle, spy-hole fitted into the cubicle door. If this observation strategy is adopted the child remains unaware of the interest in his behaviour. However, the observer does run some risk of being deafened if the child is pounding on the door!

If a cubicle is to be effective it must be robust enough to withstand the most violent onslaughts of the strongest child. If, for example, the trainer has to remove a child from a flimsy cubicle because it is about to collapse, has to struggle to hold a door shut because no lock has been provided or has to take the child out because she is afraid that a window or light within the cubicle will be broken, then the procedure will be ineffective because the child will have received attention for unwanted behaviour. We are convinced that many of the problems and failures reported concerning use of time-out have arisen because unsuitable rooms or cubicles have been used.

Time-out cubicles must be readily to hand. The act of escorting an obstreperous child upstairs to his bedroom, or to a cubicle adjoining the head teacher's study at the other end of the school, seems to us to be fraught with risks to everyone and potentially rewarding to an attention seeking child. Such an excursion also means that an already disrupted group of children is left short staffed – the more so since, ideally, the person who decided that time-out should be used should be on hand to see the entire episode through. Here we include continual undetected observation of the child during the period in the cubicle. We are aware that in many units such observation is delegated to junior or ancillary staff, or else it may be completely neglected because no one else is available and the person in charge has to dash back to settle the group. When this happens children can be left for considerably longer than the maximum five minutes that we advocate.

The classroom has a one-way screen. This is of generous size and has our only purpose-built observation area on the other side. There is a microphone socket in the classroom, so that with a microphone plugged in and the amplifier on, sound is transmitted to the observation room. The 'mirror' side of the one-way screen is very useful for teaching children to use Paget-Gorman and

Makaton signing language. They are able to check whether their reflection matches the model provided by the instructor.

There is ample storage space in the classroom. A wide range of equipment must be available because the children educated in Beech Tree House have such divergent skills. For example, the classroom teacher may be tackling the very earliest number concepts, say one-to-one correspondence, with a mentally handicapped sixteen year-old, while teaching complex phonic blending to a relatively bright seven year-old. The storage problem is exacerbated by the fact that each school to which we send a child seems to have different number and reading schemes. To help a child transfer we purchase the appropriate materials and subsequently have even more to pack into the cupboards.

When the classroom was first opened a sink was provided. This was later removed since it was a very potent distractor, took up a great deal of room and was rarely used. Many creative activities take place in Beech Tree House during evenings and weekends. It was therefore concluded that it was a waste of very valuable training time for the teacher to pursue similar activities during the day. The reader will remember that the classroom was established to train children how to cope with 'classroom' activities, not to provide a rounded education. The latter is offered by the Beech Tree House experience as a whole.

The Playroom
New entrants to Beech Tree House usually start their education in the playroom teaching group. The goals here are very different from those pursued in the classroom group, being largely concerned with the removal of 'education blocks': either behaviour which impedes learning or the absence of skills which would normally facilitate learning. Examples of the former type are violence to others or self, attacks upon the environment, chronic delayed continence and stereotyped behaviour; examples of the latter type are inability to attend visually, fleeting attention span and inability to follow spoken, signed or symbolic instructions.

The playroom teaching group is so called because much of the children's education takes place in the playroom, *not* because they *play* there during school time. The room presents more problems for the staff and children than any other room in the unit. It is certain that no teaching area in our new unit will have so many faults. I recount the main ones here so that the reader may avoid similar pitfalls. I believe that it is worth noting that our problems arose out of converting an existing building with only limited funds; the problems experienced by colleagues working with handicapped children in the recently completed glut of open-plan schools came about as a direct consequence of misguided planning. Reference to Figure 8 will clearly show the major drawback – the room has five doors. It is also the main circulation area for house seventeen and the only internal route to house sixteen. Although all staff are aware of the disruption caused by walking through a teaching area and therefore keep such intrusions to a minimum, the children in this room nevertheless suffer many unavoidable interruptions.

As well as being a teaching area, the playroom is used as the main dining room and, of course, for playing in. This poses additional problems, not least of which is the speed with which it has to be cleaned up after breakfast and lunch in readiness for teaching sessions. Such changing-over makes settled teaching difficult and we have resolved to have separate dining room facilities in our new unit.

The playroom has a time-out cubicle similar to the one in the classroom and a closed circuit television mounting facility identical to the one in the toilet training area. The camera point is positioned so that it can record what happens in the kitchen. As in the classroom, high cupboards are provided to store equipment.

Playroom

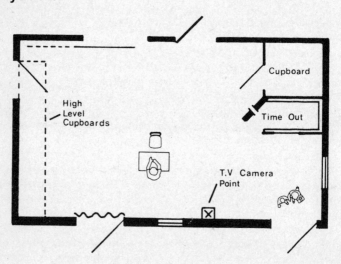

Figure 8.   Plan of Playroom.

It has become clear to us that one of the most potent distractions for children in any group teaching situation is the acting out behaviour of other children. If more space had been available we would have constructed within the playroom two partitioned teaching areas with fixed tables. Such semi-private areas would have reduced the problem of mutual distraction; they would have been a second stage in teaching 'attending' behaviour, the first having taken place in the distraction low room which is described below.

Despite these disadvantages, there are certain features in the location of the playroom which work to the advantage of the children educated there. As stated earlier, it tends to be the new-comers who need most help with toilet training, attention to task training, self-help skills and so on. Reference to the ground floor plan of Beech Tree House (see page 24) will show that the play-room is located between the kitchen, the distraction low room and the children's lounge. Just down the corridor is the toilet training area, while the stairs are handy for certain aspects of mobility training and access to the bedrooms. Obviously it would be inappropriate to transfer the playroom teaching group to the class-room because they would be forever traipsing around the house to get to the rooms where practical sessions take place.

The Distraction Low Room
Some children, when they arrive, appear to have absolutely no ability to concentrate on even the simplest task. One may wander aimlessly about fingering equipment briefly before moving on; another may dash, twirl and leap about the room, bouncing from walls, jumping on furniture, apparently driven by some inner dervish; a third may sit rocking, flapping her hands, fiddling with her clothes and periodically emitting piercing screams; a fourth may appear consumed with lethargy and lie across a table or curl up on the floor. If they are to benefit from the training offered in Beech Tree House, such children must learn to attend, be still, look at the task being presented and, above all, co-operate.

Experience has taught us that such children learn the initial steps most easily in a distraction low environment where the materials to be manipulated stand out from the bland background. In the early days we used a bedroom for 'attention-to-task' train-ing, but this had obvious disadvantages. Two years after Beech Tree House opened, the parents, staff and friends of the unit raised sufficient money to build the distraction low room depicted in Figure 9.

It is easy to describe the distraction low room because there is so

Distraction Low Classroom

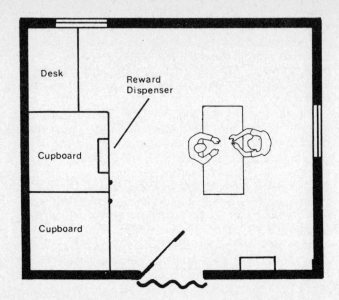

Figure 9. Plan of Distraction Low classroom.

little in it. The windows are high so that the children are not visually distracted by what is happening outside. The door has a Makralon panel to enable rudimentary observation to be made. (A one-way screen would have been better, but there was too little money available to provide one and we have learned to make do without.) There are curtains on the outside of the door so that events happening in the playroom can be shut out. The large storage cupboard is painted white to match the walls and the 'desk' is simply a shelf at which the teacher can sit to make notes. The only other permanent item is the bright blue token-operated reward dispenser which is built into the cupboard door. This is described in Chapter 3.

Use of the Observation Areas

The recorded progress of children and the techniques used to teach them are our 'bread and butter' and rich topics for study. All our reports to parents and local authorities are statements about change in behaviour, or the lack of it. We strive to offer objective data and rarely include subjective surmises about changes in 'attitude' or 'emotional' state. For example, in the case of an 'improved' child we might report fewer tantrums, more laughter, greater co-operation and a marked decline in stereotyped behaviour – these in addition to a list of newly acquired skills. Although much of the information upon which such reports are based is collected while training is in progress, detailed studies are conducted without disruption to the child, by means of observations via our one-way screens or the closed circuit television. The same facilities, particularly the closed circuit television, are used to train the staff. Many of the lectures and workshops that we run are illustrated by videotaped material.

The Observation Annexe
The observation room, shown in Figure 10, is approached through the observation annexe. The annexe has a fixed bench beneath the large observation screen which gives a view into the classroom. All surfaces in the annexe are painted matt black to avoid reflections on the one-way screen. Readers unfamiliar with such screens should note that they are made from glass coated with a very thin

Observation Room

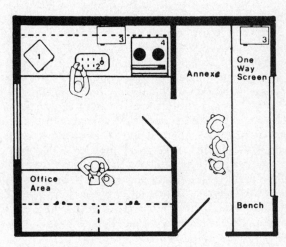

1. CCTV Monitor
2. Control Unit
3. Speaker
4. Video Recorder

Figure 10. Plan of Observation Room and Annexe.

silver layer. From the well-lit side such glass acts as a normal mirror, while from the darker side it is like a slightly tinted window. If the relative balance of light is reversed there is a tendency for the screen to work the other way round and for the observers to become the observed. It is for this reason that the annexe is dark and painted matt black.

A speaker is provided in the annexe to relay sound from the classroom, and an observer can plug a headset into the speaker circuit without disconnecting it. This is useful when visitors enter the annexe to receive explanations about classroom activities. Ensuing conversations, which might easily distract an observer, are effectively shut out by the headset and the observer can continue working uninterrupted.

It is possible to video record the classroom through the one-way screen. However there is considerable light loss due to reflection back into the classroom from the partially silvered glass. We have used this technique but cannot recommend it. In our new units each classroom will have a remote-control closed circuit television camera bracket and connection box of the type described earlier.

The Observation Room
The observation equipment is confined to one side of the room (see Photograph 9). A bench runs the length of the room, with a well on the right to accommodate a black and white reel-to-reel video recorder, while a similar well at the other end protects a record player deck which can be used to play music into the adjoining children's lounge. In the centre of the bench is a remote control unit for the video camera and lens. This enables the operator to pan and tilt the camera; zoom the lens in for close-ups and out for wide-angle shots; focus the picture and open and close the lens aperture in order to cope with changing levels of light. All these operations can be watched on a monitor which usually sits on the cover of the record player well. Beside the control box is a picture signal switch which allows the apparatus to be changed rapidly from the record to the replay mode. Behind these items is a series of removable panels concealing the cabling which comes to the observation room from many parts of the unit. These cables are terminated in a number of labelled sockets into which the operator can plug equipment.

Above the bench, to the left, a vertical tape recorder and a five-channel amplifier are built in. The amplifier is used in conjunction with the record player, tape recorder and video recorder and is switched accordingly; the tape recorder can be used to make sound recordings of events in various parts of the house. Because it has a choice of speeds, it can be used to 'collapse' time by recording events on a slow speed and replaying them on a fast one. This can be a useful technique for analysing a night time screaming behaviour, for example, when eight hours' behaviour can be compressed into a little under two hours' listening.

Numbered and indexed video tapes are stored beside the tape recorder: reel-to-reel tapes in three categories – Micro-Teaching, Data and Lecture Tapes – and cassette tapes containing mainly Off Air Programmes thought to be useful for staff training and Entertainment Tapes for both children and staff.

Cupboards for storing infrequently used audio-visual materials, spare cables and so on, complete the space to the ceiling.

The opposite side of the observation room has a similar bench and shelves, plus two small filing cabinets. This area is the office of the head of unit. Unfortunately the room is too small for all its functions. It is particularly difficult to seat five staff comfortably for the weekly, hour-long micro-teaching sessions (see Photograph 29) which give members of staff the opportunity to study themselves teaching and the chance to discuss their conclusions with colleagues. It is likely that, in our new unit the closed circuit television side of our observation and staff training work will be located in the multipurpose rooms.

The reader who glances back to the plans of the unit will see that many of the rooms have not been mentioned in this chapter. This is because they have little that is special about them. The office serves as an office, ordinary bedrooms serve as ordinary bedrooms, and so on; there seems little to be gained from describing them. What needs to be said is that we endeavour to keep all rooms as bright and as pleasant as possible by using attractive wallpaper, colourful curtains, gay bedding and furnishing, and by displaying children's personal photographs, work and pictures on the walls.

3 EQUIPMENT

While it is probably true that most of the work carried out in Beech Tree House could be done without our technical aids, many more staff would be needed to achieve the same results. In the course of visits to other units we have been struck by the amount of potentially useful, and no doubt expensive, equipment which ends up in the back of cupboards or on high, dusty shelves. Many reasons are given to explain this waste but the common factor seems to be that few units have a philosophy which embraces the use of technology to enhance teaching and the care of children.

Although most establishments claim that they could do more for their children if they had more staff, economic reality dictates that such increases are unlikely to occur – in many situations a reduction in staff is more probable. An alternative is to use the available staff more effectively. A number of measures can be taken: staff morale should be kept at the highest level, staff should be trained to peak efficiency and be prepared to exchange roles, and *technical devices* should be introduced wherever they will enhance staff performance or release them to work with children.

In Beech Tree House equipment is used to perform five distinct functions: releasing staff from routine work; monitoring children's behaviour and alerting staff to the occurrence of certain key events; rewarding children for appropriate behaviour; enhancing staff's ability to collect data; and presenting certain aspects of programmes to children.

Releasing Staff from Routine Work

I include in this category washing machines, vacuum cleaners, dish washers and the like; all readers will appreciate that such equipment saves staff time. One small caveat is worth adding: heads of units should not allow the type of equipment installed to be determined by the organisation's supplies officer whose brief will probably be to equip schools and units as cheaply as possible. We have experienced the false economy of installing domestic quality equipment when industrial quality should have been specified; Multi-programmed domestic washing machines and plastic vacuum cleaners with their plethora of fancy brushes tend to end on the scrap heap within a few months.

The choice of commercial machine is also vital. Until we

received a vacuum cleaner that could suck up water, staff were spending very disagreeable hours cleaning up vomit, thrown food, urine and such like; the new machine both saved time and boosted staff morale. The dish washer which was introduced in the third year of the project was small enough to fit under the sink. It released from the chore of washing piles of dishes a member of staff who was subsequently able to work with a child at the sink on a dish washing programme, using a small number of plates, while at the same time supervising the dish washer which did the bulk of the work. In short, careful selection of equipment can free staff to work with children. It should not be introduced to ensure progressively longer coffee breaks. The goal is to use the energies of the staff productively, not to 'feather bed' them.

Monitoring Children's Behaviour
This second function has proved very fruitful, the collaboration between unit staff and Ken Ketteridge resulting in some quite outstanding devices. Two of these have enabled us to monitor night time behaviour with great accuracy, without increasing the number of staff involved. We claim that few units are able to run night time behaviour improving programmes as efficiently as we can. The equipment used is described below and a case study will be found in Chapter 9.

The Bed-Bug and Nocturnal Eneuresis Alarm
Every bed in the unit has a Bed-Bug, but not the crawling type. These Bed-Bugs are the electronic kind, designed to alert staff when a child has got out of bed and to indicate which child is concerned. There are two basic elements, the detector at the bed end of the system and the display panel with the member of staff (see Photograph 10).

The display panel is shown in Diagram 3. This part of the system is portable and can be plugged into sockets strategically placed around the unit, enabling staff to perform other duties while monitoring the children. When a child gets out of bed the device bleeps and the child's bed is indicated by a flashing light. Reference to Diagram 3 will show that a plan of the first floor of the unit is a feature of the display panel, every bed being indicated by a small red light.

Each bed has a switch on the panel which can be set in three positions. When pushed to the left, 'in bed' behaviour is monitored and, if the child gets out, the sequence described above occurs. The member of staff then has a number of choices: she can move the child's switch to the central position, so turning off that

Bed-Bug

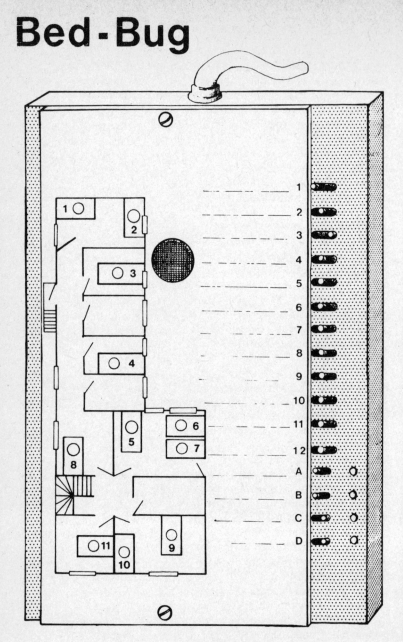

Diagram 3.   Bed-Bug display panel.

particular bed, and go and see what is happening (this would be the appropriate action for a physically handicapped child who might have tumbled out of bed); she can push the switch to the right hand position which sets the machine to monitor 'out of bed' behaviour knowing that the moment the child gets back into bed the panel will emit a different tone (this would be appropriate for an ambulant child known to be capable of coping with his own toileting needs); finally, if for some reason she does not respond within three minutes to the tone and light – perhaps because she is fully occupied dealing with a child having a fit – a loud alarm rings in the staff residential quarters and all her colleagues will arrive at the gallop.

The control panel is also used to monitor nocturnal eneuresis. Up to four beds can be coupled to the system. Commercially produced pads are used in the beds (see Photograph 11), and as soon as one of these becomes wet the Bed-Bug display panel emits a distinct tone, while the appropriate yellow light at the bottom right of the display lights up.

The detectors, which signal to the display panel the presence or absence of children in their beds, are modified scales. In essence these compare the weight of the unoccupied bed with its weight plus the child and inform the electronics which of the two conditions prevails. They can be easily adjusted by staff to take account of different weights of children and beds (see Photograph 12). In bedrooms where children might tamper with the scales they are either incased in a metal box or built into the base of the bed. The latter is the case in the safe bedrooms. Portable versions with very simplified display panels have been produced for use in children's homes.

Purpose Built Safe Beds

Diagram 4 shows the beds that we have developed for children exhibiting difficult night time behaviour. These were mentioned briefly in Chapter 2. I have included them in the 'monitoring' section because they have been especially designed for use in conjunction with the Bed-Bug system. The base of the bed is screwed to the floor and is of very solid construction, with a lockable door at the head end of the base giving access to the Bed-Bug scales. The solid tray in which the mattress rests is fixed to the base at three corners with steel, counter-sunk screws passing through rubber door stops. This method of mounting ensures sufficient flexibility for the bed to move when a child gets in and out. The fourth corner has a leg which goes inside the base and rests on the scales of the Bed-Bug, thereby activating the mechanism.

Purpose Built Bed

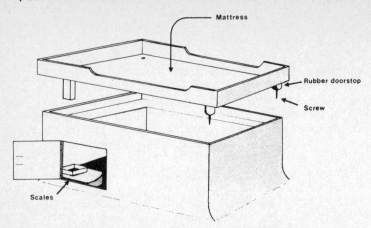

Diagram 4.   Purpose built bed.

This design has proved to be exceptionally successful. No bed has sustained any damage in two years and the Bed-Bug mechanisms only need checking and adjusting at the start of each term. Our physiotherapist is enthusiastic about the firm sleeping surface provided, and we have also been pleased to note that the lack of spring in the beds has reduced the tendency of children to use them as trampolines.

The Sound Activated Monitor – SAM
The Sound Activated Monitor is used to listen to children in their bedrooms. It replaced an adapted baby alarm system which gave continuous sound from all bedrooms at once. This worked reasonably well when only one child was making a noise but it was impossible to listen selectively – moreover it delivered sound to the duty staff member throughout the night, providing a continuous background of heavy breathing, coughing and bed springs. SAM has eliminated these problems.

Like the Bed-Bug system, SAM has a portable display panel, shown in Diagram 5. It too indicates, by means of small red lights, where significant events are happening, in this case from which room a noise is coming. Once a noise has triggered the system for a particular room the light remains on for five seconds and the sound is relayed via the speaker in the SAM display panel. The system then shuts down until another noise occurs. If the member of staff considers the sound to be of significance she simply moves the

Sound Activated Monitor

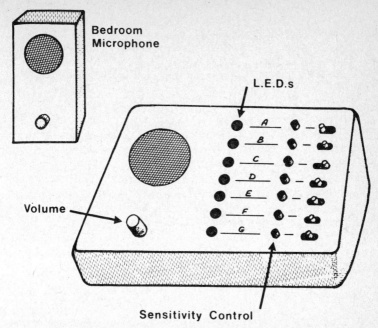

Diagram 5. Sound Activated Monitor (SAM).

three-position switch on the display panel to the right and the device monitors sound from the selected room until it is switched off. Photograph 10 shows SAM in use with a Bed-Bug.

In each bedroom there is a small blue box screwed to the ceiling. This contains a microphone, some circuitry and a small black knob. The knob is used by staff to set the sound level at which the microphone switches on the system, allowing very different levels of sound to be chosen to trigger the system in different rooms. A further knob is provided for each room on the display panel, so that staff can make fine adjustments to any microphone's switch-on threshold without entering the room and disturbing the child or children concerned. This ability to set sensitivity thresholds is very useful – particularly so in the case of epileptic children who may have fits while asleep. So long as their fits are reliably accompanied by noise, perhaps a panting or gagging sound, the bedroom microphone can be set to a level which will detect this and SAM will alert the member of staff on duty. If on the other hand a child is fond of singing loudly as soon as he wakes in the morning, the sound level at which the microphone in his room activates the system can be set much higher.

If for some reason it is important to monitor a room continuously, the automatic features of the system can be overridden completely. This alternative is usually selected if a child is unwell and remains in bed during the day. SAM is then placed in the classroom so that the staff can keep in touch with what is happening.

The Wee-D (Urine Detector)

The Wee-D or Urine Detector is a small, battery powered, box-like gadget from which forty centimetres or so of soft wire protrude. This wire is attached with press-studs to the outside of a child's pants and the box is pinned to the child's outer garments in a position where it cannot be fiddled with (see Diagram 6). When the child's pants are wet the Wee-D makes a whistling sound to alert staff (see Photographs 14 and 15).

The value of the Wee-D is three-fold. When planning a toilet training programme it is important to establish whether or not

Wee-D

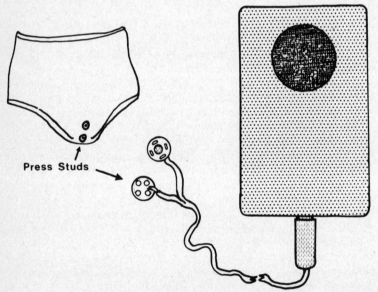

Press Studs

Diagram 6.   Wee-D Urine Detector.

there is a pattern to the child's wetting, and if there is, it will obviously make sense to take the child to the toilet when urination is likely. It is equally important to have a clear picture of the extent of the problem before training starts. Such 'baseline' data act as a reference point against which to measure any future progress. A third, and more controversial use for the Wee-D can arise during training itself: to let staff know the moment the child is urinating in the wrong place. Disapproval follows immediately – perhaps a token is taken away or the child is 'told off'. We have rarely used the Wee-D in this punishing manner because we have found that rewarding children for performing in the correct place is an effective and of course happier procedure. Furthermore, there are occasions when the Wee-D gives 'false-positive' signals: that is, it indicates children are wet when, in fact, they are dry. This tendency increases in summer when children perspire, and quite obviously, they would be confused if they were punished for something they had not done.

The Pedestal Urine Detector – PUD

The Pedestal Urine Detector, or PUD, shown in Diagram 7, is used in toilet training programmes. It is a form of switch, activated by urine and faeces, which triggers a buzzer to alert staff that a child has 'performed'. Alternatively it can be used in conjunction with a Switching Timer, described below, which turns on a toy enjoyed by the child.

The PUD is simply two pieces of stainless steel wire which pass through a small plastic block resting against the inside of the toilet pedestal, where it will be splashed by urine. The ends of the two wires protruding through the block are about two millimetres above the surface of the water, so that they are briefly submerged if any ripples occur, while the other ends clip round the rim of the toilet pedestal beneath the seat. A flexible twin-core wire leading from these to the Switching Timer or buzzer is routed behind the false wall at the back of the toilet, thereby preventing children from fiddling with it. As soon as urine strikes the plastic block or faeces ripple the surface of the water, the PUD triggers the system to which it is linked.

Closed Circuit Television

Closed circuit television is an immensely valuable monitoring aid if it is used correctly. We claim that correct usage should include non-intrusiveness of the camera, rapid deployment to the desired location, simple controls and an efficient means of retrieving data stored on tapes. In discussion with visitors we often discover that

Pedestal Urine Detector

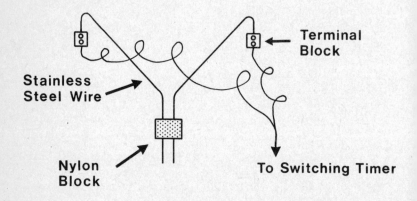

Terminal Block

Stainless Steel Wire

Nylon Block

To Switching Timer

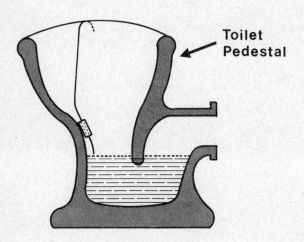

Toilet Pedestal

Diagram 7.   Pedestal Urine Detector (PUD).

their video equipment is used almost exclusively for recording and replaying off-air materials, although the more adventurous occasionally branch out into 'filming' the school pantomine and the parents' egg-and-spoon race! Just occasionally we hear of units where attempts have been made to record children at work; these efforts are usually abandoned because of the effort involved in setting up tripod, camera, video-recorder, microphone, mains leads and so on, not to mention the serious disruption to the session caused by the operation. Staff therefore become disenchanted and a valuable aid is neglected.

Diagrams 8 and 9 show the solution we have adopted. The camera is mounted on a pan/tilt unit permanently screwed to a metal plate with a slot in it. This plate can be slipped onto a solid wall bracket and secured by a single knurled nut and the various leads from the camera and pan/tilt unit plug into their appropriate sockets on the connection box. The equipment can be installed and running within a minute. Because the camera is high on the wall and there is no one fussing over it, children and staff are not distracted.

Rapid Use CCTV System

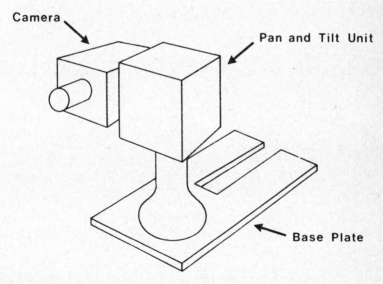

Diagram 8.   Rapid Use Closed Circuit Television System on pan/tilt unit.

Rapid Use CCTV System

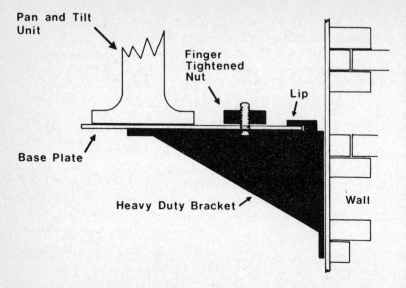

Diagram 9.   Rapid Use Closed Circuit Television System – side view showing wall mounting.

   Operation of the camera is very simple. The member of staff working the controls in the observation room can see from the television monitor the effect of every action. Whatever appears on the screen will be recorded, so a fuzzy picture can be corrected by adjusting the focus button, an overbright one by moving the iris control, and a too small one by pressing the zoom button. The simplicity of the system means that any member of staff can work it, so avoiding the necessity for special staff to produce recordings.
   Video tapes are not simply used to monitor behaviour. They are used to teach staff, parents and participants at lectures and workshops. They can also be a very valuable record of progress.

Rewarding Children's Appropriate Behaviour
There are several different types of reward which a child can receive for doing something correctly. Some of these cannot be mechanised – for example, praise, smiles, cuddles and a host of other social signals which indicate the correctness of a given action. There are, however, certain rewards which can be mechanised with advantage, and the gadgets we have evolved in

Beech Tree House for this purpose are described below.

Many of the devices are operated by 'token', in much the same way that vending machines and juke boxes are triggered by coins. Most of our children participate in the Beech Tree House 'token economy', a scheme similar to the world economy where people receive metal and paper tokens which they can exchange later for

Token Bank

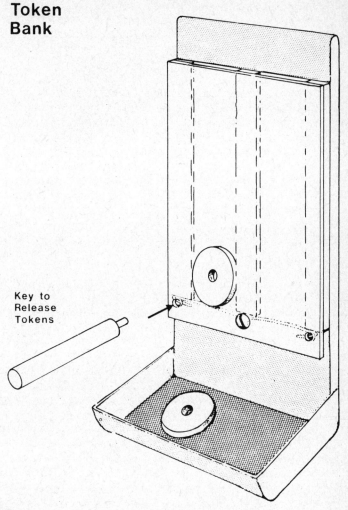

Key to Release Tokens

Diagram 10. Token Bank showing how tokens are stacked and released.

goods and services of their choice. Ours is a very simple economy in which all tokens have the same value, and they are given to the children the moment they have completed a task, rather than at the end of the week or month.

Each child has tokens of a different colour in order to limit the possibility of stealing from each other. They are made of plastic, three millimetres thick, of the same diameter as a two pence piece. The thickness of the tokens allows them to be stacked on edge in the Token Bank, while their size ensures that two pence pieces can be used to work token operated devices. This latter design feature helps children to learn to value and use money.

The Token Bank

Just as participants in the world economy have banks, so do the children in Beech Tree House. Their banks are rather simpler and they keep track of their accounts by noting how many tokens are stacked on edge behind their bank's perspex front (see Diagram 10). Many of our pupils have perceptual problems and would find it difficult to detect any increase in the height of a pile of tokens if they were stacked flat, so it is a great deal easier for them to see an increase in height if the latest token deposited contributes its full diameter to the pile. Withdrawals are made with the help of a member of staff: a special 'key' is pressed into a small hole at the bottom of the child's 'deposit' column and the tokens fall into the tray beneath. Photograph 16 shows a child withdrawing her tokens.

The Token Operated Sweet Dispenser

The Token Operated Sweet Dispenser is usually the most popular machine in the unit. It gives one sweet per token, plus flashing lights and chiming bells while doing so. Some children appear to find the machine's performance quite as rewarding as the sweet they receive. A very valuable feature is that it can deal with any shape of small sweet; not knowing which type will come out probably heightens the children's interest.

The sweets to be dispensed can be seen beneath the perspex top. As shown in Diagram 11, a light flashes continuously while the machine is switched on and the dispensed sweet falls onto a small tray in front of the machine (see Photograph 17).

By means of a Switching Timer it is possible to link battery-powered versions of the Sweet Dispenser to the PUD, in order to deliver a sweet mechanically to a child as a reward for using the toilet. The battery version can also be attached to the A4 Tutor to give a sweet reward when a sheet of questions has been answered

Sweet Dispenser

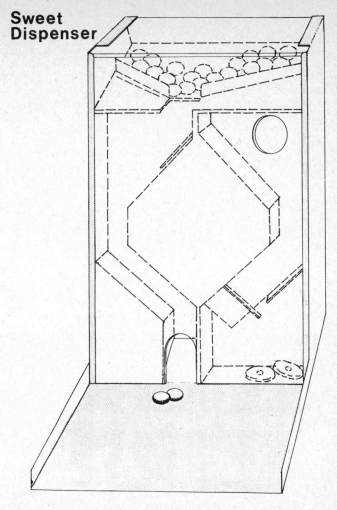

Diagram 11.   Token Operated Sweet Dispenser.

successfully. The Sweet Dispenser, which is used all day, every day, is mains powered. It is of very robust design and is screwed to the bench in the observation annexe.

The Token Operated Music Dispenser
The Music Dispenser is a cassette recorder controlled via its remote control socket by a Switching Timer, both gadgets being

Music Dispenser

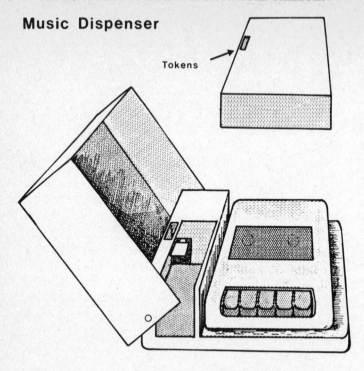

Tokens

Diagram 12.   Token Operated Music Dispenser.

protected by a metal case. The timer is activated by putting tokens into the slot in the metal case, and the duration of music per token can be preset between one and five minutes.

Pre-recorded pop and nursery music is the most popular. Because the cassette recorder is used in the battery mode children can take the machine and play it in the privacy of their own rooms if they want to (see Photograph 18). The very straightforward design, with locking lid, is shown in Diagram 12.

The Token Operated Television

Staff in Beech Tree House are very wary of using television to entertain children, being all too aware of its misuse as an electronic baby minder, with handicapped children planted in front of it to 'watch' the most unsuitable programmes. For years we did without one and the children spent their time actively involved in doing things, but despite our prejudice, we do realise that there are a few programmes which are suitable and that some

Token Operated TV

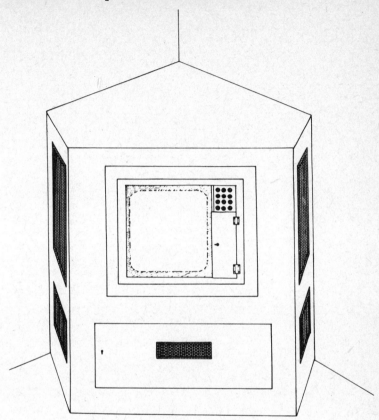

Diagram 13. Token Operated Television.

of our children enjoy watching them. We have also come across one or two children who have a passion for watching television – one was sufficiently undiscriminating to find the test card worthy of rapt attention. All in all, we felt that one-minute spells watching whatever happened to be on, in return for twenty minutes' work, was a reasonable bargain. The Token Operated Television was duly created (see Diagram 13).

The machine is built into a metal box with a Makralon screen across the front, and children obtain the picture by inserting a token into a slot on the front. Thirty seconds before the picture disappears a whistling sound is heard to indicate that another token should be inserted. A recent development has enabled the machine to be used in conjunction with a video recorder, so that we can now provide suitable programmes. One young man, who is not particularly interested in watching television, but is keen on cars, now uses his tokens to watch recordings of motor racing (see Photograph 19).

The Switching Timer
The Switching Timer is a device used to turn battery driven toys and equipment on and off, the running time being preset with a small knob within the Timer. Diagram 14 shows the front panel. The 'input' socket enables a switch to be connected to the timer by means of a cable and a 3.5mm jack plug. These switches can be either a simple button or an adapted switch for use by a handicapped person; or the contacts can be built into a form board which then acts as a switch when an insert is placed correctly: or a PUD can be clipped into a toilet, or whatever can be adapted to 'make' a circuit when a child does something correct. The two sockets labelled 'toy' are used to control a toy, tape recorder or

Switching Timer

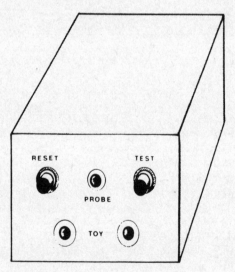

Diagram 14.　Switching Timer.

other battery driven device. Most toys have the twin cable wired to either side of the on/off switch, so that the toy can be used as it was originally designed, as well as in conjunction with the Switching Timer. In the case of a cassette recorder the connection is made via the remote control socket.

The 'reset' button can be used to turn off the Switching Timer and the device attached if this should prove necessary. Its main function, however, is to 'prime' the timer ready to respond to a signal from whatever switch is attached. This design feature means that a child cannot repeatedly obtain the reward of a working toy without the intervention of a member of staff. It is, of course, easy to override the reset button if repeated operation is desired. The 'test' button enables staff to test that the system is working without using the switch. This is an obvious advantage when the Switching Timer is connected to a PUD.

The Token Operated Reward Dispenser

Two variations of this versatile piece of equipment have been produced, one free standing, the other built into the door of a cupboard. This latter design is generally more satisfactory for use with our 'playroom group' children because it cannot be hurled about the room. Before we changed the design hurling was used as an alternative strategy to obtain the reward by some of our most difficult children. See Diagram 15.

The top part of the Token Operated Reward Dispenser is a box with 1500mm sides. It has a Makralon door which slides down to allow children to take out whatever reward has been placed inside. The door is released when a preset number of tokens have been fed into a slot – the Dispenser has a great deal in common with a vending machine. The door-mounted version has been amalgamated with a Token Bank so that children can clearly see the tokens mounting up towards the target number which will open the door the moment the final token is added to the column.

The door-mounted Token Operated Reward Dispenser is used in the Distraction Low Room where, apart from equipment in use during a teaching session it is the only salient item. The idea is that children who have learned how to use tokens to operate it should work with their reward in sight through the Makralon door of the Dispenser and see their tokens accumulating in the Bank columns (see Photograph 20). Children who do not understand the device work with their backs to the cupboard.

The Token Operated Reward Dispenser is extremely useful because it means staff can be very flexible in the rewards they offer to children – small toys, film-wrapped food, drinks, books, items

Built-in Reward Dispenser

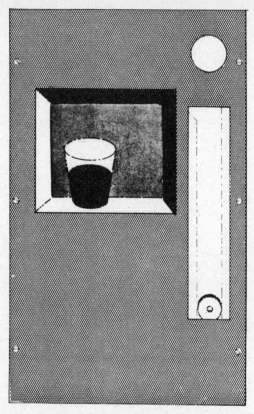

Diagram 15.   Built-in Token Operated Reward Dispenser.

of clothing, plants to be set in the garden, plus a host of other favoured items, can all be dispensed automatically. With bright children 'contracts' can be made: the child selects a reward of an agreed token value, has this placed in the Dispenser, and then works to obtain it.

Data Collecting
The straightforward data collecting techniques which we use in Beech Tree House are described in Chapter 8; the devices themselves are discussed here. Certain of these we have developed ourselves and consequently they will be described in more detail.

Watches, Kitchen Timers and Tally Counters

One commonly used form of data collecting is that of counting how often something happens. Although it may seem quite easy to make a small mark on a sheet of paper each time the 'something' occurs, this can be a cumbersome approach when the person collecting the data is involved in teaching as well. Because this is often the case in Beech Tree House, we have found it much simpler to use Tally Counters. These small, lightweight devices, which can be pinned to staff clothing, have a display similar to a car odometer. Each time the button on top of the Tally Counter is depressed the number displayed increases by one. At the end of the observation the total shown is transferred to a data collecting schedule and the Tally Counter is reset to zero by turning a small knob. We have found it a useful precaution to stick a self adhesive label to each Tally Counter and note which type of behaviour it is being used to record. This avoids confusion when more than one type is being observed.

When collecting 'frequency' data it is essential to know the period of time during which the recorded number of occurrences of a behaviour pattern take place. If head banging is the subject of study, very different types of intervention are indicated by ten bangs spread over an hour and ten bangs per five minutes. It follows that staff involved in collecting data need a reliable method of timing their observations. Watches and clocks appear to be the obvious answer but in practice cause great difficulty because staff become engrossed in what they are doing and forget to look at them. This results in frequency counts being recorded for differing periods of time. A far more reliable approach is to use a Kitchen Timer which can be set to ring as soon as the observation period is over. It is a simple matter for the member of staff to note down the number shown on the Tally Counter, reset the Kitchen Timer for the next observation period, and then carry on with her duties (see Photograph 21).

The Fixed Interval Timer – FIT

The Fixed Interval Timer (FIT), is a small, light, battery-powered device (see Photograph 22). It may be used in much the same way as the kitchen timer described above. However, it has two distinct advantages: it is small and may be pinned to staff clothing and it can be preset for a given time interval which may be repeated at the touch of a button. Because FITs are so accurate and convenient to use we only resort to kitchen timers when all FITs are in service.

Diagram 16 shows the simple controls of the FIT. The switches

Fixed Interval Timer

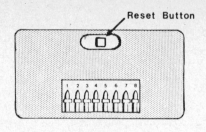

Diagram 16. Fixed Interval Timer (FIT), showing the whole device and a view of the control panel.

numbered 1 to 6 are for selecting different units of time – for example, if 'Switch 2' (one minute) and 'Switch 4' (four minutes) are moved into the 'on' position, the FIT will be programmed to signal five-minute time intervals. By choosing appropriate switches any period from 0.5 minutes to 31.5 minutes may be set in half minute increments.

When a preset period of time has elapsed the FIT emits a buzz. The wearer can either turn it off by moving 'Switch 8' or, if 'Switch 7' is on, press the 'reset' button on top of the FIT. This turns the buzz off and restarts the Timer from zero for the preset period, at the end of which it will buzz again.

The Teacher Prompt

It is comparatively simple, when working in a one-to-one situation, for a member of staff to record a child's correct behaviour by making simple notes; in a busy classroom, however, or during social skills training sessions, it is much more difficult, particularly if staff wish to focus on 'good' behaviour. 'Good' behaviour simply does not stand out when staff are helping other children with problems and redirecting them to their tasks. However, if staff are periodically alerted to observe and record a particular child's behaviour, exceptionally useful data may be obtained.

The Teacher Prompt has been developed to facilitate the observation of non-salient behaviour in a busy setting. It is a battery-powered device no bigger than a packet of twenty cigarettes and may be pinned to the lapel. By means of an unobtrusive ear piece, the 'teacher' is cued by a tiny buzz to look at a chosen child forty times in a ten-minute period, the end of the time being signalled by a continuous buzz. Each observation lasts one second. By pressing a tally counter the observer records each occasion, out of forty, that the child is judged to be behaving correctly. Professionals would call this 'behaving in an "on-target" manner'. At the end of the observation period the teacher is able

Teacher Prompt

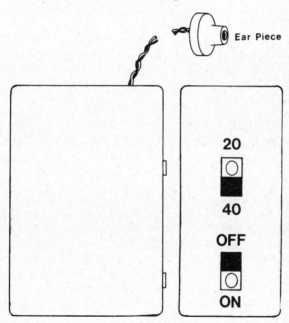

Diagram 17. Teacher Prompt, showing side and front panels and ear piece.

to read off the tally counter the number of occasions the child has been observed to be 'on-target'. This figure may in turn be expressed as a percentage of the total number of observations.

This data is a *sample* of the child's behaviour; a *continuous* observation procedure would be necessary to give a full record. Studies that we have undertaken, however, have produced results indicating that an accurate picture of a child's behaviour can be obtained using the Teacher Prompt and a tally counter in the manner described. Children have been video recorded and the tapes have been analysed using both a continuous observation procedure, where the child's 'on-target' behaviour is noted every three seconds, and the sampling technique described above. When both sets of data have been converted to percentages showing the proportion of 'on-target' behaviour, the difference between the results derived from the two techniques has rarely exceeded seven per cent. By using this sampling procedure a member of staff, preoccupied with teaching a group of children, can obtain a precise measure of one aspect of one child's behaviour. This information, which would normally require the cooperation of another member of staff observing on a continuous basis, is consequently obtained economically.

The version of the Teacher Prompt shown in Diagram 17 has a '20–40' switch in addition to the 'On–Off' switch, activated when the Teacher Prompt is used to cue staff to reward children for 'on-target' behaviour. This aspect of the device is described in the final part of this chapter.

Closed Circuit Television
Video recordings of children's behaviour enable a vast amount of information to be gathered at one go. When observations are made 'live' the observer has to be very selective about what is being recorded; if speech is the focus of interest it is unlikely that there will be time to record, for example, the child's visual behaviour as well. If the session is video recorded, all these and many more aspects of both the child's and teacher's behaviour can be teased out, including whether or not the member of staff conducting the session was reinforcing the child for each correct response. In fact it would be possible for the person working with the child to observe, collect data and also analyse it.

Video recordings do not sort out data; that still has to be done by an observer. The great advantage the system bestows is that the same sequence can be reobserved many times, not only allowing the material to be analysed in different ways, but also opening up to other staff, parents, professional colleagues, students and so on, what is usually a very private interaction between teacher and pupil. Within Beech Tree House this video-stored data is used for staff training at weekly Micro Teaching sessions (with the knowledge and consent of the 'performers') when colleagues discuss and analyse the teaching skills employed.

Programme Delivery
In this final section devices which themselves play an important part in actually presenting the training programmes will be described. A number of the devices have been mentioned earlier because they can be used in other ways – for example, the FIT is used both to collect data and to train children to sit and work progressively longer periods of time.

The Potting Primer
The Potting Primer is particularly useful when children who wet unpredictably are being toilet trained. Such children usually start their programme by being toileted at half-hourly intervals. As they improve they graduate to hourly visits and finally progress to going after meals and at break times. When such programmes are in progress it is a problem for the busy 'Toilet Trainer' – and in the holidays the parents – to remember exactly when to take the child to the lavatory, with the ever-present risk that they may become absorbed in another activity and completely forget the child's needs. We have tried using kitchen timers to remind the trainer when to toilet children, but these are fiddly to set and bulky to carry round – apart from the fact that their continual ticking makes the trainer sound like the crocodile from Peter Pan!

The Potting Primer is a small battery-powered device very similar to the FIT. It has a switch which can be set to three positions: 'Half' (an hour), 'One' (hour) and 'Off'. Like the FIT, the electronic countdown is started by pressing a small button on the top of the device. As soon as the preset time is reached, a continuous, high-pitched tone starts and the unit can then be reset by pressing the button again, usually when the child leaves the Toilet Training area. The Potting Primer also serves as a badge of office indicating who the toilet trainer is.

The Fixed Interval Timer
The FIT has been used successfully on a number of occasions to teach children to behave in a desirable way for progressively longer periods of time. Greg provides the most straightforward example: he found it exceptionally difficult to sit down and attend

to a task for more than a few seconds unless an adult was working
with him, although he was a relatively bright little boy and readily
understood that if he remained in his seat working until the little
box on his table started to buzz, he would be rewarded. The training strategy was very simple. The teacher set the FIT for half a
minute and explained to Greg that he would receive a token if he
worked continuously until it buzzed. During the first FIT-assisted
lesson Greg received five such training sessions, during each of
which he sat and worked for the required half minute and earned
all his tokens. The next lesson saw Greg completely successful for
five one-minute periods. The programme continued for two weeks
by which time Greg had no problem working for ten-minute
periods without leaving his seat, calling for his teacher or disrupt-
ing the class in any way.

Used in this way, the FIT appears to help children scan time by
giving them a goal which they know they can achieve. This
confidence is generated by the initial training time being very short
and subsequent increments being equally small. We have found
that the FIT can be used in a similar manner to reward children for
refraining from producing violent and destructive behaviour.

The Teacher Prompt
The Teacher Prompt can be used to cue staff and parents to
reward a child for desired behaviour, so increasing its frequency.
The bleeps, which cue them, occur in a random sequence so that
the child in question cannot predict when he is likely to be
observed or reinforced.

When the Teacher Prompt is used as an aid to changing
behaviour, a number of decisions have to be made. The most
important of these concern:

a) The target behaviour which is to be increased.
b) The kind of reinforcement that will be given if the
    behaviour is on target when the adult is cued to observe.
c) The nature of the adult's response to off-target behaviour.
d) The criterion for success (at which point training will
    terminate).
e) The criterion for failure of the programme (at which point
    an alternative strategy will be tried).

Having made these decisions, the training procedure is straightforward. The Teacher Prompt is switched on and each time the
buzz is heard the teacher, or other adult, observes the child for one
second and asks herself, 'Is he on target?' If the answer is 'Yes',
the reinforcement is given. If the answer is 'No', the on-going

behaviour is ignored or treated in a previously determined manner.

The adult uses a tally counter to record the number of times the child is reinforced, and the total shown at the end of the session should coincide with the number of times the child has been observed to be on target and thus received reinforcement. Since this data is directly comparable to that collected in earlier 'baseline' observations made with the device, (see the information concerning the Teacher Prompt on page 73) it will be clear whether or not the training procedure is working. If it is proving successful a progressive increase in the amount of on-target behaviour will show up.

As children improve and produce progressively more on-target behaviour, the staff can become overburdened with doling out reinforcement – even if this is only in the form of brief words of praise. It is for this reason that the Teacher Prompt has the '20–40' switch: moving it to the '20' position halves the number of observations in the ten-minute period. Such a change is usually the first step in weaning the child off the initial high level of reinforcement (the technical term for this procedure is 'Fading').

The A4 Tutor
The mains powered A4 Tutor is the only teaching machine used in Beech Tree House (see Photograph 23). It is robust, cheap and simple for children to understand and operate; it requires no technical skill to set up; it is very easy to programme; it uses no expensive programme materials since the teacher requires no more than a pen and sheets of A4 paper and it can be linked to other devices in the unit – all essential features. Every other teaching machine that we have looked at has failed on at least two of these counts. It also folds down into a convenient package for carrying – a very useful attribute if not absolutely necessary. To date it has been used mainly with mentally handicapped, cerebral palsied children and in consequence certain features of its layout reflect this. However, there is no doubt that it could be very suitable for young normal children as well.

In operation the machine is simplicity itself. A question sheet containing up to eight questions is positioned on the vertical display panel and the answer selection sheet is placed on the horizontal response panel (see Diagram 18). A light comes on behind the first question and the child is required to select and touch the correct answer. If this is done successfully the machine acknowledges the correct response with a chime bell and the light moves to the second question. The machine ignores incorrect

A4 Tutor

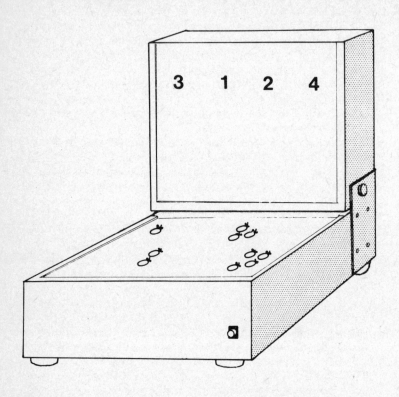

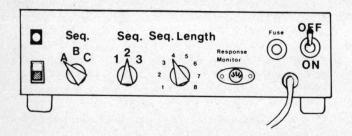

Diagram 18.   A4 Tutor – general view and control panel.

responses. When the child has completed all the questions correctly, the machine chimes until either the teacher or the child presses the reset button.

The machine is designed so that a given answer position does not regularly correspond to a given question position; the location of the correct areas on the response panel can be set in nine different configurations by simply turning two knobs at the rear of the machine. This prevents children from learning a trick, instead of thinking about the question.

An additional feature is the provision of a socket which can be used to activate another piece of apparatus. The attached device might take the form of a recorder which charts a child's response pattern, or perhaps an electrical toy which works when a child makes one or more correct responses. We have developed both types of module and have found that a reinforcing toy, controlled through a Switching Timer, is very effective in motivating certain children to use the A4 Tutor.

The Loop Aerial

It would probably be true to say that most investigators into the processes of education have, at one time or another, longed to have a robot teacher. Such a 'colleague' could be programmed to teach in different styles and might thereby enable the investigator to discover which teaching strategies were the most suitable under given conditions. Although I have yet to produce a robot teacher, I have worked with equipment which enables a very significant level of control to be exercised over a teacher's behaviour without the experimenter being in the classroom: a one-way screen and a Loop Aerial system.

Effectively, a Loop Aerial system performs like a short range radio transmitter, although it functions on rather different principles. Sounds picked up by the microphone connected to the system are sent via the amplifier and loop to hearing aids within the loop field, the latter being determined by the area enclosed within the wire loop itself. This is usually the room in which the system is installed. No cables are required between the hearing aids and the equipment because the aids act as radio receivers to whatever is fed into the loop aerial.

Normally this technique is employed in classrooms for hearing-impaired children, to eliminate the unwanted sounds of the class-room itself and the inevitable noises produced by body-worn equipment; the system is also installed in certain progressive places of entertainment to help the hard of hearing. In our work the system allows the observer to communicate with the teacher or residential therapist without disturbing the children. The technique has been referred to as the 'Bug in the Ear' approach.

In some of our earliest work we were able to demonstrate how important it was to interact with children when they had done the 'right' thing rather than when they were off target, although the latter course is the one adopted by most staff in group training situations. We were able to report dramatic improvements in work behaviour when a teacher praised children for being on target, and this was a surprise to some of our critics who predicted that such a strategy would disturb the children's concentration.

The Programmable Picture Clock

Some children find it very difficult to understand that time has elapsed, or that a task has to be completed in a given period. One boy presented us with a problem whenever he had finished his five minutes on the most popular of the Beech Tree House tricycles; like many young children he would claim that he had more time left (see Photograph 24). He was completely unable to understand even the passing of five minutes as shown by a normal clock. A girl in the unit was perfectly capable of dressing herself, but usually took so much time that breakfast had been eaten and cleared away before she appeared downstairs. Like the boy, she was unable to understand clocks, and so an alternative method of representing time had to be found.

The face of the Programmable Picture Clock takes the form of a circle with a wedge cut out. It is made of card and alternative faces can easily be substituted. On the face is drawn a series of pictures which are known to be understood by the child for whom the programme is designed. When the clock is started the mechanism turns the face in an anti-clockwise direction and the pictures are progressively drawn into the slot in the front of the machine. Eventually all the pictures disappear.

The reader will no doubt see the advantage of such a device. In the case of the boy, once all the tricycle riding pictures had gone, there was no more tricycle for him. The girl's programme and pictures were slightly more complicated. Her clock face had the various courses of breakfast depicted: cereal, main course, toast and cup of tea. As each of these disappeared, so she missed that course of the meal. After a couple of days of the programme it was clear that she recognised the significance of the disappearing pictures and her dressing speeded up dramatically.

In addition to the visual stimuli, the clock produces auditory reminders that time is passing. Throughout its running time it gives a loud, slow tick until it reaches the end, when it emits a loud, deep buzzing tone. It can also be set to buzz loudly for ten seconds, at times chosen by the programme makers. This option is usually selected to indicate when a picture is about to disappear. Thus it would occur whenever a course of the girl's meal was lost.

The speed at which the face disappears can also be predetermined, the range being from five minutes to approximately three quarters of an hour.

The Automatic Token Dispenser
Some children react badly to having tokens taken away from them by staff, and yet seem able to cope with a machine doing exactly the same thing. It is not suggested that they like losing the tokens in either situation, but that the latter is less traumatic. Perhaps it is a reaction akin to that of normal adults who usually find it more acceptable to be corrected by a teaching machine than by another adult. Possibly the 'error maker' is spared embarrassment when a machine makes the correction.

Certain behaviour occurs over such protracted periods of time that it is difficult to commit staff to observe and record it; this is especially true of in-bed behaviour at night. Ideally one needs a machine which can dispense tokens periodically for remaining in bed and take them away if the child gets out. The Automatic Token Dispenser meets both these requirements and those in the preceding paragraph.

The Automatic Token Dispenser is virtually a Token Bank with a built-in Fixed Interval Timer. It can be triggered to empty the accumulated tokens in the bank column into an internal reservoir by means of an ultrasonic tone or a pulse from another device (see Photograph 25). We have used it in two ways.

Firstly, the device has proved valuable in the classroom where it sits on a child's desk and periodically dispenses single tokens into the integral bank. Once a preset number have been given, the device whistles and the teacher goes to the child, praises him and releases the tokens from the bank column for the child to spend. If, on the other hand, the child displays unacceptable behaviour while the machine is in operation, the teacher can unobtrusively point her ultrasonic 'torch' at the machine and all the tokens disappear. She can then go and sympathise with the child and discuss what he might have done to cause the machine to behave in the way it did. If the teacher were seen to be responsible for the loss the child's resentment might preclude this opportunity for counselling.

The second way we have used the device is in conjunction with the Bed-Bug system. It is placed beside the child's bed so that he can see the tokens accruing in the bank column, and he is taught that if he gets out of bed he will lose the tokens earned up to that point. The device is triggered completely automatically by the Bed-Bug system itself and once set may be left for the night. The reader should note that the longer the child stays in bed the higher will be the cost of getting out.

In both examples the tokens are dispensed at regular intervals, the range being from one per minute to one every one and a half hours. The number dispensed before the machine signals the end of the session can be varied from one to ten. A gentle whistle can be set to accompany each token as it is dispensed, as can a subdued light behind the bank column. This latter feature was included to enhance the machine's effectiveness at night.

The Automatic Token Dispenser is a delightful device which has been of great value, but only on a very small number of occasions. I chose to feature it as the final item because it exemplifies what appears to be a rule about equipment: the more complicated a device is, the less likely it is to be used. The Automatic Token Dispenser has probably spent more than twice as long on the shelf as it has in operation. This is in contrast to most of our simpler gadgets which are in daily use, and resembles some of the other 'bright ideas' which we have abandoned and which, therefore, have not been described here.

4 TREVOR – A BOY WHO RESPONDED WELL TO A TOKEN ECONOMY

When I lecture I am aware that it is all too easy to lose an audience by forgetting to talk about children. Data, statistics and graphs are very important, as are the organisation of staff and the layout of buildings. But all of these details are secondary to the stories of Trevor, Emma, Peter and the rest of the children. This chapter should redress the balance. It is about Trevor – his problems, his successes and the methods we used to help him. Photographs 26 and 27 dramatically portray how he changed in a little over eighteen months: in the first we see a child drowsy from the effects of Largactil prescribed to dampen down his behaviour, and virtually bald from having plucked out his hair; in the second photograph he is shown peeling potatoes for lunch; he is clearly happy and alert, and his hair has regrown.

Trevor is Excluded from Meldreth Manor School

The story of our work with Trevor starts before Beech Tree House opened, for he was one of the children who convinced us that such a unit was needed. He was admitted to Meldreth Manor School in the autumn of 1976. It was known that he had only partial hearing, no speech, and that he neither signed nor used a symbolic communication system; there were suggestions that he had autistic tendencies. He had been assessed as severely mentally handicapped. At that time we were unaware that he had a range of difficult behaviour patterns and that he received medication to control them. Two months later the staff were all too familiar with his 'wickedness' and he was excluded from Meldreth Manor School.

The report which I prepared immediately after he left included the following information about the problem behaviour he displayed:

a) Breaking light fittings – by climbing up to them and hanging on, or more frequently by throwing shoes or toys at them (£62 of damage was reported in one eight-day period – 1976 prices).

b) Pulling threads from clothes, curtains, bedding, carpets, etc., and then eating them after playing with them. His faeces were found to contain an unbelievable assortment of such items.

   c)   Deliberately vomiting small amounts of food. This occurred in his bedroom – onto the floor, not into the bed; onto the dining room floor if he liked his meal, and across the table if he did not; and in other assorted locations.

   d)   Fiddling, almost ceaselessly, while awake with string, wool or whatever he could obtain of this nature to the virtual exclusion of other activities. He often threaded materials, swung or twirled them in an intricate way, paying rapt visual attention to these activities.

   e)   Avoiding contact. This included both eye and physical contact, and he appeared not to respond to either praise or correction.

In addition, he was the physiotherapists' public enemy number one. He located all their giant inflated therapy balls and bit irreparable holes in them!

Drugs to Control Behaviour
Beech Tree House opened in January 1977 and Trevor moved in on the seventeenth of the month. Notes made at the time were as follows:

> On arrival in Beech Tree House he was minus his hair and receiving a high drug dosage – 75 ml Largactil × 3 per day and 50 ml Disipal × 2 per day. The dosage was regarded as high by medical colleagues because Trevor was a very undersized eleven year-old.

In Peter Parish's *Medicines – A Guide for Everybody* the author states that 'Largactil, or Chlorporo-mazine Hydrocholoride, is a phenothiazine major tranquilliser.' Among the adverse effects he lists 'drowsiness, depression, indifference, dry mouth, pallor, weakness, nightmares and insomnia.' The reader is again referred to Photograph 26. Parish further recommends that 'doctors, pharmacists, nurses and anyone who handles the drug frequently should wear masks and rubber gloves,' and gives a list of side-effects including 'sensitivity of the skin to sunlight and muscle tremblings and rigidity (Parkinsonism and dystonias).' Perhaps this in part explains why Trevor received Disipal or Orphenedrinal Hydrochloride as well, for Peter Parish notes that this drug is used among other things 'to treat Parkinsonism.' However, among the adverse effects of Disipal are listed 'Insomnia, mental excitement, increased trembling (tremor) and nausea.'

There are, of course, differing views about the wisdom of using drugs to change children's behaviour and, some would say, ethical considerations as well, both for and against. I shall simply state that we do not use them to control behaviour in Beech Tree House. It seems clear to us that if drugs are effective in dampening down unwanted behaviour then we will have difficulty in establishing its full extent and exact nature. Furthermore, if a drug is effective it is likely to be so across the full spectrum of behaviour, including the child's ability to learn. Most teachers will be well aware how difficult it is for children to concentrate on a hot summer's day after a good lunch, and will sympathise with the following extract from my report describing Trevor on arrival:

> He spent most of his time during the day fitfully asleep but rose frequently to go to the lavatory where he strained and pressed the area of his bladder, presumably in an attempt to pass urine . . . He showed none of the destructive behaviour familiar from his earlier stay in the junior part of the school. We presume this was because he was heavily sedated. The lethargy exhibited by Trevor made it virtually impossible to commence any training programme.

In order to reduce and eventually eliminate the drugs which we felt were a barrier to Trevor learning new skills, we contacted the medical staff at the subnormality hospital from which he came. They would not agree to any reduction in the prescribed dosage. We explained that Trevor was now in a special unit modified and staffed to deal with children like him, but permission to make any changes was still refused. Fortunately, we were able to obtain a second opinion. We therefore contacted the Spastics Society's Consultant Psychiatrist who examined Trevor and provided us with a programme to fade out the drugs completely. Trevor responded well and, as the term neared its end, I again contacted senior staff at his former hospital (to which Trevor, in the ordinary way, would have returned during school holidays) and described the boy's improved behaviour. I pointed out that he now received no drugs and asked if they would continue this regime or at least use only minimal dosages. The reply was that he was 'written up for what he had when he left and that is what he will receive when he returns.' Nothing I said would change this attitude which was apparently shared by the doctor and senior nurse alike.

We responded by informing the local authority that we would look after Trevor in our own homes on an informal basis during the Easter holiday. Future holidays could be spent at the Spastics Society's Family Help Unit at Bury St Edmunds, an arrangement we saw as a tremendous advantage to Trevor because the head and staff at the Family Help Unit were very talented, and prepared to continue our training procedures. Eventually they became extremely fond of him.

Destructive Behaviour May Fill Void

As the first weeks in Beech Tree House passed and Trevor was eased out of his drug-induced trance, we attempted to reduce his problem behaviour by the simple expedient of offering a stimulating, home-like environment in which there was a great deal for him to do. Our premise was that if he was busy doing something useful and appropriate he would be unable to indulge in his repetitive, destructive time-filling behaviour. Professionally such behaviour is known as 'Stereotyped Behaviour'. The training strategy itself is known as a 'Competing Behaviour Strategy'.

We assumed that, rather as a prisoner of war in solitary confinement will resort to activities, often apparently bizarre, to occupy his time, so Trevor had learned to manipulate wool and string skilfully in order to fill similarly long, bland hours. This will not appear to be such an improbable suggestion to those who have worked in subnormality hospitals or who have seen the TV film *Silent Minority*. This documentary vividly protrayed the plight of some children in subnormality hospitals and contrasted this with what happened to similar children in Beech Tree House. Further support for the notion that Trevor had learned a way of occupying his time which was not particularly extraordinary is suggested by the many hours that young children spend playing cat's cradle games with string.

It seems distinctly possible that fiddling with string served a useful purpose for Trevor when he had little or nothing to do. For similar reasons we believe that much of the apparently bizarre behaviour shown by mentally handicapped people is, or has been, equally satisfying for them. The young man who beats his head against the wall, or the child who screams, will periodically gain the attention of nearby staff. The sad thing is that, when large numbers of handicapped people are herded together, each one has to 'up the stakes' to get a share of the adult attention.

Love, a Stimulating Environment and Education – Not Enough to Reduce Trevor's Behaviour Problems

Once he had settled in Beech Tree House, Trevor began to perform well when he was involved in household tasks under supervision, and later in certain classroom activities. After further psychological testing had indicated that he was possibly only moderately mentally handicapped, it was arranged that he should spend most days in a Meldreth Manor School class for the least severely mentally handicapped children. This continued for the first two terms. During his third term he spent most afternoons in a class of moderately mentally handicapped, partially hearing boys who communicated by means of the Paget-Gorman Signing System. It was hoped that this environment would encourage him to use the small amount of Paget he had learned in Beech Tree House.

By January 1978 it was clear that, although Trevor had learned many new skills, these had not replaced his passion for fiddling with string, wool, cotton, and so on. He was still inclined to damage his clothes to obtain the necessary threads. It was for this reason that one of the goals listed in his first Annual Report was as follows:

> Trevor will be put on a token economy. For the first two weeks he will be rewarded for appropriate behaviour, task completion, etc. During the subsequent phase his *clothes damaging* behaviour will be punished by removing tokens that he has earned. If he responds positively to this programme, we shall probably try a similar approach for his hair.

A Token Economy is Introduced
The idea that a coloured plastic disc has value is taught by showing the child what happens when one is put into a particular dispensing machine; we select one which gives the child something he really likes. Next, the child is taught to insert tokens for himself. Later, he has to complete tasks at which he is already adept and is immediately given a token to pop into the machine. Both the tasks and the rewarding are done in close proximity to the machine. The fourth stage is to get the child to do similar tasks in a room away from the dispenser. He carries the token to the machine and spends it and returns to his task. Only after this stage has been successfully negotiated for a week or so is it reasonable to expect the child to delay gratification by 'banking' his token.

Banking itself is also taught in simple stages. The child has to learn that a token put into the bank is available later. The first step involves one token remaining in the bank for a minute, and this time is gradually increased until finally it will remain there for five minutes. Once the child accepts this delay before being able to spend his token, two tokens will be saved for five minutes, and so on. Eventually tokens are only exchanged at the end of a lesson or when a target number is reached – indicated by a small picture of the desired 'purchase' stuck in the appropriate position on the perspex covering the token column. Thus a picture of a telephone might be stuck over the fifth token position on Jane's bank column, a picture of a jam-filled pancake on the seventh position of Ivan's and that of a car on the tenth position of our other Ivan's bank.

Trevor was trained exactly as described above to understand that tokens were valuable. However, he was not taught about 'banks' because in 1978 we had not invented them. He grasped the token concept and procedure very quickly, and it was an equally rewarding time for staff. A smile would transform Trevor's usually 'dead pan' expression as he received his token, and he would then gallop to the Sweet Dispenser to spend it. His willingness to wash and dry up, help lay tables, pick up scattered toys, and so on, improved dramatically. Prior to tokens being introduced he had joined in such activities, but with little apparent enthusiasm.

Both Reward and Punishment are Used

All these improvements were very encouraging, but they were merely bonuses along the way: our goal was to use the tokens to stop Trevor damaging his clothes. We decided to try a combined reward and punishment strategy. Each morning after Trevor had chosen his clothes and was bathing, a member of staff examined them very carefully to ascertain whether any were imperfect. This was important because it would have been unjust to punish Trevor later for damage he had not done. Trevor then dressed and his day continued as before.

In the unlikely event of someone catching Trevor in the act of damaging his clothes, he was 'told off'. Because he was partially hearing, this was done by the member of staff putting on an angry face, cupping his chin in her hand and making him look at her while she emphatically signed 'No!' in Paget. Having done this she would grip Trevor firmly by both shoulders and give a very brief backward and forward movement of two or three centimetres distance – a sort of rudimentary shake – before immediately pointing to the damaged item, again cupping his chin in her hand and once more signing 'No!' Trevor usually responded by looking crestfallen, then sheepish. All interactions of this sort were recorded.

As it turned out there were few such notes. Over the years Trevor had learned to be very circumspect about damaging things – indeed, we wonder if his swallowing of wool and string had any parallels with the behaviour of folk heroes like James Bond. We all cheer inwardly when Bond swallows the secret formula to prevent it falling into the hands of some dreadful enemy. Swallowing the evidence of a damaged curtain or carpet might have saved

Trevor from punishment on many occasions. If we are correct in our surmise, then this apparently peculiar aspect of his behaviour can be seen as functional – it got rid of the incriminating evidence.

Only when Trevor was observed through a one-way screen was it possible to see how he set about acquiring a length of wool, for he gave the impression to the staff with him that he was industriously involved in whatever task he had been given to do. He would watch the member of staff attentively out of the corner of his eye and as soon as it was clear that she was involved with something else, he would begin to 'worry' at a cuff or the waist band of his jumper. The moment he saw her turning towards him his hand would flash back to what he was supposed to be doing. The concentration and skill he put into both watching her and working to loosen a thread was startling. Having got sufficient thread he would quickly stuff it into his pocket for later use. It has to be admitted that there was often great, but suppressed, hilarity among the observers who could see so clearly how Trevor was able to outwit the adults trying their best to catch him in the act of unravelling his clothes.

At bed-time, after Trevor had taken off his clothes and laid them on his bed, he put on his dressing gown and went to the bathroom. Meanwhile, a member of staff checked each item of clothing carefully and placed them on one of two piles, the undamaged and the damaged. When Trevor returned, the pantomine of giving and taking away tokens took place.

The first of these sessions (which I observed and recorded from behind the partially closed bedroom door) was the first time Trevor had ever had a token away from him. On this occasion there were four undamaged items out of seven. When Trevor returned to his bedroom he found Alison sitting on his bed with the two piles of clothes beside her.

She signed for him to sit next to her and to turn and face her. She wreathed her face with smiles, held up the first undamaged item, signed 'Good', rubbed Trevor's cheek and gave him a token. Trevor received this with what appeared to be mingled surprise and pleasure. When the next item was held up and the second token was similarly given, this time accompanied by an emphatically signed 'very good', Trevor could hardly contain his pleasure. He grinned, rocked to and fro and rubbed the side of his nose with his forearms – always a reliable sign that he was pleased. His smiling, rocking and gentle nose-rubbing increased as he received two more tokens.

Trevor was still gently rocking, suffused with pleasure, when he noticed that the situation had altered dramatically. Alison's face

DAMAGE TO CLOTHES SCHEDULE

DATE .... T.E. DAY .... TOKEN COLOUR ....

Item	A.M. Condition	P.M. Condition	Tokens Given	Tokens Withdrawn
Jacket				
Cardigan				
Jumper				
Shirt				
Trousers				
Pants				
Vest				
Sock				
Sock				
Handkerchief				

Checker's Initial Entries

Figure 11.   Trevor's clothes tearing record sheet.

had changed; she was now glaring at him ferociously. He lowered his eyes and sat still. Alison cupped his chin in her hand, pointed accusingly at the unravelled sleeve of his jumper, signed 'No!' emphatically, then took the hand in which he clutched his so recently acquired tokens, uncurled his fingers and removed one of the tokens. Trevor went pale. Alison snatched up a sock, jabbed with her finger at the torn top, signed 'No!' and 'Silly!' and removed a second token from his hand. Trevor's eyes watered and a tear trickled down his cheek. As Alison started to hold up his torn shirt he appeared to grasp the full significance of the situation and, flinging his two remaining tokens at Alison, he lay on his bed and sobbed. 'Got the young monkey!' I whispered to Alison from behind the door.

Are the bureaucrats grabbing for their pens to condemn this dreadful punishment? Shall we see the following headlines, 'Mentally handicapped boy fined for damaging clothes,' 'Bedtime punishment for deaf child'? Probably not. But some readers may be worried, some may feel we overstepped the mark. All I can say to reassure them is that, within three months, Trevor rarely lost a token. After all, the remedy was within his own hands. He could stop damaging his clothes, and he did.

Unfortunately he continued to eat other people's jumpers and socks, and fairly tucked into curtains and carpets! This is known as a problem of 'Generalisation'. I shall return to this and how we dealt with it later in the chapter.

Recording Progress
Whenever we run training programmes we collect data. This is important if we are to keep track of progress, or the lack of it; if there is no progress it is clear that the programme has failed. We believe that it is vital to clarify this point – it is programmes that fail, not children. We do not take this stance out of false sentiment but rather because it is the only practical way to look at the situation. The fact is we cannot change the physiological make-up of our children, particularly their neurological make-up, so if a programme designed to teach Trevor to tie his shoe laces fails to work, it is no help to moan about how very 'dim' he is. Even if this conclusion were true it could not be changed. The remedy is to re-examine the programme and redesign it so that he does eventually succeed. Perhaps, for example, the steps within the programme should be made smaller and therefore easier for him to master. Figure 11 shows the schedule we used to collect data regarding Trevor's performance on the programme to stop him spoiling his clothes.

The 'A.M.' column was used to note any damage to clothes before Trevor put them on. If no further deterioration took place he was rewarded for that item in the evening. The 'P.M.' column was used to record any damage that had been done during the day. The 'Tokens Given/Withdrawn' columns were used to note the number of tokens involved with each item. Warmhearted readers should be reassured that the token giving ceremony was always calculated to leave Trevor with at least one token: if he had damaged five out of eight items he would receive two tokens for each of the three undamaged ones and lose one token for each of the five that were damaged. Our reasoning, however, was motivated less by warm hearts than by the conviction that it was important not to 'turn off' Trevor's interest in the nightly sessions. He had experienced so much failure, it was vital to ensure that his successes were predominant.

Once Trevor had reached the point when damage to his own clothes occurred no more than once or twice a week, we started the generalisation programme. Now he was to learn to refrain from damaging anything.

Generalising the Improved Behaviour
Our strategy was simple: we introduced the 'Ripping Box'. This intriguing-sounding device was made of stout brown cardboard and had the following words on the side: 'One dozen boxes Weetabix'. We kept this in the office during the day and anything that Trevor damaged was put into it. If he was caught actually doing damage he was remonstrated with as described earlier, the item was taken away and went into the box. In the evening the Ripping Box was taken upstairs and brought out once Trevor had received his tokens and praise for his undamaged clothes. Like an irate conjuror pulling rabbits from a hat, the member of staff would take out each damaged item, sign to Trevor how bad he was and fine him a token. The procedure worked within two months and we were able to enter the next phase of training, designed to stop Trevor plucking out his hair.

Here we were confronted with a different problem – we rarely found any of the hair Trevor removed, and then only a few hairs under his pillow. If we were going to use the Ripping Box approach we needed a good visual aid to pull from its depths. We resorted to other people's hair, kindly donated by the local hairdresser.

The training procedure was very simple. Once Trevor had received his tokens for not damaging his clothes the Ripping Box would appear. The member of staff would point at Trevor's head with apparent horror, tap the area from which it appeared that more hair had been removed, pull the small bunch of hair from the box, sign 'No' emphatically, match the hair to the most recently plucked area, sign 'No' emphatically again and finally take away two or three of Trevor's tokens. It has to be admitted that Trevor usually looked surprised, particularly when the tuft of hair was produced. Perhaps he remembered disposing of it safely and was amazed we had discovered it. We shall never know. What we do know is that the programme worked and he stopped removing his hair within two weeks of its commencement.

It would be easy to stop at this point and allow the reader to assume that the tokens and the programme as described were alone responsible for the progress that Trevor made. Possibly they were, but other strategies were being employed which no doubt influenced the outcome. Some of these were deliberately designed to increase Trevor's chances of succeeding, others were features of daily life in Beech Tree House which probably played their part. Readers who have picked up this book anticipating a series of 'clean' behaviour modification case histories, in which a specific strategy can be credited with certain changes in a child's behaviour, had better put it down. We see our work as embracing the whole child, using as many methods as possible to effect change as rapidly as we can. 'Uncontaminated' programmes in which all factors not in the programmes remain fixed, thereby ensuring that the programmes themselves can be seen to be responsible for whatever changes occur, are rarely used – ours is an educational setting, not a laboratory. It follows that in Trevor's case we were doing our very best in a variety of ways to enhance the outcome of his token programme.

H.G. Wells once said something to the effect that, 'One of the most exquisite pleasures is to pick at a small scab on one's scalp!' I have often quoted this remark at lectures and many audiences have nodded knowingly. I confess to sharing this fascination. In a very small way we can consider this behaviour self injurious and yet we indulge – particularly when our hands are less than fully occupied. Another self injurious habit which is incredibly difficult for the reformed addict to refrain from is that of smoking; this is true long after the drug withdrawal phase has ceased. Although I have not smoked once in the past five years, I still experience strong urges to 'light up' after virtually every meal and whenever I enjoy a pint. The behaviour is obviously deeply ingrained and certain settings, sometimes called 'discriminative stimuli', evoke a very strong urge to revert to it. We considered that Trevor might well have been experiencing similar problems, especially when he lay in bed, this being the only place where we had ever noted evidence, of hair plucking. If this was the case, in order to make it difficult for him to gain sufficient purchase on his hair to pull it out, and also to reduce the temptation to fiddle with it – a possible precursor to plucking – we had what remained of his hair crew-cut. It was kept in this fashion for some weeks after we were satisfied that the plucking behaviour had ceased. In this way we reduced the saliency of the long hair discriminative stimulus.

Rechannelling Former Problem Behaviour

We reached similar conclusions about Trevor's clothes unravelling behaviour. In this case we decided that he would be taught to make Readicut rugs. This activity, which he was very keen on, was available to him whenever he was not involved in class, mealtimes, jobs around the unit or organised games. An activity using wool and material was selected because we were well aware that Trevor had had a passionate interest in fiddling with wool and thread for a number of years; we were looking for something which would capitalise on this. A variety of tasks, including knitting, weaving, French knitting, sewing and tapestry work were tried; Trevor preferred to make rugs and rapidly became very adept at this. His interest was so great that eventually he was prepared to pay tokens to be allowed to do the work! He became so proficient that when we ran out of funds to buy any more rug-making materials staff invested in kits which Trevor made up for them to give to their relations for Christmas. Once this happened, he could enjoy both the pleasure of using the kits and the bonuses he earned in the form of boxes of sweets and trips out to select new rugs, with the obligatory meals at the Little Chef. Having nothing to do had previously been a discriminative stimulus to clothes damaging behaviour. Now it triggered Trevor to get his rug making kit.

Are Children 'Cured'?

The success that Trevor achieved prompts me to consider whether or not we *cure* children of problem behaviour. This seems most un-likely. Often visitors put us into a Catch–22 situation when they comment on the behaviour they witness. If the children are 'good' when visitors meet them they naturally conclude that they are not like the difficult children *they* work with in their school or hostel or ward. If, on the other hand, the children act out their problem behaviour, the visitors decide our methods do not work. In response to the first conclusion, we explain that, in our experience, if good children are returned to their previous environments without any changes being made there, the behaviour which brought them to Beech Tree House is likely to recur. We go on to stress that in many cases those apparently bizarre habits which brought them to us were in fact functional, in other words, in the environment in which they were learned they served a purpose for the child.

Trevor Slips Back

Trevor's later progress in Beech Tree House demonstrated the reversion phenomenon very clearly indeed. Some months after his hair had regrown and his unravelling behaviour had all but disappeared, he had to spend a holiday in a unit unfamiliar to him. We took the normal steps of forwarding reports, discussing Trevor with the staff and visiting with him so that he could meet them and explore the environment; sending rug making kits, having Beech Tree House staff visit him at the start of the holiday, and so on. Despite these preparations the placement went wrong. We understand that, although a great deal was laid on for the children, Trevor failed to 'opt in'. We also understand that he lost the tool for pegging his rug. It seems likely that he spent considerable periods of time isolated by his inability to communicate and his reluctance to participate and that he had little or nothing constructive to do. Tragically he resorted to his old time-filling patterns. At the end of the holiday he had destroyed over £120-worth of new clothes and had only a track suit made of tightly woven nylon to come home in. Approximately one third of his hair had been plucked out (see Photograph 28).

Figures 12 to 15 have been prepared to illustrate what happened to Trevor. They should be seen as true in essence for most of our children, although the detailed behaviour will of course be different.

Figure 12 refers to the reader's present behaviour (i.e. reading this book) and a number of alternatives that he or she could produce. It is suggested that at any moment there is for each of us a hierarchy of possible behaviour which we could emit, and that past experience combined with the prevailing situation determines which of the many possible behaviour patterns will be displayed. The hierarchy of behaviour Trevor would produce in an under-stimulating environment on his arrival in Beech Tree House is shown in Figure 13.

What we try to do when training our children is to give them a new hierarchy of behaviour to cope with situations in which they formerly produced anti-social or unacceptable patterns. If necessary, as in the case of Trevor, the unacceptable behaviour at the top of the hierarchy with which they arrived is made less

Hierarchy of Possible Behaviour for the Reader of This Book

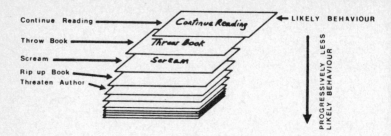

Figure 12.   Hierarchy of possible behaviour for the reader of this book.

attractive by being punished. More usually we ignore this behaviour while rewarding alternative patterns, so relegating the earlier, unacceptable patterns to the 'basement'. Unfortunately they will be dragged out again if the newer behaviour ceases to be rewarded. It will be seen in Figure 15 that Trevor was taught a very acceptable and functional loop to cope with 'boring' situations. If he tired of a particular activity he packed it away and took out something else, usually a Readicut kit or a Lego assembly toy. If

Some of Trevor's Problems which came to the top of His Hierarchy when he had Nothing to do

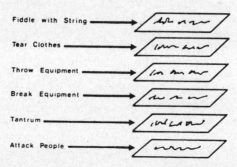

Figure 13.   Hierarchy of behaviour displayed by Trevor in an under-stimulating situation.

Replacing Unwanted Behaviour With Acceptable Alternatives

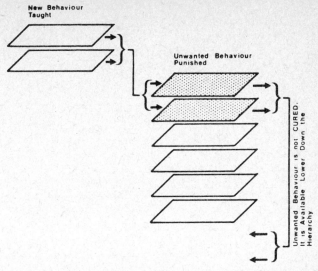

Figure 14.   Replacing unwanted behaviour with acceptable alternatives.

New Functional Loop and Possible Reversion Loop

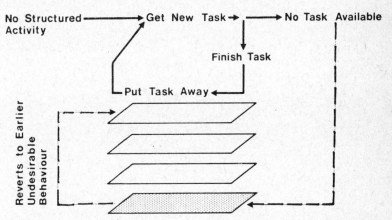

Figure 15.   The new functional loop and possible reversion loop, showing how near the surface was Trevor's old, unacceptable behaviour.

necessary he would involve staff in getting him something new. The reader should also note from Figure 15 that only a few steps further down the hierarchy is the 'basement'. If the loop is broken, that is, if no alternative activities are available, the old behaviour patterns are perilously close to re-surfacing to fill the vacuum. It is because we realise these dangers exist for each of our retrained children that we work so assiduously to pave the way for each of them to return home or to their new school. It would be totally unrealistic to expect them to transfer their new skills without considerable help.

Once Trevor was back in Beech Tree House the token economy was re-established. There was one major difference, however: all three aspects of his destructive behaviour were treated at once – clothes unravelling, damage to the fabrics in the unit and removal of his hair. He resumed his good patterns within days and there were no relapses. He eventually transferred for two terms to the Independent Living House at Meldreth Manor School where he lived with two staff and five other children. From there he attended a local Adult Training Centre one day per week. In September 1982 he transferred so successfully to the Spastics Society's Dene College for a further two years' education, that we have reason to be guardedly optimistic about his future.

5 STAFFING

Many of our visitors remark on the organisation of the staff in Beech Tree House, for, in their experience, it has unusual features. None of the practices described below, however, arise out of 'philosophical whims' of the staff who established the unit – on the contrary, they are practical alternatives to methods of staff organisation which currently obtain in many centres for handicapped children – methods which we believe undermine the possibility of establishing the most favourable environment for the children. If we have made any significant contribution to the understanding of methods of helping handicapped children, it will probably be in this area of our work. We believe that a number of our methods of organising staff could usefully be tried in other units.

The Structure of Staff

Figure 16 shows the hierarchy of responsibility within Beech Tree House. It should be noted that the Deputy Head is not a teacher but a member of the care worker team. This is a most important feature of the staff structure because the appointment endorses our conviction that care workers play a key role in training our children. Teachers are, of course, very important, but they are contracted to work considerably shorter hours with the children on a face-to-face basis than the care workers: in addition, there are fewer of them. It follows that care workers spend a great deal more time with the children than any other staff do and that as a group they are likely to be the most potent in changing the children's behaviour. Such a preponderance of care workers is typical of most residential units for handicapped children and it seems very odd that, as a rule, this, the potentially most influential group, is the least regarded, the lowest paid, the hardest worked and the least involved in decision making. In Beech Tree House we have attempted to redress the balance in a number of ways, the most obvious of these being the appointment of the most senior care worker as Deputy Head. This demonstrates our high regard for care workers to outsiders and new colleagues alike. In theory it might be possible to appoint a suitable care worker as Head of Unit; in practice this cannot be the case because the Department

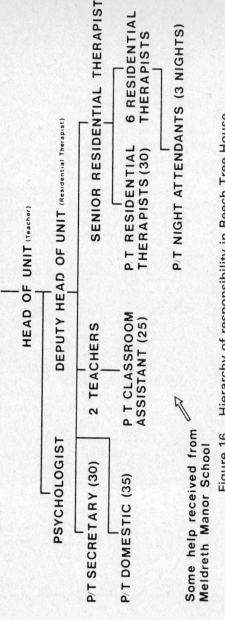

Figure 16.   Hierarchy of responsibility in Beech Tree House.

Notes: a) The Psychologist and the Project Co-ordinator are the same person. b) The hours/nights quoted in brackets refer to the total input from all part-time staff in a given category per week. c) Meldreth Manor School is reimbursed for the professional help and services received.

of Education and Science understandably requires that the Head
of a school is a qualified teacher.

Our care workers are known as Residential Therapists, a title
for which we are indebted to Roger Burland, Principal of Chelfam
Mill School. We were unhappy with the term care worker, and
with other commonly used terminology such as house mother, care
staff or residential social worker, for we did not feel that they did
justice to the contribution which can only be made by this group of
workers. On the contrary, calling them care workers can imply that
they are only able to mind children and deal with their bodily
functions as though they were low-level tasks requiring little or no
skill. While this may be true of many care workers who are given
no opportunities for developing understanding and expertise, such
a narrowing of their role is really a waste of a potentially valuable
resource. It is particularly regrettable when this results from the
attitude of professionally trained colleagues who jealously guard
their own areas of interest, for such pettiness diminishes rather
than enhances their status. Our experience clearly indicates that,
given opportunity and in-service training, care workers can excel
in a wide range of therapeutic skills.

Initially, however, we were cautious about using the term
Residential Therapist, owing to the proliferation in recent years
of helpers of the handicapped who have chosen to style themselves
as Therapists: Music Therapists, Art Therapists, Horticultural
Therapists, Drama Therapists – to name but a few. In certain
instances we feel that the term 'therapy' is a rather grand way of
describing the activity involved and that the consequent use of the
'therapist' title to describe the person who organises the activity is
somewhat at odds with the quality and importance of the work
undertaken by the paramedical therapists – Physiotherapists,
Speech Therapists and Occupational Therapists. If spending an
hour or so a week making music with children is considered to be
therapeutic (and this we can accept) how much more so is the
training in the everyday aspects of children's lives that our
Residential Therapists are responsible for. We feel their case is a
particularly strong one because they do not restrict themselves to
dealing with one isolated and arguably low priority activity but are
centrally involved in developing, implementing, modifying and
evaluating detailed training procedures essential to each child's
future well being. Beech Tree House children receive training, or
therapy, throughout their waking day and the major part of this
training is carried out by Residential Therapists. It therefore
seems very reasonable to us to clarify the important nature of their
role by the Therapist title.

The Myth of the Multidisciplinary Team

Perhaps the greatest barrier to the efficient implementation of training programmes in most schools, development centres, hospitals and other institutions working with handicapped children, arises out of divisions between different groups of staff. Many head teachers and consultants are guilty of self-deception when they describe their staff as forming a multidisciplinary team. On close examination, lines of demarcation will usually be found between sub-groups of staff who make up the supposed team, and the members of each sub-group will tend to function within these circumscribed boundaries. Communication between the sub-groups will typically be ritualised by memos and meetings.

Frequently the sub-grouping structure is officially endorsed by departments being formed. Such departmentalisation normally serves to ossify the demarcation lines between the sub-groups. Along with the autonomy that department status confers upon its members, there tends to go an inward regard that focuses upon the department rather than the organisation it was formed to serve. There is a frequent closing of department ranks against 'them'. The fragmentation of staff into groups is often exacerbated by membership of unions and professional organisations which reflect levels of training and by widely differing salaries and conditions of service.

As organisations grow larger, so departments increase in size, and it is not uncommon for distinct physical premises to be established on a departmental basis. When this happens the client is usually obliged to trek from department to department to receive the full range of services offered by the organisation.

In Beech Tree House we have recognised the possibility that sub-grouping of staff could occur and have striven to avoid it. The relative smallness of the unit and its family-like atmosphere appears to be one significant bulwark against fragmentation into departments. The unit was opened to cater for six children; it expanded to cater for nine. Pressures to take more have been resisted for it has been decided that this would run counter to our philosophy. In our opinion any expansion of the service should take place in new Beech Tree Houses located elsewhere. It is proposed that these should continue the intimate, family approach pioneered in the first unit.

We have given considerable thought to the problems plaguing establishments that bring together different disciplines to train handicapped children, and our conclusions have influenced many aspects of the staff training and ethos established in Beech Tree House. It is hoped that our departures from more traditional staff training formulae will be recognized as the result of careful rationalisation. They are directed to maximising the service we offer to our children.

Multidisciplinary Teams Contrasted with Client Centred Teams

I am sure I am not alone in finding that so-called multidisciplinary teams frequently devolve into interdisciplinary sparring matches. This terrible waste of talent is particularly common when staff are organised into professional hierarchies with the most senior members of each professional pyramid having no direct involvement with the clients. The majority of subnormality hospitals and large residential schools are organised in this way (see Figure 17).

In such an organisation the front-line staff have their professional or union reference point outside the group in which they work. The pitfalls of such a method of organisation are obvious: change on the shop floor will rarely occur without involved, time-consuming interdepartmental discussions at the

Traditional Organisation of Management of à Ward or Small Residential School for Handicapped Children

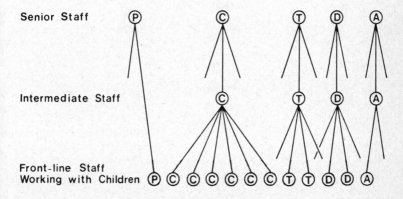

Figure 17. Functional organisational hierarchy in a ward or small residential school for handicapped children.

In this figure five groups of staff and their respective management structures are shown. The workers depicted are: P = Psychologist; C = Care staff; T = Teachers; D = Domestics; A = Administrative staff. Members of each of these groups make a specific and restricted contribution to the care of the children and responsibilities do not overlap. While this division of labour avoids duplication of effort it serves to fragment any team ethos. The staff are organised into management hierarchies according to their function. The staff who work face-to-face with the children do not make decisions about the nature of their work or the role that they play on an inter-professional basis. Decisions of this type are left to senior staff who play an administrative role. Interdepartmental matters are likewise settled at senior staff level.

highest levels; disagreements at shop floor level will embroil heads of departments who may have little idea of the special needs prevailing in a particular ward or school 'house'; nationally negotiated conditions of service may be uniformly applied and may, as a result, impose inflexible lines of demarcation between colleagues of different professions; and so on.

An alternative method which neatly avoids the problems inherent in hierarchical organisation-by-profession or organisation-by-function is one in which all the staff who work as an identifiable group, say on a ward or in a school 'house', are, regardless of profession, made responsible to one member of the group itself. They form a Client Centred Team and only the team leader has a formal organisational reference point outside the group. This type of structure tends to focus each worker's attention within the group because it is only by within-group activity and negotiation that each person can attain his or her day-to-day professional goals. Likewise, changes in conditions of

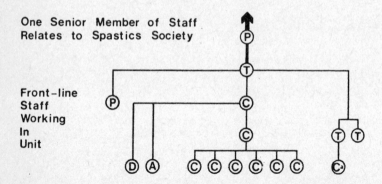

Client Centred Staff Structure – After B.T.H.

One Senior Member of Staff Relates to Spastics Society

Front-line Staff Working In Unit

Figure 18.   Client centred staff structure on the Beech Tree House model.

Six types of staff are shown. They are: P = Psychologists; T = Teachers; C = Care Staff; D = Domestics; A = Administrative staff; Ca = Classroom assistants. The model shown is based directly upon the Beech Tree House model (see Figure 16). Each person has a primary role but will, from time to time, undertake duties normally done by colleagues of a different discipline. There is no division into hierarchies on the basis of different functions performed by staff. The most senior member of the team is the Head of Unit who is a teacher. Professional balance is maintained by the Deputy Head being a Residential Therapist (Care Worker). Most decisions concerning the running of the unit are taken at the weekly Team Meeting which all full-time staff attend. The Psychologist has a dual function: he works as the unit psychologist and in this role takes directions from the Head of Unit; he is also the co-ordinator of the Beech Tree House projects and is the link in the line management between the unit and the Spastics Society. In this role he is regarded as the most senior member of staff.

work, rotas and so on are agreed internally within the constraints laid down by the employing authority. Beech Tree House is organised in this manner. See Figure 18.

Democracy and the Team Meeting
Client Centred Teams of the type described above may be organised on democratic or authoritarian lines. In an authoritarian Client Centred Team a small elite group of staff makes the majority of decisions; in an extreme example of authoritarianism, the team leader makes virtually all decisions. In a democratic organisation all staff, or their elected representatives, are involved in taking decisions in collaboration with each other. Beech Tree House strives to follow the democratic model, not for any philosophical reason but because during the past years it has proved to be the most efficient method.

Before the Team Meeting had evolved to its present form, treatment programmes were devised by experienced senior staff. They were explained to junior staff who would be urged to follow them meticulously: sometimes they did, and sometimes they did not. Today we are confident that programmes are implemented unit-wide by all staff, simply because all staff are involved in formulating programmes, evaluating the staffing implications, determining data collecting procedures and assigning a team member to co-ordinate the collective effort. This approach takes considerably longer in the discussion stage than the programming-by-edict method adopted initially; however we feel that the additional time spent in talking through every aspect is fully justified by the enthusiasm and insight with which each programme is eventually carried out. In the long run time is saved.

The Team Meeting is not limited to evolving programmes: any topic can be raised for discussion by any member of the team. It is a weekly meeting, lasting two hours, which all full-time staff attend. The children are looked after by part-time colleagues who later attend a briefing session of about forty-five minutes. The agenda may include items on rotas, timetabling, equipment, criticism of the way an activity has been organised, suggestions for fund raising, a formal staff training lecture, a budget report, items raised by part-time colleagues, and so on. It is the forum at which information is shared, problems are dispelled and decisions are reached. It is the core of Beech Tree House democracy. Through it we achieve a team-wide sharing of goals.

Encouraging Consistent Staff Behaviour
A question frequently levelled at the Head of Beech Tree House

is, 'But aren't you too well qualified and highly paid to be washing up or toilet training or cooking?' The answer is a categorical 'No'. Each member of the team must know the skills and deficiencies of each child and the strengths and weaknesses of each colleague if she is to contribute fully in planning, programming and teaching. If the team leader denies herself this knowledge she becomes a mere consultant or administrator. The more remote the head of an institution is, the less likely her goals will reflect the needs of the clients and the staff who work directly with them. We advocate leadership by example as well as by direction, for, apart from any other considerations, inexperienced staff pick up good practices most quickly when they work side by side with skilful colleagues.

All staff are aware that mistakes can be made in carrying out programmes. Such mistakes may occur because a colleague missed a Team Meeting at which a particular strategy was revised; because a colleague is under the weather and is running out of patience; because a colleague has simply forgotten the agreed strategy or because some vital detail was overlooked at the planning stage. Whatever the reason, the friendly relationships between staff enable non-threatening help to be offered or advice given. The ease with which such mutual support is offered and received is particularly striking when it is a junior member of the team who helps a senior colleague.

Visitors are sometimes surprised at the friendly and confident manner with which all staff speak to each other. We believe that such ease of communication is vital if ideas are to permeate freely and high standards are to be maintained. It is fostered, in part, by staff with different backgrounds working alongside each other: through this they learn to perceive each other as friends involved in the same job rather than as professional associates with different responsibilities doing rather different things, albeit with the same children and to the same end. The following recent example nicely clarifies this point. A residential therapist who had left the unit to study for a diploma in residential care was visited by three of her friends from Beech Tree House. One of these was a teacher. Her fellow care worker students expressed great surprise that such a close inter-professional friendship had developed; it was something that none of them had experienced. We do not find such friendship patterns at all surprising: in Beech Tree House, staff with very different professional backgrounds are as likely to holiday together, attend leisure activities together and so on as those with the same basic qualifications; the professional barriers have been broken by equality in decision making, joint participation in staff training and by role sharing.

Each member of staff is appointed to the unit to play a primary function: teachers teach, typists type and domestics clean. However, if interdisciplinary understanding is to be promoted it is appropriate to timetable staff to sample each other's duties. This policy has been vigorously followed, and consequently the Head of Unit teaches and does care work and domestic duties; the residential therapists spend a lot of time in the classroom helping children learn self-help skills, as well as joining in other classroom activities, and they also share in administrative duties; the secretary, likewise, spends what small amount of time she can spare with the children and thus knows the subjects of the reports and programmes that she types. This pattern is repeated for all staff.

The value of shared roles and the consequent mutual understanding can often be detected at the Team Meeting. For example, as training programmes are evolved and their staffing implications are considered, everyone readily appreciates the impact that the proposed strategies will have on themselves and their colleagues; similarly, when timetable revisions are being considered, the entire staff can participate. Over and above such practical considerations is the fact that the act of role sharing contributes to a team ethos. Working together on the 'shop floor' has another advantage, too: more experienced staff can demonstrate methods of teaching to less experienced colleagues without the stultifying atmosphere that can infect even the best workshops and lectures.

Staff Turnover
In analysing staffing at Beech Tree House we have found it useful to speak in terms of Core Staff and Transient Staff. Core Staff are those members of the team who, it is anticipated, will stay for two or more years; typically they are the qualified members who have already embarked on their careers, are usually relatively well paid and frequently have a post with considerable responsibility. We include among the Core Staff the Head and Deputy Head, the Senior Residential Therapist and the teachers. Part-time staff of all disciplines tend to fall into this category as well, because they are normally married and live in the local community, and therefore stay for a number of years. They are exceptions in that they rarely earn high salaries and do not hold senior posts, but they certainly help to maintain continuity. Transient Staff are usually junior Residential Therapists and our expectation is that they will work for one year. Many of them see their appointment to our staff as an opportunity to obtain experience. A significant proportion have been graduates who have left us to study for post graduate

qualifications in an allied field, for example, in psychology or social work.

During the early phase of our work we did not make the Core/-Transient distinction because we felt that all staff should be prepared to remain for at least two years to 'give the children stability'. We had not bargained with the exhausting nature of the work done by the junior staff, and had to revise our expectations when faced with a significant number of individuals whose work deteriorated in their second year of service after an initial outstanding one. So the concept of Transient Staff was born. We feel that the rapid 'burning out' can in part be explained by the fact that junior Residential Therapists spend virtually all their working time in face-to-face contact with the children. More senior staff have periods of administration, supervisory and preparatory duties. There have of course been remarkable exceptions where junior staff have continued to make a major contribution into their third year. When the Transient Staff leave they tend to gain promotion or to undertake further training. A small number have concluded that they were mistaken in wishing to work with handicapped people and have moved into other types of work.

We do not regard the annual change in the Transient Staff as a problem since the core and part-time staff provide the necessary stability. We begin each year with an influx of enthusiastic young people, and because each new team is appointed before the autumn term starts, we have an opportunity to run an intensive, resident, staff training week towards the end of the summer holiday. By means of video recordings, slide presentations, role play sessions and formal lectures, the new team members have a very clear idea of what to expect and how to react when the children walk through the door on the first Sunday of term.

Fortunately, we have found that staff changes are not as unsettling as we had foreseen. It is important to remember that Beech Tree House pupils are not admitted for long term education – they are there for as brief a period of training as will enable them to settle into special schools which cater for their primary handicaps. Such short stays are unlikely to be disrupted by one change of approximately a third of the staff. The situation is further eased because changes in staff usually coincide with the long summer holiday during which the children no doubt begin to forget about last year's staff, and when they return there are of course many familiar faces to welcome them back.

A final important point is that we always undertake not to displace the parents in their children's affection. This possibility has worried many families and it is a topic which we discuss with all parents before a child is admitted to the unit. We explain that we will always try and keep memories of the family fresh in the child's mind by talking about events at home, by reading and rereading the weekly letters from parents, brothers and sisters, and by encouraging use of the telephone; we do our best to ensure that when parents stay in the unit the visits are enjoyable. A useful spin-off from our efforts to preserve the family as the children's emotional focus is a consequent reduction in the untoward impact of any changes in the staff. Children rarely appear to develop close emotional ties with staff, although there is usually a fairly super-ficial but happy and friendly relationship. It has to be admitted that closer ties have developed where children have had no families or where the home situation has been an unhappy one and, according to the circumstances, this is a contingency for which special provision has to be determined.

Staffing Levels

Below a certain staff-to-child ratio the quality of care in any institution becomes less than adequate. The staff-to-child ratio that marks the transition from inadequate to adequate care we have termed the Minimum Adequate Level of Care (MALC). Discussions with staff from other institutions suggest that in a worrying number of instances the MALC point is rarely reached. There is a second staff-to-child ratio of importance: the point when all care needs are fully met and additional increments of staff can be devoted to education, in its broadest sense. This we have termed the Transition to Education Level (TEL).

When children with different needs are being catered for, the two staff-to-child ratios will vary; more able and responsible children will require fewer staff. Hypothetical, but not unrealistic figures are given in Table 1 to clarify this point. They are based on the typical staff-to-child ratios found in good schools and residential centres and they match current professional recommendations.

Problems arise when comparisons are made between staffing levels in different units. In order to be meaningful, like must be compared with like and unless this elementary precaution is taken the staff-to-child ratios in a unit such as Beech Tree House will be regarded as profligate luxury by the head of a unit for bright mildly handicapped senior children.

How useful is each additional member of staff who is added to a particular situation? The proverb concerning cooks suggests that there can be a level of staff where additional people reduce efficiency. The proverb is no doubt true if there is insufficient

Comparative Staff-to-Child Ratios for Different Groups of Children. Figures for the Minimal Acceptable Level of Care (MALC) and the Transition to Education Level (TEL) are Given.

	Normal Senior Children	Normal Infant Children	Bright Mildly Handicapped Senior Children	Multiply Handicapped Children	Multiply Handicapped Children With Behaviour Problems
Minimal Acceptable Level of Care	1:100	1:40	1:20	1:5	1:3
Transition to Education Level	1:30	1:15	1:8	1:3	1:2

Table 1. MALC and TEL ratios for children with different needs.
The table shows the different staffing levels required by various groups of children. The MALC levels quoted for non-handicapped children refer to playtimes; the TEL levels are for classtime. The infant TEL figure of 1:15 is calculated on the basis of classroom assistants working alongside teaching staff.

work for all the cooks or if they get under each other's feet while they do it. However, if the cooks recognise the likely problem and the hotel management is willing to let the 'idle hands' do other types of work, then each additional cook can be productively employed. On the other hand, if there are rules stating that cooks are not permitted to turn their hands to other tasks, the proverbial predictions will indeed come to pass, and exactly the same thing could happen in Beech Tree House if Residential Therapists were only permitted to undertake care duties. As more participated in a

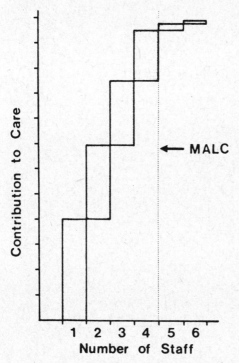

The Diminishing Contribution of Each Additional Member of Staff to the Overall Care Level.

Figure 19. Decrease in the contribution to care from additional staff after MALC is achieved.

This figure shows that each of the first four care staff contributes marginally less to the total level of care than her predecessor. As soon as the Minimal Acceptable Level of Care is reached additional care staff contribute virtually nothing to the overall level of care. It is possible that such additional staff may actually detract from the level of care by gossiping and getting under their colleagues' feet.

Optimal Grouping of Children According to the Number of Staff on Duty

Essential Care Duties	Optimal Grouping of Children with Staff					Staff on Duty	Comments
1	1:2	1:2	1:2	1:2	1:1	6	TEL achieved for all children
1	1:3	1:2	1:2	1:2		5	TEL achieved for 2/3 children
1	1:3	1:3	1:3			4	MALC achieved
1	1:5	1:4				3	Below MALC
Not Done	1:5	1:4				2	Seriously below MALC
Not Done	1:9					1	Dangerously below MALC

Table 2.   Optimal distribution of children into groups for various levels of staff.

The table shows the effect of increasing the number of staff on duty in a unit of nine multiply handicapped children with behaviour problems. The notes in the Comments column are based on the MALC and TEL figures quoted in Table 1.

given session the care duties would be completed more rapidly
and the staff would become progressively less productive. Each
additional member of staff would then be seen to contribute less to
the situation. Figure 19 shows that the fifth and sixth residential
therapists to come on duty add virtually nothing to the quality of
care received by the children. They are coped with very
adequately by the first four staff, each of whom can be seen to
make a major contribution. The MALC therefore occurs when
four staff are on duty.

The bottom two rows of Table 2 show why the MALC is not
achieved until four members of staff are on duty. One person has
to be available for 'care duties': coping with fits; running the toilet
training programme; organising meals, laundry and cleaning; dealing with accidents; answering the telephone, and so on. She cannot
be regarded as being with the children. This being the case, the 1:3
MALC ratio specified in Table 1 for multiply handicapped
children with behaviour problems is not achieved until four staff
are available. (See the fourth row from the bottom in Table 2.)

If staff and management agree to flexibility in roles, then it is
possible to use each additional 'cook' productively. Instead of the
fifth member of staff making a minimal contribution, as indicated
in Figure 19, this additional person enables most of the
team to shift gear and six of the children to be put into small
enough groups to receive structured education. The third row up in
Table 2 shows that the TEL staff-to-child ratio of 1:2 is achieved
for six of the children when the fifth member of staff comes on
duty.

It is interesting to consider what would have happened if the
unit had not practised flexibility in staff roles. This is indicated in
Table 3 where the fifth member of staff to arrive is a teacher. She
takes two children from the care setting and works at her TEL
ratio of 1:2, leaving one member of care staff with one child. This
would be very acceptable if the care worker had the inclination or
the right to train the child, but since this would not be the case it is
likely that she would be underemployed and the child would
receive no more than he would have done when he was with two
other children. Similarly, if the fifth member of staff had been a
care worker she would have been 'spare', because her presence
would have only marginally improved the care offered to the
children. In fact, she might well have reduced the overall level of
care by distracting other staff, by interfering or by gossiping.

The top line of Table 2 shows the ideal situation, when all
children are in groups where the TEL has been achieved, and all
staff are actively engaged in educating them.

Wasteful Use of Care Staff When a Teaching Group is Formed Without Involving Them in Teaching

Essential Care Duties	Alternative Groupings of Children When a Teacher Forms a 1:2 Teaching Group and Other Staff are Restricted to Caring.				Staff on Duty	Comments
a 1	1:3	1:2	1:2	Teaching Group 1:2	4 + Teacher	TEL achieved for 6 children. ONLY 2 taught
b 1	1:3	1:3	1:1	Teaching Group 1:2	4 + Teacher	TEL achieved for 3 children. ONLY 2 taught
1	1:3	1:3	1:3		4	MALC achieved

Table 3.   Effect of an additional member of staff (teaching) in a unit where role flexibility is *not* practised.

Rows A and B indicate two ways of dividing the children into groups when the fifth member of staff is a teacher. It is interesting to note that is there is no role flexibility, then even in the advantageous grouping shown in row A, where six children are in groups small enough to be taught, only two children are fortunate enough to receive tuition. Again the MALC and TEL figures are for multiply handicapped children with behaviour problems.

Waste of Staff Resources Due to Departmentalisation

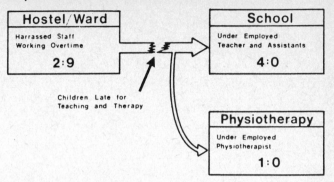

Figure 20. Departmentalised unit – MALC not achieved despite sufficient staff being available.

This figure depicts a residential school or hospital for children at 10.15 am on a day when sickness among the care/nursing staff has reduced the care situation to a level 'seriously below MALC'. (see the second row from the bottom of Table 2.) Because the children are late arriving at their departments, the staff have nothing to do. Their role and physical location prevents them from helping in the care setting. On the other hand, if they had all pooled their efforts, not only the MALC but also the TEL would have been achieved and no children would have been late for lessons or therapy.

Figure 20 shows an even more worrying situation which commonly occurs when organisations have become departmentalised, as described earlier. For clarity only three departments have been indicated – Care, Teaching and Physiotherapy. The situation portrayed shows an incredible waste of manpower. Because, as a result of sickness, the care staff have not reached the MALC, they have not completed dressing and feeding their children and it is already 10:15. The teachers, the classroom assistants and the physiotherapist have been sitting impatiently in their respective departments for over an hour waiting to get started. Clearly if the three departments had pooled their staffing resources at nine o'clock the MALC would have been amply achieved on the care side, and the children would have been to class and physiotherapy by nine thirty. Sadly, such pooling of effort is rarely the case in departmentalised schools and hospitals.

In Beech Tree House we have solved this particular problem by ensuring that all staff have a multi-role capability and that departments as such do not exist. Whenever the children are awake we have four staff on duty and increase this to a minimum of six during the 'teaching day'. Thus MALC is always achieved and between eight thirty in the morning and six at night the TEL is achieved or exceeded.

The TEL Transition and How it Reduces the Need for Staff to Act as Care Givers

An intriguing phenomenon occurs in Beech Tree House as the staff-to-child ratio passes the Transition to Education Level: there appears to be an absolute and very significant drop in the proportion of staff time needed for care duties. Clearly this is because small-group and individual training activities obviate the need for staff to play a custodial role. It follows that because all staff have multi-role capability, examples of the following type occur. A young woman reading a story to four potentially difficult children in a pre-TEL period – say during the rest after lunch – transforms herself into a teacher instructing two children how to break eggs and make a cake in the post-TEL situation. Her colleague, whose arrival made the transformation possible, assists two children as they prepare sentences with their 'Breakthrough' materials.

Staff Selection

We have had very few unsatisfactory members of staff; those who found the work too demanding have readily appreciated their problems and resigned. It appears that even weaker colleagues identify closely with the team and are well aware that they are not contributing as fully as the other members. Good initial selection is obviously very important in creating and perpetuating a successful staff, and to this end we have gratefully adopted successful staff appointment practices from a number of sources which I have not identified because to do so might affect their staff selection procedures. We have also developed a number of selection strategies ourselves.

There are six stages in selecting staff once an advertisement has appeared. The first is a process of self selection. Each person who responds to an advertisement receives, together with an application form, a very detailed description of what the job involves and a frank summary of behaviour problems of children who have been educated in the unit in the past. No punches are pulled because we do not wish to waste our time or that of candidates by depicting the work in a glamorous light. We rarely receive completed application forms from more than a third of those who responded initially, and on a small number of occasions we have had uncompleted application forms returned with a letter thanking us for being so helpful with the job description!

The second stage is carefully to scrutinize the application forms. This is undertaken by a senior residential therapist and a senior teacher – regardless of the nature of the post advertised – and a shortlist of candidates is drawn up. The third stage starts when written references are sent for. We require these for our files but because we are convinced that more precise information can be obtained by speaking to referees personally we also telephone them. The shortlist may be revised on the basis of the references obtained and the candidates who remain on it are invited to attend for interview. The letter they receive explains that they should bring clothes suitable for playing with the children, in addition to their choice of clothes for the more formal interviews. All candidates are offered the opportunity of an overnight stay so that they have a longer time to get the feel of the unit and meet the staff informally.

Stages four and five are reached on the 'interview' day when candidates are assessed for practical skills – the way they relate to the children in a free play and a structured teaching session and their ability to make observations and turn these into a written report. The fifth stage involves two interviews with each candidate, the first conducted by teachers and the second by residential therapists. It is explained to the candidates that these interviews carry equal weight.

In the final stage, every full-time member of staff ranks the candidates in order of preference, the slips are collated and the applicant with the highest score is offered the post. This ranking is done once the staff have been given summaries of the references obtained and the impressions created by the candidates at the interviews. Obviously the Head of Unit has the right to overrule a decision – but this right has never been exercised even when the Head's favoured candidate has not been selected.

The selection procedure is designed to identify people who have a number of qualities which we believe are important for success in the Beech Tree House situation. Certain appointments require that specific qualifications are held by applicants – for example, a teaching post or a senior residential therapist post – but while possession of such qualifications necessarily narrows the field, it does not exempt candidates from meeting our other requirements. We are interested in four broad areas: Work Related Qualities; Personal Qualities; Skills, Experience and Habits and Commitments Beyond Work. The reader may consider the items included under the four headings to be fairly arbitrary but they do appear to be the key elements predictive of success in Beech Tree House. Staff who have resigned within a term or so because they were experiencing difficulty with the work have invariably had a weakness in one or more of the qualities discussed below.

The Work Related Qualities we are looking for include intelligence, stamina, a good health record, literacy, common sense, a stable work record and proof of an ability to work hard. Candidates are aware of our interest in these qualities because on their application form we ask them to rate themselves for these characteristics against the general population. We ask the same question of the referees and of course compare the answers. Literacy is tested by the practical observation and report writing exercise on interview day. We attempt to explore each candidate's common sense by posing a series of questions at the formal interviews. For information concerning health and work record we depend upon the referees and the candidate's word.

Visitors often ask us what Personal Qualities we look for in staff and are usually surprised when we commence by enumerating what we are not particularly excited about. For example, we find that references which waffle on about someone being kind, loving, dedicated, wonderful with children and exceptionally patient are usually describing a fairly dim, unexciting, unambitious individual entirely content to play the 'orifice minding' role of the traditional care worker. The reader should not be surprised that we are not looking to employ such worthy but undynamic people. The Personal Qualities we do require include tolerance, humour, friendliness, ambition, candour and commitment. The first three are vital if harmonious relations are to be maintained between the eleven full-time staff, particularly because the majority 'live in'. It should be noted that tolerance does not mean the holding of middle-of-the-road beliefs. At the time of writing a committed Christian, an atheist, a vegetarian and individuals of all political hues make up a very harmonious team. Discussion centred upon the varying views adds 'flavour' to the Beech Tree House experience, it has not led to divisions of intolerance. That staff should be candid is of importance in many contexts but none more so than at Team Meetings and Micro-Teaching sessions. Often staff can help colleagues work more effectively by offering advice sympathetically; similarly, help can be received if staff admit frankly to any problems they are having. This latter point is particularly important with regard to liking and disliking children within the unit. All staff are taught that it is perfectly normal to dislike a child and that when this happens to them they should declare it. Once everyone knows that a colleague finds a particular child really irritating they can do a great deal to ease the situation. It takes a considerable amount of candour to admit to what at first sight appears to be a failing in someone who has chosen a career working with children.

The Skills, Experience and Habits area is a rag-bag of items which we look for in applicants. The importance of certain of them is determined by the activities the children are offered. If staff are appointed who cannot drive or swim, or who are afraid of horses, then trips out and swimming and riding will be restricted. For similar reasons we prefer staff who have practical skills, who can turn their hand to cooking and who have outdoor interests. Unless staff can do simple art and craft work the children will have less to do in their leisure time; unless they can prepare meals the children will lose this experience at breakfast and tea time when they are expected to help prepare their own meals; and unless staff are prepared to go camping, canoeing and the like, camping trips and the Lake District adventure holiday will be impossible. The importance of relevant experience and qualifications is obvious – but neither is absolutely essential: we have appointed staff from entirely different fields who have proved to be outstanding. Smoking is included as an undesirable habit! Three years or so after the unit opened it so happened that we found ourselves with an entire staff of non-smokers; it was unanimously agreed that smoking would not be permitted anywhere within the unit, with the exception of staff bedrooms, and this civilised rule has been endorsed by a majority vote each ensuing year. The only exceptions allowed are parents whom it is appreciated are often under stress when visiting the unit. They are allowed to pop down to the Multipurpose room for a quick puff, but they are not permitted to smoke when with children.

Commitments Beyond Work are an important consideration when appointing staff. Young people who have a fiancé many miles away can find the situation very unsettling; likewise a daughter can find herself in a difficult dilemma if she leaves aging parents to take a resident post in the unit. We are always careful to probe such areas of potential difficulty, but hopefully with sympathy and in such a way that the candidate is not offended. We rarely have applications for full-time residential therapist posts from married people because the hours are so very unsociable. However, married women do apply for part-time posts, particularly those who have school age children, because Beech Tree House closes for the holidays. Obviously we have to discuss in detail what arrangements can be made to look after young children when they inevitably fall ill. We have lost some exceptionally able part-time staff because of family commitments.

We always encourage staff to work an 'academic year':

Appointments commence in September and end in August. One great advantage of this arrangement for the unit is that we are able to run an intensive week-long staff training course during the summer holiday when there are no children about. The year period chosen also has advantages for staff, many of whom join the team directly from college and leave Beech Tree House to take further training. Their appointment in June/July usually coincides with the end of any course they might be studying, while the August leaving date enables those undertaking further study to start most courses at a convenient point. This mutually beneficial annual flow of staff cannot always be maintained, but it is a target that we work towards and achieve most of the time. We are convinced that an appointment strategy of this sort is a great help in planning the admissions of children (none in the autumn term when new staff are finding their feet); in the training of the team (intensive in the autumn term and in the week preceding it); in the recruitment process itself (this can be accomplished in one major effort and with a single issue of expensive advertisements); and in the way it meets the needs of staff (quite a number of whom see their work in Beech Tree House as part of their training/-experience for a career in the caring professions).

Staff Training
Staff training in Beech Tree House is a pragmatic exercise. Through it we aim to achieve three objectives:

a) efficient day-to-day running of the unit.
b) consistent around-the-clock implementation of child train-
     ing programmes by all staff.
c) harmonious relationships between staff.

We do not attempt to teach in detail the nature of child development, the theory of behaviour modification, the psychology of handicap or any of the many interesting topics that touch upon our work. Study of these subjects in depth is more properly undertaken on a professional course. However, staff are encouraged to read the many relevant books available to them, and an annotated reading list is given to each new member.

The primary goals of Beech Tree House staff are to teach children to abandon dangerous, destructive and disruptive behaviour patterns and to adopt more acceptable ones; the training we give our staff equips them to do just that – it does not attempt to turn them into teachers, residential social workers or psychologists. Having said that, the majority of staff who have left the unit report that the training and experience they received while with us proved valuable in their later studies and careers.

Staff are Trained to Share Roles

The likelihood that staff with varied experience and a wide range of professional skills will devolve into partisan groups has been squarely faced in Beech Tree House. Perhaps the most significant step taken to prevent such fragmentation has been the decision that all staff undertake duties performed by colleagues with different roles. Thus residential therapists teach, teachers do care duties and psychologists 'sleep in'. Such a practice makes it essential that each member of staff is familiar with the duties of all other colleagues.

Equipment-Based Training

Most of the equipment-based duties carried out by staff are familiar to them on arrival and therefore little in the way of training is required. However, in a number of instances unfamiliar equipment will be involved in completing a duty and it is necessary to demonstrate to all staff how it works. Use of the washing machine and the dishwasher are good examples of such equipment-based training, and failure to run programmes for new staff leads to inefficiency, invites damage to equipment and increases the risk of accidents. Staff joining the team in September are taught these skills during the August course; any staff who join during the year have to be taught 'on the job'.

Staff are Trained to Involve Children in Their Work

Many of the new staff's strategies for completing duties are inappropriate in Beech Tree House; for example, newcomers frequently overlook the possibility of involving children in their duties. It may be true that the tea time washing up can be completed by a member of staff in half an hour and that it takes two children and the member of staff three quarters of an hour to do the same thing; however, it is likely the children will benefit more from what at first sight appears to be the inefficient alternative.

All too often the time 'won' by staff who complete jobs 'efficiently' by themselves is not passed on to the residents of an institution, and even when it is, there is a tendency for the staff to use the minutes saved in what amounts to 'time filling' activities. If one of the major goals of those working with handicapped people is to train them to the point where they can be independent, it seems self-defeating to exclude them from washing up and preparing food in order to have time to teach them to weave tea-pot stands and shake tambourines to Schoenberg.

The involvement of children in domestic activities is a funda-mental practice that is expressly taught to all staff. Because of this the teacher sorting the laundry or the psychologist preparing the breakfast will, as a matter of course, involve children in the task.

All Training is Staff-Wide
Staff training is never undertaken in 'professional' groups; teachers and residential therapists learn together. To approach staff training in any other way is to invite division. Because the training we offer makes no assumptions of previously acquired information, no one is left floundering as a result of limited previous training, and because the skills we teach the staff are practical rather than theoretical, they rarely have any problems in assimilating them.

Staff are Encouraged to Understand Variations in Conditions of Service
There are certain differences between categories of staff which no amount of training can eradicate. Differential rates of pay, variation in hours worked and divergences in holiday entitlement are all potential points of friction which need to be discussed, accounted for and understood by all members of the team. For example, it is ironic that by far the longest and least sociable hours are worked by the worst paid. Reconciliation of this apparently unfair situation can only be achieved by a shared appreciation of such factors as the justice of financial reward for qualifications hard won and the many hours of work contributed to the team effort out of 'statutory working time' by the teachers, psychologist and other staff with favourable conditions of service. An under-standing of these potentially divisive factors is usually achieved in Beech Tree House.

The Encouragement of Freedom of Expression
From the time of their appointment, all staff are encouraged to question established practice, to offer their own ideas and, when the need arises, to remind colleagues how it has been agreed that programmes should be implemented. Having stated the obvious – that staff are told they should express their ideas – it has to be admitted that it is difficult to be precise about the way this freedom of speech is taught. One factor may be that all contributions during training sessions and Team Meetings are welcomed and sympathetically considered, and likewise that all criticisms are

talked through by the team. The chairperson of each meeting has the responsibility of drawing comment from all present and this ensures that normally retiring members of the team become familiar with making a contribution.

All staff have to prepare reports about children and from time to time undertake a project and present the results to the entire team – this ensures that each person makes a publicly acknowledged and valued contribution.

Whatever the precise reasons for our confident and outspoken staff, it has been encouraging to note the many visitors who have been surprised at the number and quality of contributions from all staff at Team Meetings and Case Conferences; equally gratifying has been the inability of many visitors to pinpoint the professions of the contributors. It seems that the problem of the 'silent care staff' and the 'effusive professionals' has been solved in Beech Tree House.

There are, then, both structured and 'covert' training processes in operation to make each member of staff an articulate individual within our blend of professionals. It is hoped that the label with which each member of staff arrives will be seen eventually as of secondary importance in the light of the goals shared with all the members of the team.

Initial Training

Most staff are recruited during June and July and start work when the autumn term commences. At interview it is explained that one condition of employment is that successful applicants will spend the week preceding the children's return for the autumn term at the Beech Tree House induction course. It is pointed out that serving staff also attend this course and they, in their turn, will be expected to do likewise in subsequent years.

There are fourteen clear goals to be achieved during these four days:

a) The foundations of the 'team ethos' will be laid.
b) All staff will know what their primary roles and duties are.
c) All staff will know the names of the children, their parents, their immediate family, their pets and so on. They will be able to recognise them when they arrive.
d) All staff will know the broad patterns of behaviour to expect from each child, how to calm them, how to control them, and their modes of communication.
e) All staff will know the key programmes being following by each child.

f) All staff will know how to use essential equipment in the unit – the washing machine, the 'Bed-Bug' System, the Sound Activated Monitor and so on.

g) All staff will know how to use the Report Book, the Accident Book, the Contact Book and the more frequently used data collecting schedules.

h) All staff will know what to do in the event of a fire.

i) All staff will be aware of the range of duties that they will learn during the first six weeks of their employment. For example, weekend and evening leadership, the dispensing of drugs, each role in the six week rota and so on.

j) All staff will know Lists One of the Makaton and Paget-Gorman vocabularies. These lists cover the minimum signing vocabulary staff need to direct and encourage children in Beech Tree House.

k) All staff will know how to obtain data from files and will receive outline instructions on how to compile reports.

l) A number of case studies will be presented to give a rounded idea of the scope, the failures, the frustrations and the successes of the work undertaken in Beech House.

m) All new staff will receive copies of rotas, fire instructions, schedules, staff training notes, reading lists and so on for their individual files.

All new members of staff are issued with a file and paper which they bring to subsequent meetings, and all in turn take the minutes of the Team Meetings and other meetings which they attend. These are then typed and distributed to all staff for inclusion in their files, new staff receiving backdated copies so that they can familiarise themselves with the format, and they are given help, if necessary, in compiling their first minutes.

During the induction course part of the time set aside for 'relaxation' is used to familiarise staff with local facilities. The minibus is used twice: the first trip to show them where the local bus stops, railway station, shops and pubs are; the second trip to Cambridge where the very broad range of leisure facilities, shops and so on are pointed out. An informal meal or drink outside the unit is arranged for the entire team on each of the training days. This allows staff to mix in a relaxed atmosphere and hopefully friendships will begin to form.

Term-Time Training

Once term starts staff training takes a variety of forms. Because it is impossible to get all the staff together at the same time the

Induction Course approach cannot be used. The following sections outline the strategies that we have adopted to continue staff training.

Record Keeping
In order to keep track of the participation of each member of staff in training a simple record sheet has been devised. It is a general-purpose schedule and is used to note participation in lectures, practical sessions, micro-teaching sessions, viewing of videotaped material, individual signing training and so on. Attendance at courses is also noted. The name of each member of staff is recorded, together with his or her role in the unit, and the names of visiting students on placement and any outsiders who are invited to training sessions. This gives us a clear idea of the number of people involved in our staff training efforts.

During the year 1981–82 a small number of staff were appointed before September. Since it was impossible to offer them the initial training course for new staff, which is usually taught as a unit during the last days of August, formal training was given as the duty rotas allowed, informal training being offered on-the-job. Although this was not an ideal alternative to the organised course, it was undertaken in an orderly manner thanks to the information kept on the Staff Training Record.

Micro-Teaching
Micro-Teaching sessions enable staff to observe their own teaching performance with children and provide opportunities for staff to discuss teaching strategies in a small group. Teachers and Residential Therapists attend the weekly Micro-Teaching sessions four at a time according to their rota, participating on an equal footing. (see Photograph 29).
Prior to starring as the instructor whose performance will be monitored on closed circuit television, the chosen member of staff completes a schedule which details key aspects of the brief teaching session, the goal being selected by the 'star'. The maximum time available for working with the child is ten minutes. The session is observed via closed circuit television by the remainder of the group and a recording is made which is then shown to the 'star'. Meanwhile the observers, who watched the live performance on the television monitor, fill out questionnaires about the session. A discussion of strengths, weaknesses and possible alternative strategies follows, based upon notes made in response to items on the questionnaire. The total session lasts one hour.

On-the-Job Training

We recognise that, despite the value of lectures, practical demonstrations, role playing, micro-teaching and so on, real mastery of any skill is achieved through practice augmented by feedback of success and failure. For this reason new staff are regarded virtually as apprentices and their performance is monitored by experienced staff. Good performances are reinforced and less well executed ones corrected – better alternatives being modelled. The Deputy Head and the Senior Residential Therapist work rotas which ensure that they share every aspect of their staff's work; they are therefore able to observe the performance of their colleagues, correct one-off problems as they occur, and take more general issues to the weekly Residential Therapists' meeting.

In September, when most new recruits start, *all* senior staff share in working alongside them, helping to enhance good standards in a way similar to that adopted by the Deputy Head and the Senior Residential Therapist. During the initial weeks of the autumn term, in addition to the Residential Therapists' meeting, the weekly Team Meeting is used to discuss the refine techniques for handling children, organising activities, relating to parents, using the Report Book, dispensing medication and so on.

Staff Training at the Team Meeting

From the moment staff join the unit they are encouraged to share with their colleagues at the Team Meeting any problems they have in handling children, completing duties, with their conditions of service, and so on. An open agenda sheet is posted on the staff notice board throughout the week and any member of staff can add items to this.

Each year there is a pattern to the items put on the agenda – a progressive shift from relatively straightforward items requiring a factual answer to more thought-provoking issues which touch upon such matters as staff motivation, values and emotional involvement with the children and the work. This is not to imply that Team Meetings devolve into T-Groups. However, each year certain themes have cropped up. For example, most years we have had to explore whether or not it is realistic for each member of staff to like all the children. This particular subject is usually precipitated by a new member of staff offering her resignation because she has discovered that at least one child's behaviour makes her angry to the point where she feels she might lose control. So far we have never felt that such frankness should be rewarded with our accepting the offer to resign. In a private session we counsel that many others have been shocked to discover that they, too, actively dislike a handicapped child, and that the first steps in coming to terms with this apparent failing are the ones they have taken – namely, acknowledging the strong emotion and seeking advice. We continue by explaining that to date, presumably because no two members of staff are the same, we have never had a situation in which a particular child was disliked by every member of staff. If the member of staff comes to me privately, I usually describe an aversion I had to one particular boy who was in the unit and how this was resolved. I explain that I, too, had to acknowledge my feelings to all members of staff at a Team Meeting and invited them to help by dealing with this lad in the event of any likely friction between the boy and myself. I then encourage the member of staff to share her problem in a similar way with her colleagues at the next Team Meeting. It is this topic which usually sets in motion a process in which new staff adopt the standards of frankness and mutual support which we believe are a hallmark of our successful teams.

Periodically, part of the Team Meeting is used to teach specific topics; on other occasions newly compiled lectures for general use are tested on the staff; new equipment is demonstrated, explained and at a later meeting evaluated. Occasionally visiting speakers contribute. For example, a talk by Jan Porterfield, Senior Research Officer at the Mental Handicap Wales Applied Research Unit, in May 1982, led directly to changes in classroom management strategies. These were evaluated by the class teacher and a visiting Italian psychologist six weeks later and the report of the evaluation was given at a subsequent Team Meeting. Similarly, staff report their own projects at this time.

All programmes are developed by the staff at the Team Meeting. It is noticeable that newcomers initially contribute little, but as both their knowledge and confidence increase, they take a bigger part. A recently compiled lecture which details the steps followed in Beech Tree House from assessment, through the mooting of overall objectives, the setting of precise target behaviours and the evolution of teaching strategies to be used, appears to have great value in clarifying for staff the very important part they play at every stage. The fact that there is an expresssed expectation that all staff will contribute appears to enhance the probability that they will.

Staff who have attended courses are expected to present a brief resumé at the Team Meeting; however there is no expectation that they will return and teach Beech Tree House staff the material presented to them on the course.

Individual Counselling and Training Sessions

It is considered important that the Head of Unit meets with each member of the Residential Therapy team individually for half an hour once a week. This special treatment for Residential Therapy staff is thought to be necessary for the following reasons:

a) They are usually the youngest members of staff.

b) They are usually the least experienced members of staff. Often their job in Beech Tree House is their first full-time appointment.

c) They work face-to-face with the children for at least 40 hours each week and are therefore exposed to more physical and emotional buffeting than any other group of staff.

d) They tend to be at Beech Tree House for shorter lengths of time than other staff, so there are more occasions when sympathetic correction of inappropriate child handling is necessary. It would be invidious to single out individuals for periodic visits to the Head of Unit for such guidance. Routine individual sessions are the chosen alternative.

Individual sessions also provide an opportunity for teaching the various sign systems used in the unit, and for assigning and supervising the projects which each member of staff is expected to complete twice during the year, presenting the results at a Team Meeting.

We believe that direct contact between the Head of Unit and the junior staff is a key element in preserving our strong team ethos. The individual counselling/training sessions are an important adjunct to the many occasions when the Head of Unit works alongside and often under the direction of junior colleagues.

The individual meetings with the Head of Unit are written into the staff rota and so become part of a familiar routine, helping to dispel any anxiety staff might have if instead they were told to report to the Head and so felt themselves to be on the carpet. The teachers meet with the Head of Unit on a weekly basis at the Teachers' Meeting. This is a small group which discusses educational matters and also serves a similar function to the individual counselling/training sessions for Residential Therapists.

Classroom Training

All residential therapists work in the classrooms. This is particularly important because class time is used to teach the children many self-help skills. We capitalise on our teachers' abilities to formulate training programmes and on their skill in instructing their colleagues to adopt uniform teaching strategies.

1 The original Beech Tree House.

2 Children serving lunch in the kitchen. Note the 'target' area for sweeping up on the floor.

3 Parents observing their son at lunch through a one way screen.

9   Observation room equipment bench.

10   Recording night time behaviour with a Bed-Bug and a SAM.

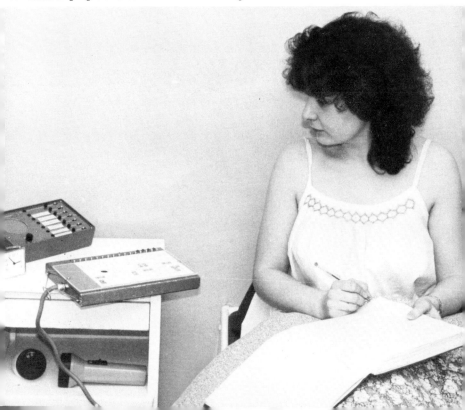

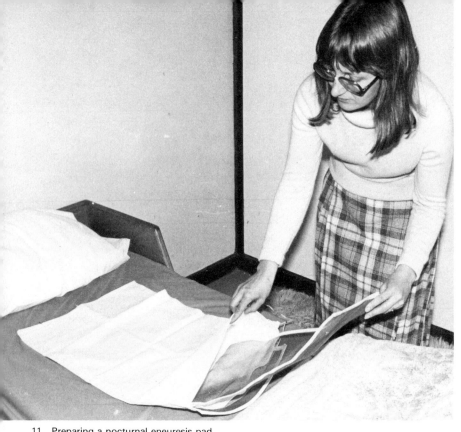

11 Preparing a nocturnal eneuresis pad.

12 Adjusting the sensor of a Bed-Bug to the weight of a particular child.

13 A senior member of staff helps with the mending — all roles in the unit are shared.

14 Wee-D connected with press studs to a pair of pants.

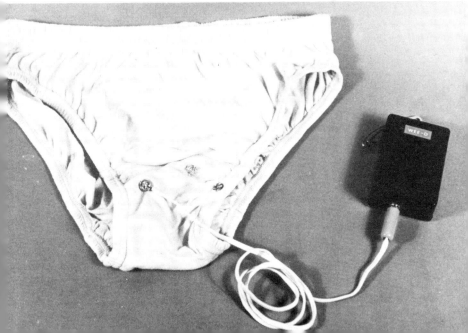

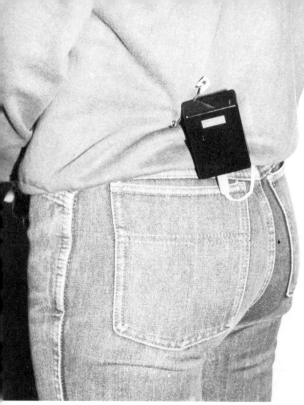

15 Wee-D pinned to the back of a child's jumper.

16 Jane waiting to receive her tokens from a Token Bank.

17 Ivan using the Token Operated Sweet Dispenser.

18 Philip using a Music Dispenser in his bedroom.

19　Richard watching the Token Operated Televison.

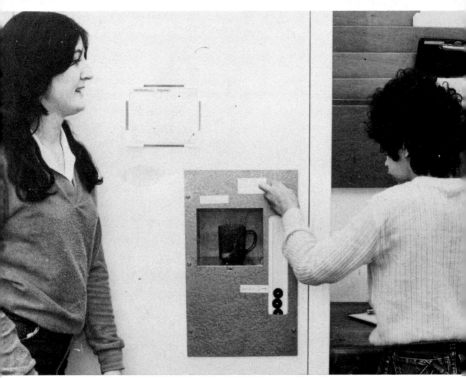

20　Daphne using the Token Operated Reward Dispenser.

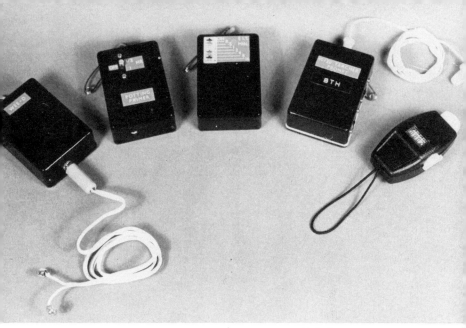

21 From the left: Wee-D; Potting Primer; FIT; Teacher Prompt; Tally Counter.

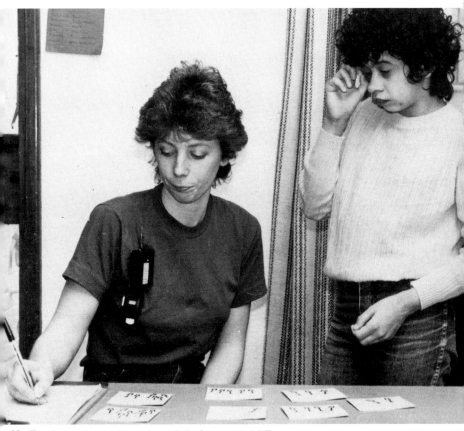

22 Teacher recording data using a Tally Counter and FIT.

23 Philip working with an A4 Tutor.

24 Programmable Picture Clock which indicates to Ivan when his tricycle ride is over.

25 Automatic Token Dispenser. The remote control is out of sight in the teacher's pocket.

26 Trevor on arrival at Beech Tree House. Notice the lack of hair and haunted expression.

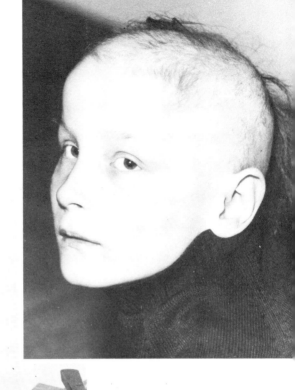

27 Trevor 18 months later, helping to peel potatoes for lunch.

28 Trevor with his hair plucked out again after inappropriate holiday placement.

29 A Micro Teaching session — staff making the initial observation of their colleague working with a child.

30 Parents and staff relax over a drink.

31 Peter learning to use his Rebus communication board. Note the token card on the teacher's right — once he has earned four tokens he can go outside to play.

32 Emma crying as her parents leave.

33 Emma at infant school.

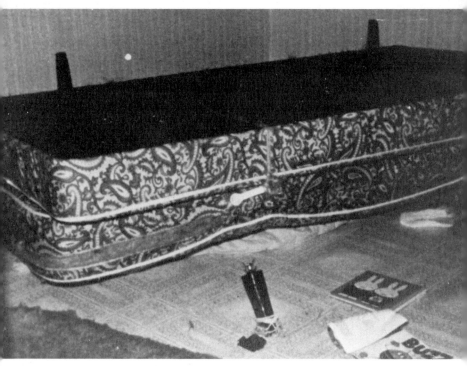

34 Emma's bed overturned during the first attempt to transfer her improved night time behaviour to her home. (This photograph was taken immediately after the disruption by Emma's mother.)

The Playroom Group

Residential therapists spend the major part of their classroom time involved in the Playroom Group. This is because the children in this group require the most favourable staff/child ratio. They are normally the least able and most disturbed children, and the skills they learn will typically be practised daily throughout their lives in the unit. It is therefore important that staff have the experience and information to ensure consistent training, in order to help the children acquire such skills at all times and in all places.

The group is located with immediate access to the distraction low individual teaching area, a time-out cubicle, the toilet training suite, the kitchen, the lounge, the bedrooms and the garden. It is a very suitable environment for the distractable, disruptive, delayed continent children with limited self-help skills. The residential therapists work with the children out of classtime in all these areas. The climate for the generalisation of both staff and children's skills is enhanced by this arrangement.

Because the children's training programmes evolve and change, the Playroom Group teacher spends a significant amount of time training and retraining her colleagues – this is a continuing aspect of her work. It has been described as strikingly different by a number of visitors who are usually familiar with the typical classroom assistant, expected to go through a routine of set tasks with children, presumably designed to keep them occupied rather than to extend their skills. The rationalisation of this approach is that any extension of skills requires teaching and that teachers, rather than classroom assistants, are employed to do that.

Nevertheless, although the Playroom Group teacher has the final responsibility for what goes on in her classroom, residential therapists are not passive recipients of her training. They are expected to suggest goals, assist in devising programmes, help evaluate progress and so on. As in other areas, they contribute more as their experience and confidence grows.

The Classroom Group

The Classroom Group is staffed by a teacher, a classroom assistant and a residential therapist, the latter being timetabled to undertake a one-week placement in the Classroom Group once every six weeks. The residential therapists are trained by the teacher to carry out classroom duties when they start their week-long placement, and the training concentrates on the limited number of tasks that they are to teach the children.

Although the tasks may be challenged as being less obviously useful than those taught in the Playroom Group, they can be justified as being related to placement. Most staff find it enlightening to help children with rudimentary reading and number skills. The Classroom Group rota is welcomed as a very different aspect of Beech Tree House work by the residential therapists; in terms of staff training they are exposed to different goals – although the teaching strategies are similar.

The Training Role of the Deputy Head and Senior Residential Therapist

Residential Therapists are the backbone of the team. In the year 1982–83 they formed eight elevenths of the full-time establishment and each week they contribute 301 out of a total of 393 hours of unit-based work put in by full-time staff. Virtually all their work time is spent with the children, so it follows that if they get things wrong all the efforts of other staff will have but marginal impact. The very best programmes can be devised, but if they are not implemented correctly and with enthusiasm by everyone, they will have little prospect of succeeding.

To ensure that standards are maintained, the Deputy Head and the Senior Residential Therapist follow a rota which involves working alongside their staff in every aspect of their job. They are familiar with every task the junior staff are expected to do because they do them themselves each week; their presence on the shop floor enables them to share and therefore fully appreciate any problems, to correct errors as they arise, to praise well executed duties and to note matters suitable for general discussion at the Residential Therapists' weekly half-hour long meeting.

The Deputy Head and Senior Residential Therapist meet the Head of Unit once a week for an hour. At this meeting problems are identified and, where appropriate, suggestions framed for presentation to the full staff at the Team Meeting. On many occasions training will be seen as the solution to a problem. Even occasional inter-staff difficulties can be presented in a training guise, particularly if the protagonists can be encouraged to work through their problems at the Team Meeting.

Part-Time Staff Training

There are two broad categories of part-time staff employed in Beech Tree House: those whose primary role is to work with children (the part-time Residential Therapists, the part-time Classroom Assistant and the part-time Night Attendant) and those whose primary role is to provide ancillary services (the part-time Secretary and the part-time Domestic Staff).

The training offered to part-time staff is much less than that given to full-time staff; it is also different for the two groups.

Despite the more limited input from the part-time members of the team, it is vital that they have up-to-date information about all that is happening in the unit. For this reason, the part-time staff 'Briefing' takes place immediately after the Team Meeting, in a forty-five minute session which all part-time staff attend. The title 'Briefing' is used to denote that the meeting is essentially to pass on information rather than to reach decisions through processes of discussion. Questions are of course asked and part-time staff do add points to the Team Meeting agenda. When this occurs the person is invited to attend the Team Meeting for discussion of the particular point.

There have been a number of occasions when Team Meetings have gone on longer than scheduled and the Briefing session has been lost. This is unsatisfactory. Part-time staff can rapidly feel insecure, particularly if they are unaware of changes in child training programmes.

Most of the part-time staff who work with the children receive their training 'on-the-job'. This is not because they are excluded from such sessions as the Pre-Autumn Term Course – they are invited but cannot always attend. Their problem is generally one of what to do with their school age children while they participate. Occasionally, when new staff are appointed during the year, part-time staff have the opportunity to join the newcomers when they receive an abbreviated version of the Pre-Autumn Term Course. However, mid-year appointments are rare and so such sessions are infrequent.

Part-time staff tend to remain in the job for lengthy periods. This is probably because they live locally; moreover they do not become emotionally and physically exhausted by the work and they value a job with school holidays. Long service enables them to accumulate considerable practical experience which tends to compensate for the limited formal in-service training offered to them.

Ancillary staff bring with them the skills they require. Their training amounts to little more than guiding them when and where to do specific tasks and how to operate the various machines they use.

The Secretarial post is an exception. Over the years this job has increased in complexity. Only one change has occurred since the unit opened and then the departing secretary trained her successor. It would be very difficult for any other member of staff to do this training thoroughly! It is hoped that any future change will be executed in a similar manner.

Professional Sessional Staff

The unit staff are assisted by a Physiotherapist, a Speech Therapist and Nursing staff who are part of the establishment of Meldreth Manor School. There are no formal opportunities to involve these professionals in the unit's staff training programmes, although invitations to attend the Pre-Autumn Term Course have been taken up on some occasions. In addition, at the start of each Autumn Term each of the professionals attends a Team Meeting and gives a talk about his or her work within the unit.

When these professionals are involved in treating or assessing a child a member of Beech Tree House staff is usually present and advice is given on how the child is likely to behave before the encounter takes place. Problems are rare because the staff involved have been helping the unit for a considerable number of years and have attuned themselves to our children and our techniques.

The Theory and Vocabulary of Behaviour Modification

Although I have stated that we do not teach the theory of behaviour modification in detail, we have found that great advantages accrue if all staff have at least a working knowledge of the key concepts and an ability to use the more familiar terms. We believe this to be important for the following reasons:

a) Communication between staff is enhanced by a shared theoretical framework.
b) If all staff understand and use a precise (if somewhat restricted) vocabulary for describing behaviour and the techniques used to change it, then communication is further enhanced.

Without a shared theoretical framework and the terminology appropriate to it, misunderstandings of a quite serious nature can occur. Of course, few of our new recruits arrive with fully fledged theoretical explanations of problem behaviour, nor with the habit of using descriptive language exactly. They do, however, come with 'commonsense' theories. These can be as incompatible with our essentially behaviourist approach as, say psychodynamic views would be. For example, an attention-seeking child who manipulates situations by bursting into tears might well be given a cuddle by a new member of staff, whereas experienced colleagues would refrain from encouraging behaviour they did not think was in the child's interest. Similarly a newcomer who interprets the misuse of toys and the breaking of them by a severely handicapped child as the result of deprivation, is likely to overwhelm the child in the name of enrichment. Our strategy would probably be to teach constructive play skills.

At the Pre-Autumn Term Course lectures illustrated by video recordings and slides describe each child currently in the unit and serve to introduce a number of key behaviour modification ideas. Additional lectures which review earlier cases serve to emphasise other aspects. In one lecture token economies and reinforcement scheduling are dealt with, in another negative reinforcement, and so on. Finally, three rather more formal lectures bring together the theoretical issues and explain the meaning of the most commonly used terms.

Once the lectures have been given, staff evaluate their understanding of the behaviour modification information presented to them. They do this by completing a simple, and hope-fully mildly amusing self assessment schedule. A copy of part of this is reproduced on the following pages.

BEECH TREE HOUSE STAFF TRAINING SCHEDULE
BEHAVIOUR MODIFICATION SELF ASSESSMENT
STORY 1

1 John, who is completely deaf, is running along the pavement apparently not looking where he is going. A nervous driver hoots at him.

    Would it be correct to say that for John a Stimulus Event had occurred?———————

In two sentences explain why you answered 'Yes' or 'No'.

    —————————————————————————

    —————————————————————————

    —————————————————————————

    —————————————————————————

    —————————————————————————

2 John continues his walk into the town. List three different types of Stimulus Event which might make him think of food (in three different sense modalities).

    —————————————————————————

    —————————————————————————

    —————————————————————————

3   John was once run over by a red bus. As he goes round a
    corner just such a bus draws alongside him. His hair prickles
    with fear.
        Is this a case of Operant or Respondent Behaviour? In two
    sentences say why you chose the answer you did.

    _____
    _____
    _____
    _____
    _____
    _____

4   John starts to make a very loud wailing sound because of his
    fright. Mrs Evans, a well known impatient busy-body, comes
    over to him, fussing and telling him to be quiet – John
    continues to wail. After a couple of minutes, Mrs Evans
    bustles off muttering about the nasty brat, his nasty noise and
    the embarrassment caused by such children.
        Should the walking away behaviour of Mrs Evans be
    categorised as an Operant or Respondent behaviour (for
    Mrs Evans)? One sentence to explain why.

    _____
    _____
    _____
    _____
    _____
    _____

5   Mr Evans has been watching these events from the nearby
    pub. He sees his wife walk off angrily and notices John wave
    two fingers after her as she goes. Mr Evans downs his pint,
    dashes out of the pub, rushes over to John and begins to shout
    and leap about with rage in front of him. John stops his noise,
    stares at Mr Evans and then begins to laugh.
        Has a process of Positive Reinforcement, Negative Rein-
    forcement or Punishment occurred for John's wailing (for
    John)? You should consider 'Intent' in your two sentence
    answer.

    _____
    _____
    _____
    _____
    _____

6   If you chose the answer Operant to question 4, say which
    process you think was at work. Positive Reinforcement,
    Negative Reinforcement, Punishment. If you chose
    Respondent do likewise.

    _____
    _____
    _____
    _____

7   The more Mr Evans shouts and leaps about the more John
    laughs. Suddenly Mr Evans lashes out and smacks John's ear.
    John stops laughing for a few minutes but begins once again
    when Mr Evans shouts and leaps about once more. Mr Evans
    grabs him and hits him again and again.
        Is this Negative Reinforcement for John? One or two
    sentences to give reasons for your answer.

    _____
    _____
    _____
    _____
    _____

8   John struggles violently and manages to escape from Mr
    Evans. He runs off down the street.
        Is this Negative Reinforcement? Two sentences please.

    _____
    _____
    _____
    _____
    _____
    _____

9   Eventually John comes to the Panda crossing near his school.
    He looks at the light which is red. He stands at the kerb until
    the green man appears at which point he crosses the road.
        The traffic lights could be termed as one of the following:
    A Negative Reinforcement   A Punishment
    A Positive Reinforcement   An Operant
    A Discriminative Stimulus
    In two sentences, indicate why you chose as you did.

    _____
    _____
    _____
    _____

10 Pick out two Operant Behaviours produced by John in the preceding story. Describe what Stimulus Events followed them and how the behaviour might have been modified by them.

_____
_____
_____
_____
_____
_____
_____
_____
_____

Write three very brief stories about children. The first should illustrate Positive Reinforcement, the second Negative Reinforcement and the third a Discriminative Stimulus.

_____
_____
_____
_____
_____
_____
_____
_____
_____
_____
_____
_____
_____

Please continue on your own paper.

6 THE PARENTS

In a recent survey of all parents who have had children educated in Beech Tree House we included the following three questions:

a) What help have you had with your child's medical problems?
b) What help have you had with your child's educational problems?
c) What help have you had with your child's behaviour problems?

Most families said that medical matters had been well attended to. Contrary to expectations, few felt that they had learned of their child's handicap in an unsatisfactory manner, although they were all understandably shocked and distressed at the news. However, one or two exceptions give cause for concern. Educational problems were generally less well catered for. Individual teachers and heads were singled out for praise but the service as a whole, for most parents, appeared to be fragmented, and teachers were defeated by the children's problems. Professional intervention specifically designed to help with behaviour problems was virtually non-existent. In one or two cases psychologists had made suggestions for programmes at home, but follow-up was appalling. In three or four cases social workers gave emotional support to parents or obtained attendance allowances or the like, but they were out of their depth in advising about the difficult behaviour.

The general impression is that there are few people qualified to help parents whose handicapped children have behaviour problems and that those who are available are prevented from working effectively because of the multitude of professionals and departments who would have to co-ordinate to meet the families' needs. Our survey suggests that, in this country, the least well catered for are families with multiply handicapped children with severe behaviour problems.

The dismal picture is only relieved by the remarkable resolve and energy displayed by many of the families we know. We are often asked if there is a class bias, in favour of middle class families, in the children educated in Beech Tree House, based upon the fact that middle class people are usually more successful at getting access to statutory rights and services. The middle class trend is not evident in Beech Tree House but there is a very marked bias towards what might be termed 'fighting families', that is, families determined to get the very best education available for their disadvantaged child.

It is worth noting that while the practice of placing handicapped children in subnormality hospitals continues there will always be an economic incentive for education departments to do just this in preference to sending children to specialist schools out of the local authority area. The reason is that a child in hospital costs local ratepayers nothing – the National Health Service foots the bill. On the other hand, a child placed in a school not administered by the responsible Local Education Authority will incur a fee to the Authority. When a child poses problems which require very specialised help the cost can be relatively high – so if an authority can convince a family that a hospital placement is appropriate (and its officers can square their own consciences), then the department budget will look healthier.

At the time of writing a growing number of Local Education Authorities are changing to a policy of 'no out of county place-ment' for any child. Where this happens a family with a handi-capped child with behaviour problems is likely to be faced with a limited range of special education provisions, none of which has been developed with the education of such children in mind. The education offered will probably be inappropriate and the child's behaviour problems will increase. Eventually the authority will attempt to place the child in a hospital or may make an exception, given the 'special circumstances', and try for an out of county placement.

This 'strategy' of coping until a child is quite unmanageable both at home and in the Local Education Authority special schools, is reflected in the steadily rising age of children who have been referred to Beech Tree House over the years. The case notes almost invariably trace a history of unsuccessful attempts to remediate the problem behaviour in inappropriate settings, with staff who are unfamiliar with the techniques that can be used with benefit. Some families are even faced with their child being withdrawn from satisfactory 'out of county' placements. The suggestion is that they should return to facilities which were regarded as less than optimal at an earlier date. Needless to say, some families are prepared to fight such decisions which have clearly been taken on economic rather than educational grounds.

The Parent Contract

The parents whose children are educated in Beech Tree House

make a contract with the unit staff. It is a contract of involvement and friendship and contains the following clauses:

a) The parents will call all staff by their first names and will themselves be referred to in the same way.
b) The parents will attend all case conferences and other major discussions concerning their child.
c) The parents will collect and return their child at the beginning and end of each holiday and will be prepared to talk with staff about the preceding half term's work or the holiday.
d) The parents will carry out programmes, collect data and report on holidays as requested by the staff.
e) The parents will live and work in Beech Tree House for at least one weekend per term.
f) The parents will visit their child as frequently as they can. They will expect to be welcomed at any time so long as they have telephoned to check that their child will not be out on a trip.
g) The parents will write to their child at least once per week and where appropriate will make frequent telephone calls.
h) The parents will have a member of staff to live with them at home for periods of two or three days in order to help their child transfer skills learned in Beech Tree House to their home.
i) The parents will attend the twice yearly Parents' Forum (our governing body) to discuss with staff and among themselves the workings of Beech Tree House.
j) The parents will be prepared to help in running the unit in the event of any emergency, for example if sickness lays low too many staff.
k) The parents will attend the long weekend at the end of the children's adventure holiday in the Lake District.

Obviously it is impossible to legislate for friendship, but by giving parents a clear obligation to come into the unit, to work alongside staff, to relate to them as friends and to share in the responsibility of maintaining the unit's standards, the growth of friendship is made more likely.

First Names
We realise that most parents initially find it difficult to call the Head of their child's school by her first name. However, it is important to achieve such an easy relationship if at a later date the Head or one of her colleagues is going to live intimately with the

family. Such a home visit is likely to be an uncomfortable one if conversations are held in terms of 'Mr This' and 'Miss That'. We are convinced that, to make the home visits work successfully, warm and relaxed relationships must exist between the staff and the parents. We have been advised by some well meaning people that to allow the familiar, first name, form of address to be used is likely to diminish the parents' respect for staff. We counter this notion by arguing that respect is earned and does not come with a formal title.

Friendship does not merely grow from sharing problems, working alongside people or addressing them by their first names – another important element is that of relaxing together. It is for this reason that we are enthusiastic advocates of the quiet pub as a therapeutic setting; everyone is on neutral territory and a drink or two relaxes parents and staff alike (see Photograph 30). Such joint trips are particularly valuable after staff and parents have spent an exhausting Saturday playing and working with the children in Beech Tree House. The trials and successes of the day prove fruitful conversation openers, and as the evening wear on so mutual confidence grows.

Key Therapists

Each child has his or her own residential therapist who is the link person between the unit and the family, the initial contact for parents if they have any queries or problems. We term each child's residential therapist his or her 'Key Therapist'. These members of staff prepare the Half Termly and Annual reports on their child's progress in the twenty-five areas not dealt with in the teacher's Education Reports. (Details of the topics covered by both therapists and teachers are given in Chapter 8.) The Key Therapist is responsible for all her child's possessions and alerts the parents when new clothes, toys and so on are needed. Whenever parents ring the unit they ask if their Key Therapist is available because they know that that person will be totally aware of all important aspects of their child's welfare. It is worth noting that no parent would use the expression 'Key Therapist' – they would ask for Rachel, Yvonne, Barry or whoever their Key Therapist happened to be.

Key Therapists are usually the people who go home to live with the children and their families, although occasionally, for example when a home visit occurs shortly after a Key Therapist has been appointed, the child's teacher will go instead. Another way in which Key Therapists help parents is by accompanying them on visits to evaluate any residential units to which their children might transfer. They are not only able to reassure the parents by giving moral support; they can also help staff at the proposed unit by describing how the child in question behaves at Beech Tree House.

Parents and the Case Conference

Parent participation in case conferences is something that we believe to be vitally important, even though decisions made on these occasions are rarely ideal solutions. They are usually compromises determined by limited funds, a dearth of suitable placements, a shortage of appropriately qualified staff or an urgent need to resolve the problem in a matter of days. When parents do not attend a case conference it can happen that such a decision is accepted by them as being a good one, taken in the child's best interests, despite the fact that everyone present knew it to be only the best of a bunch of poor alternatives. If they had been privy to the debate at the case conference they would have known otherwise.

It is not our contention that having parents present at a case conference will necessarily alter decisions – not even bad decisions made for non-educational reasons. On many occasions very unpalatable facts have to be faced by everyone concerned. If money is not available, then it is not available. If the best has to be made of a bad job, we prefer to share such facts with parents and engage their support, at least ensuring by this approach that parents are not conned into thinking the best solution to their child's problems has been found, only to have their hopes dashed a few weeks later when yet another crisis occurs. They know the score and are usually prepared to work within the limits set in collaboration with the professionals. We feel that such a rational, mutually supportive approach grows out of the problem sharing that occurs when parents participate in case conferences.

If parents choose to challenge the decisions reached at a case conference they have attended, that is of course their right. By having attended, they are aware of all the facts available to the professionals, and therefore much of the hostility that can grow out of believing information is being withheld is avoided. Our experience suggests that where such differences in opinion occur, the situation can become extremely acrimonious if parents have not attended the case conference and if they perceive it as a place where professionals 'plot' together. Such a perception can be disastrous if the child's class teacher, care worker, social worker, doctor and so on attend and become included among the 'them' with whom the family see themselves in conflict. The trust between the parents and those directly concerned with their child will then be seriously undermined, to the great disadvantage of the child.

A more obvious reason for inviting parents to case conferences is that they can usually contribute a fund of information about their child. It amazes us how many people have overlooked this point, although Dr Mary Sheridan made it many years ago. We have also learned not to ignore what parents say, nor to dismiss claims that do not match our experience of the child's accomplishments as mothers' wishful thinking or exaggeration. I can clearly remember the shock of a class teacher when she visited the home of a boy who had been in her class for two terms and not uttered a word. He had been equally mute in the care side of the residential school and yet at home was talking in fluent five- and six-word sentences – exactly as his mother had said he did. The notion that for some unknown reason the family were making it all up was rapidly revised, and instead they were consulted on techniques the school staff might use to obtain the same results! If the parents had attended case conferences and had been listened to and believed, something could have been done about the boy's behaviour a great deal sooner.

In Beech Tree House the first case conference is held six weeks after the child has been admitted. This period allows the child to settle into his new environment, to get to know the staff and other pupils and hopefully to begin to exhibit the problem behaviour which led to his referral. Likewise, the staff become familiar with the child and his problems. We always hope that the parents will visit several times during this six week period, too, so getting to know most of the staff. The first case conference is used for the parents to talk through their reactions to having their child in Beech Tree House and to raise any questions they may have. The staff report in detail on the child's behaviour and emotional reactions and a written copy of the report is given to the family. Finally, agreement is reached with the parents on the educational goals for the child and these goals are appended to the report.

Parents are encouraged to bring their child's former teacher, their social worker or a family friend to this meeting because we are very aware that they might feel a little out of their depth until they are really used to the Beech Tree House system and staff. We only ask the full range of local authority personnel to this initial conference if the parents are particularly keen on the idea.

A full case conference is held annually for each child. This involves representatives from all the local authority departments dealing with the family, a representative of each of the professional groups working with the child in Beech Tree House, staff from any other agencies involved and, of course, the parents. Despite the fact that we alert all local authority staff that parents will be at the case conference we still encounter surprise, and occasionally hostility, when the professionals arrive and find that we practise what we preach. One such professional caught a glimpse of a parent as he arrived and said, 'That was Mrs Smith and her husband wasn't it?' 'Yes. They are here for the case conference,' came back the reply. 'Ah, yes, you do that here, don't you? But do we have the *real* case conference before or after?' The inquirer was disappointed to discover that neither was the case.

One final point in support of our conviction that parents should attend case conferences: the tone of a meeting is likely to be very different from what it would be if the parents were not included – there is a pronounced tendency for professionals to refer to parents in a moralistic and unflattering manner when surrounded by colleagues. Terms such as feckless, lazy, unrealistic, rejecting, over-indulgent, dim, troublesome, immoral, greedy and so on are never used to describe parents when they are present – they are treated with a degree of respect which is regrettably lacking at many 'professionals only' conferences. We are convinced that if the only positive outcome of parent participation at case conferences is increased humanity and an awareness that human beings with feelings are being discussed rather than troublesome 'cases', it is sufficient reason to continue the practice.

Frequency of Parents' Visits
Parents meet and talk with staff at least five times per term: when the children are brought to Beech Tree House for the start of term; when they are collected for the half term holiday and returned after it; when the parents work their weekend in the unit; and when they pick up their children at the end of term. The times at which the parents deliver and collect their children are staggered so that each family gets an opportunity to talk for an hour or so with their key therapist, their child's class teacher, the Head of Unit and any other member of staff concerned with their child. Usually there are more than five meetings between staff and parents because families visit on other occasions, such as birthdays, fête days, Christmas parties, days out, Parent Forum meetings and so on.

Holidays
During holidays parents are asked to keep a simple record of their

children's behaviour, significant family events, the people with whom their children mix, any illness in the family and so on. They are also expected to continue selected programmes so that their children can begin to apply to their homes new skills learned in the unit. Arranging such programmes is normally undertaken by the home visitor who explores the feasibility of given programmes and then teaches the parents how to carry out those that are selected.

Parent Weekends
Parents' weekend visits can be great fun. Most families choose to come at the same time as another family, presumably for moral support but also for company when they take their child out for lunch or for a picnic. Some families have developed firm friendships after meeting at a parent weekend.

Parent weekends are timetabled when the Deputy Head is on duty (two weekends in three), since the residential therapist who is 'Weekend Leader' already has enough to do organising the staff and planning and supervising a full timetable of activities for the children. It would be quite unrealistic to expect her to organise the parents' job programme and look after their needs as well. The Deputy Head draws up a weekend programme for each family to include jobs, activities with children, an afternoon out with their own children and an evening with other parents and staff at a restaurant or pub.

The parents stay in the unit flat and staff hostel. They are asked to do gardening, painting and maintenance jobs; to participate in work and play sessions with the children (rarely their own); to help staff and children prepare and clear up after meals; to sew, type, tidy the loft – in fact to make themselves generally useful. A number of parents have spontaneously commented that they feel more a part of the Beech Tree House team once they have contributed to the venture by working in the unit.

Many parents cope very successfully with the children we assign to them, and we believe that this experience of success is an important therapeutic aspect of their visit; it helps lessen the blow most parents suffered to their self confidence when they realised that they could no longer cope with their handicapped child at home. The very act of sending their child to a residential special school is felt by many of them to be an admission of failure so that, if they are to succeed in the future, their confidence needs boosting. One small step along the path to achieving this is to give them the opportunity to succeed with a child whom another family found too difficult to manage. Success is possible partly because we never choose children who are not responding to their programmes, but mainly because the parents are not emotionally involved with the child. This is an important point. Often it seems that parents have made a rod for their own backs by loving their handicapped child too much; it is almost as if his physical or mental handicap has prevented them from teaching him to conform to acceptable patterns of behaviour – the handicap has been seen both as a reason for unacceptable behaviour and as an excuse for not dealing with it firmly. 'Poor little John, he doesn't know he shouldn't break the cups. It just isn't fair to tell him off.' And so John continues to break cups. This approach is of course a recipe for creating horrible children, regardless of whether they start life handicapped. At the parent weekend we are able to show families that they *can* be effective with a difficult child. In time, often after considerable discussion, they usually have similar success with their own child – once they have learned to respond to his difficult behaviour in a firmer and more appropriate manner.

It is not only parents who fall into this error. Sentimentalists often excuse one handicap in terms of another, as though to erase them both. Realists at least add the effects of the disabilities, and better still multiply them. A child who is partially hearing, partially sighted and cerebral palsied is eight times as disadvantaged ($2\times2\times2$) as a child without these handicaps, assuming that each handicap makes life twice as difficult.

Letters and Telephone Calls
Letters from home are very important for about two-thirds of the children. Although only a few can read them themselves, a significant number understand when they are read out by a member of staff and some are so delighted to hear what is happening at home that they carry their letter from one adult to another to have it read aloud. A small number of children with receptive communication disorders enjoy their letters being signed to them. There are some children, however, who do not appear to realise the significance of letters – but we persevere with reading them out to them.

Some parents initially need help in developing a simple style which their children can enjoy and understand. We suggest that they use very short sentences and simple, familiar words, and where possible, we ask that photographs or pictures be included. Parents are reassured that their children enjoy hearing about routine, homely happenings and that letters centred on such topics are always welcome. As well as reminding the children of home, such accounts are more readily understood than descriptions of unusual events. The small number of children who understand little, either of the spoken word or of any alternative communication system, usually seem pleased to receive colourful cards which they can look at. These cards are normally used by parents to send messages to the staff – in fact most parents use their children's letters to communicate with staff. This is usually done in a section at the end which is not read out to the children.

Children open their own letters – for many this is a very exciting moment, particularly if there are other little surprises included in the envelope. Those who want to keep their letters are encouraged to do so, but most children lose interest in them once they have heard them a number of times. At that point the letters go into the 'Letters File' where they remain until a reply has been sent – usually within a week. If a child wants to hang on to a letter it is copied and the copy goes on file.

Letters home are always written with the help of the child concerned. The scribe is usually the key therapist but certain children write part of their letters as a 'fun' classroom activity with the help of their teacher. Some children know exactly what they want to tell their parents and virtually dictate their letters; others manage this by signing a response to signed or symbol questions; one or two are really not aware of what is happening as the letter is written, but simple questions are put to them and attempts made to elicit appropriate responses. Like the parents, staff use the letters home to communicate with the families, and the Letters File is therefore particularly important as a reference for a parent's most recent letter. The letter home is copied with a carbon paper and the copy placed in the Letter File, so that all staff can see what was written home and, if a different scribe is involved at a later date, she can check what was said previously.

With the exception of that part of a letter which is written in class, letter writing is done at weekends and during evenings as an intimate and quiet activity, shared by each child and his or her key therapist. It is undertaken in a quiet corner and is often the occasion for a chat about the week's events between children and their key therapists.

The letters are apparently much appreciated by parents, too. On one occasion, at a Parent Forum, staff proposed that letter writing should be reduced to once per fortnight but the parents rejected the idea unanimously. They explained that not only did they enjoy the letters, but that, more importantly, they kept them up to date with everything their children had been doing. Parents with children who can understand speech or signs but whose handicap makes them poor at expressing themselves explained that because they knew what had been going on they could hold conversations with them, albeit at a rather low level; they could ask questions about events which their children could respond to by nodding or shaking their heads. Parents also found the letters very helpful for keeping brothers and sisters, grandparents and neighbours informed of what was happening at school.

Telephone calls are not appropriate for all children, particularly those with severe hearing losses. A larger number have severe communication disorders which prevent them from understanding the spoken word and for them, too, the telephone is an inappropriate way of keeping in touch with parents. One or two children who can understand speech but who can only sign, or communicate with a symbol board, have been able to use the telephone by getting a member of staff to act as an intermediary.

Parents may ring the unit to talk to staff at any time. They also have the home number of the Head of Unit. They are welcome to ring their children between six and seven-thirty in the evening and at weekends, though preferably not at meal times, and are urged not to feel disappointed if their child is unavailable, but to try again later.

Children can ring home from the pay-phone. They either use their pocket money, or in some cases, buy the necessary coins with tokens they have earned.

When a child first joins the unit parents are offered the opportunity of staying for a few days or of telephoning when and as often as they like. In one case a mother worried so much that she would wake and ring in the early hours of the morning. In another case, a father rang every day for six weeks – from Hong Kong.

Staffing Living at Home
When parents first visit the unit they do not bring their son or daughter but are usually accompanied by a social worker, a teacher or a psychologist who represents the local authority responsible for funding the child. The purpose of the visits is to enable the parents and the professional to decide whether or not the unit is suitable, so it is obviously a time when everyone has to be frank and prepared to discuss in detail the implications of education in Beech Tree House. There are obligations on all sides, one of these being the agreement of the parents that staff may live with them at home. It has to be admitted that there are some parents who hesitate at this point, but after we have explained that

this will not happen until we know them well, they have always agreed.

Some families who had children in the unit during the first year or so that it was open did not receive home visits, not because we felt they were unimportant, but because at that time we just did not have staff who could be spared. Our earliest visits took place during holidays and we were dependent upon the good will of staff to make such visits in their own time. They were so successful that we were able to make out a convincing case to the Spastics Society, and our part-time staff was sufficiently increased to allow three or four home visits per term.

It would be wrong to give the impression that all home visits have been successful and enjoyable. The parent survey shows that most families were apprehensive before the first one took place, although subsequent visits were, by-and-large, looked forward to and enjoyed. Staff reports suggest that only a small number of home visits are a complete failure. Even if all programmes fail to work at home on the initial visit, staff are usually able to spot problems and think of examples of good practices which can be fruitfully discussed. We accept the principle that a failure, carefully observed and documented, contributes information which can be used positively in gaining eventual success.

Towards the end of the home visit, parents and the visiting member of staff discuss the outcome, after which a written report is prepared by the staff member. The full text of this report is available to the parents at a subsequent meeting, generally when they visit Beech Tree House, and the discussion which follows usually culminates in agreements for action: the staff (including some senior members) suggest alternative ways for the parents to manage their child, while the parents propose new skills for him to learn and new strategies that staff might use to handle him. As mutual friendship and confidence develop through home visits, the partnership between parents and staff becomes a potent force in improving the children's behaviour and skills.

Parent Help
Parents help in a variety of ways, most predictably in raising funds. Families have worked individually and in groups to raise many thousands of pounds, using sponsored slims and runs, charity shops and jumble sales, raffles and donation seeking, all to very good effect. The money raised has provided a new classroom, the adventure holidays, toys and equipment, trips to the cinema and so on. Without parent involvement in this area the children's lives in Beech Tree House would be considerably less interesting.

Occasionally infectious illness takes its toll of staff and when this happens supervision of the children takes precedence over the upkeep of the unit. Because the children are hard upon their environment, it all begins to look very scruffy in a matter of days. On the few occasions when this has happened parents have responded to telephone calls with unstinting practical support, arriving armed with mops and dusters to revitalise the unit.

Some parents not only have very special skills but the time to become involved in a particular project. Recently the mother of a child who has left the unit completed all the interviews involved in the parent survey referred to earlier, and it is likely that she will be the key person in collating the results and co-author of the final report. It has been a great advantage to have a parent to undertake the interviews; the other parents know that she has experienced all the difficulties of having a child with severe behaviour problems and that she also has had her child at Beech Tree House. The sympathy which this shared experience brings seems likely to result in a very frank and detailed evaluation of the way parents regard our pioneering service.

Since the unit opened we have wanted to involve parents very much more in helping each other – for instance, we have always believed that it would be particularly useful if a sympathetic mother could be present when a family leaves a child in the unit for the first time. Many of them have never before entrusted their child to a residential establishment for a long period of time, and consequently they are beset with many misgivings: guilt at surrendering their child and a sense of failure. Whatever reassurances staff try and give, the parents are only too aware that we ourselves have never been through this emotional trial. We should like a parent to help at this point but have to confess that to date we have been unable to engineer it. For similar reasons we should like to have a parent present to talk to new families when they first visit the unit.

Another area where parent involvement would be very much appreciated is the selection of staff. Since we regard the Parent Forum as our governing body, it is all the more appropriate that a parent representative be present. Again, long journeys, caused by our national catchment area, and interview dates which have been inconvenient for parents, have precluded their involvement in this aspect of our work. It is anticipated that we shall solve the problem in 1983 by rescheduling interview times.

The Adventure Holiday
The holiday takes place in the Lake District at the Northern

Association for Community Care's Bendrigg Lodge. This excellent centre has met all our children's needs for the past four years. The accommodation is fairly basic and therefore there is no fuss about what our children might do – indeed, the Bendrigg Lodge staff have been quite outstanding in their help and in their understanding of the children's problems. They organise canoeing, riding, caving, sailing and so on, and provide all the necessary equipment and trained personnel. The children and Beech Tree House staff travel up on the Monday, and by the Friday the Beech Tree House staff are quite exhausted. This is when the parents arrive and virtually take over.

The importance of the weekend for most parents lies in seeing their children participating with enjoyment in potentially hazardous activities. There have been parents who have understandably expressed considerable reservations about the holiday, claiming, despite clear evidence to the contrary, that their children do not like the activities offered and that they would prefer them to go home for the week. We have explained that, as with the parents of non-handicapped children, there comes a time when they should encourage their child to move beyond the protective confines of home and family; that one of the most important steps they can take is to let their child do more and more without hovering protectively in the wings. Many of our parents appear to love their handicapped children to excess: they want to do too much for them and to hold their hands for far too long. While on the adventure holiday, they begin to appreciate the resilience of their children and this valuable experience can increase their willingness to let them grow.

After Children Leave

With most parents, continuing contact has been very encouraging for the staff. Many still visit and most ring or write from time to time. Occasionally we are contacted for advice about behaviour or appropriate action to resolve a problem concerning education or a future placement. From time to time, at the instigation of parents of former pupils, we have written reports or met with colleagues from other schools to explain the way we worked when the child was in Beech Tree House. In one or two cases we have assisted parents who were battling to reverse less than sympathetic decisions regarding their children's future. When a family crisis has occurred, or there has been a recurrance of a behavioural problem, we have sometimes been able to take a child back for further training or simply to give everyone concerned a break. An indication of the relationships formed between staff and parents is that all families who had had children in Beech Tree House willingly participated in the survey.

Children without Parents

Approximately one fifth of our children have been orphans, abandoned or in minimal contact with their parents. The majority of these came to us from subnormality hospitals, the remainder from Children's Homes. The long term prognosis for them is less encouraging than for children with parents who are involved; this is true regardless of the level of success they achieve in Beech Tree House.

The greatest problem that these children experience concerns the turnover of staff in the homes and wards to which they usually return during holidays and when they finally leave the unit. For example, there have been many occasions when the staff on a ward has changed completely during *one term*. This appears to happen because children's wards are normally regarded as staff training areas and pupil nurses rotate through them on six week placements. The problem is compounded by the high turnover of trained staff who leave to have families or to seek promotion. Faced with such rapid changes of hospital or institution staff, it is very difficult for us at Beech Tree House to be certain that someone will be available to carry out the programmes from one holiday to the next. These programmes have to be agreed, and sometimes they need to be demonstrated. There have been many distressing incidents when children have regressed to earlier patterns of violence or self mutilation when faced with staff unable to communicate with them or ill prepared to continue vital programmes. For this reason, we have decided that in future we shall only consider taking hospital children if the placing authority will arrange for the child to spend holidays in the same foster home, or other institution, with people who can maintain continuity of treatment.

While they are with us children in care are treated in exactly the same way as children living at home. Consequently, staff from the 'holiday' home receive the same guidance as parents do. Moreover, they, too, are expected to involve themselves in the work of the unit and have Beech Tree House staff live with them. This is because the children have the same problems in generalising skills from Beech Tree House to their holiday home as the other children have in transferring the behaviours they have learned to their own homes.

Perhaps the greatest difficulty faced by children in care is the absence of committed parents to fight for their rights. This observation should not be seen as an attack on the responsible professionals – most of the parentless children have come to us because they were fortunate in having a teacher, social worker or psychologist who cared for them a geat deal. That this can happen is not in question – nor is the fact that such committed individuals move on and may be replaced by colleagues with other interests and priorities. This has happened to children in our unit and their futures have taken on a distinctly less rosy hue. We have tended to carry on the battle – but we too shall leave one day, and what will happen then? We begin to share the anxiety which plagues all parents as they look into the future – what will happen when we have gone? All we have by way of consolation is the hope that the intensive training offered in Beech Tree House will be sufficient to win our pupils a warm place in the hearts of those who will help and protect them in the future.

7   BEHAVIOUR MODIFICATION

Introduction
A great many books have been written on the subject of behaviour modification, a significant number being devoted to the use of this teaching technique with mentally handicapped people. The main purpose of this chapter is therefore to show how the technique has been applied and adapted for our work in Beech Tree House and to point out, for those already familiar with the topic, where our approach differs from the established view and why we have felt it necessary to follow our own line. For the benefit of newcomers to the subject, an outline of the general principles of behaviour modification is included, together with details of the books which Beech Tree House staff have found particularly helpful. We hope that the following pages will explain to this second group of readers why it has been important to organise the unit in the manner described earlier in this book.

The Underlying Principles
Behaviour Modification is based on a very straightforward idea of learning, namely that a behaviour which is *followed* by a reward is more likely to be repeated than one which is not, and that behaviour which has an unpleasant *outcome* tends to disappear. This simple idea that behaviour is, at least in part, controlled by its consequences, has been demonstrated in many ways with both humans and animals.

When I lecture on this topic I try to keep the session light-hearted by introducing the idea of the 'Jones Box'. There is a picture of this imaginary piece of equipment in Diagram 19. The box is made from solid concrete which no sound, light, smell or other stimulus can penetrate unless I instal the necessary equipment. This I can do at the stroke of a pen. I have conducted a number of experiments in this box, all of them designed to help staff understand the principles of behaviour modification.

In the Jones Box is a little man who sits in front of three buttons, one white, one grey and one black. The little man chosen for the experiment is inquisitive; he is also particularly partial to the odd gin and tonic. The atmosphere in the box is hot and dry. The subject is strapped into his seat with a belt.

It is explained to him that once he is strapped into his seat he is

Three Button Jones Box

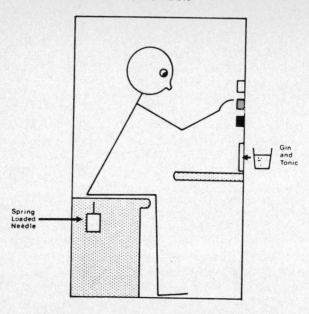

Diagram 19.   Three button Jones Box.

free, if he wishes, to press whichever of the buttons he likes during the hour long experiment. Within a minute or so he presses the white button. He waits; nothing happens. He presses it again, still nothing. After three more tries he appears to lose interest in this particular button and presses the grey one. Immediately the small door opens and an ice-cold gin and tonic pops out. Because he is warm and thirsty the little man drinks this quickly. He again presses the grey button and is rewarded with another gin and tonic. After two more presses and two more drinks his thirst is quenched for the time being. He turns his attention to the black button which he presses – and shrieks as a needle plunges into his bottom. He decides that whatever else he does he will not touch the black button again. Somewhat tentatively he presses the grey button and drinks yet another gin and tonic, this time to calm his nerves.

One important conclusion which may be drawn from this imaginary experiment is that the litttle man's behaviour was controlled by what happened to him in different circumstances. He learned that when he operated on his environment in different ways (by touching the buttons) very different things happened to him. If he touched the white button nothing occurred at all: this being the case he lost interest and ceased to touch it. If he touched the grey button there was a really pleasant outcome: he therefore touched this button frequently, only stopping when he had had his fill of the gin and tonic. If he touched the black button something very nasty took place: he did not touch this button again.

These three examples are representative of the key ways in which consequences are thought to affect behaviour. In the first case the behaviour is said to have been *extinguished* because it was not rewarded by a pleasant consequence; but it took a number of repetitions before the lack of consequences took effect. In the second case the behaviour was *positively reinforced* because it was rewarded by a repeatedly pleasant consequence; in the example the learning took place rapidly. In the third case the behaviour was *punished* because it was followed by such an unpleasant consequence that it was not risked again; this also happened very rapidly. It as an example of what is known as 'one trial learning'.

It is easy to think of simple examples from our own work which illustrate these points. A boy who formerly gained his parents' attention by screaming, eventually abandoned this behaviour when it was consistently ignored. The screaming behaviour was *extinguished* because it was no longer rewarded by parental attention. However, this lad progressively learned to use the sign for 'Look please' when we, and his parents, responded by paying attention to him; the signing behaviour was *positively reinforced* because it was rewarded by attention. Another child who frequently attempted to push objects into mains sockets stopped the behaviour when, for the first time in his life, his hand was smacked hard by his parents each time he attempted to do it. (This is not to suggest that smacking should be used for minor misdemeanours.) The extremely dangerous behaviour stopped quickly because it was *punished*.

Parents and staff who adopt behaviour modification techniques to teach children employ their understanding of how consequences affect behaviour. If they want a child to do something more often, they generally reward the behaviour. If they want a child to stop doing something they ignore it; or if the behaviour is dangerous to the child or to other people, they might choose to punish it.

Behaviour Modification is a Technique – It does not Specify what should be taught

It should be noted that behaviour modification does not indicate *what skills* should be taught; it is simply an effective method of teaching them. Nor does it tell the user *what rewards* or *punishers* to try; these have to be selected on the basis of each trainee's known likes and dislikes. Behaviour modification is nothing more than an effective tool – its purpose and effectiveness depend entirely upon the user. Many professionals and parents do not appear to grasp this point when they complain that their use of the technique has been unsuccessful. Often in such cases the problem tackled was one for which the technique was inappropriate: for example, behaviour modification is no solution if a child's acting out behaviour arises from deep emotional trauma caused by a divided and unhappy home. Such critics are as exasperating as those people who complain that screwdrivers are not much use for prising out nails! Both have missed the point: they have used the wrong tool for the job.

Data Collecting

At best, behaviour modifiers use their techniques methodically and record what is happening as they go along. They know the power of their teaching method depends to a large extent on being able to detect small, progressive changes in behaviour, for it is such accumulative changes which indicate whether or not a particular programme is worth pursuing. The reader would be misled if he believed that most people learn new behaviour as readily as the little man in the Jones Box. The process is usually much slower, with ups and downs, and initial changes are typically very gradual.

Data is usually collected in three phases. The first, known as the *Base Line Phase*, gives a picture, in data form, of the extent of a problem or the absence of a skill. This data, collected in a manner which shows the typical pattern of the behaviour before intervention takes place, is used as a standard against which any progress may be compared. The second phase is the *Training Phase* and this charts the progress of the subject during training. If the data concerns unwanted behaviour, for example spitting at people, the hoped-for trend would be downward from the Base Line level towards zero. If the data is about the acquisition of acceptable behaviour, for example making spontaneous eye contact rather than avoiding it at all times, the desired trend would be upwards. The final phase is the *Post Training Phase* when data is collected occasionally to check that there is no backsliding to the Base Line level of the behaviour. Data collecting need not be a chore. A number of methods that we have found useful in Beech Tree House are described in Chapter 8.

Rewards and Punishers
There is a tendency for mentally handicapped people to be regarded as a homogeneous group and it is often assumed that what is liked by one will probably be liked by all. This is particularly true when it comes to choosing rewards: naive behaviour modifiers may fall into the trap of offering Smarties as positive reinforcers to every child they train. Our experience suggests that while many children find this an acceptable way of being rewarded there are a few who do not; we have even come across a small number of children who have shown fear reactions to Smarties! (This puzzling behaviour became explicable when we visited the units from which they came and witnessed the unsympathetic and sometimes rough manner in which they were given pills). Again, some children simply do not like sweets and show no interest in receiving them; it follows that they will not be encouraged by being rewarded with sweets for correct responses. This seems very obvious when the example is sweets, yet we have met many, many teachers who believe that children should work for nothing more than the satisfaction (reward) of completing the task and pleasing the teacher. This is a reasonable method if the child happens to like both the tasks and the teacher – it is miserably ill-conceived if the child does not like the task and has no affection for the teacher. Unfortunately some teachers label such children as lazy or lacking in motivation because they do not fit into their simple-minded concept of motivation. By introducing extrinsic rewards which the children like we have been able to demonstrate that the same children can work enthusiastically on identical tasks. Thus a very basic rule of behaviour modification is to check the preferences of each trainee before starting any training programme.

In Beech Tree House we establish the children's likes and dislikes by *interviewing* the people who know them well; by *observing* what the children choose to eat, play with and do; and by testing preferences for various potential rewards. The last is easy to do: a range of possible rewards is set within the child's reach and he is encouraged to take something. The items which are systematically chosen in preference to others are likely to be useful as rewards. In the example of the little man, it was important to establish that he liked what popped out of the little door if we were to teach him to press the grey button. If he had been strictly teetotal the gin and tonic would not have acted as a reward – in fact he might have regarded it as a type of punisher.

It is important to remember that *tastes for rewards change* – even within a training session. This can be caused by the trainee becoming saturated with the reward, for example too full of gin and tonic, or simply wanting a change. We have had children who worked far more readily when edible rewards were taken randomly from a selection they were known to like, rather than when just one initially liked reward was given throughout each training session. It appears that anticipation and variety are in themselves potent in enhancing rewards given for correct behaviour.

Rewards should not be given in large 'dollops'; *little and often* is a much more successful strategy, particularly at the start of a new programme. For example, if a child likes music it is usually much more effective to let him listen to a favoured tune for fifteen seconds after each correct response than for four minutes after nine or ten correct responses. The same holds true for most rewards.

A perfect reward may be defined as 'something which the trainee is very keen to have, is easy to give and disappears immediately it is given.' I have already suggested ways to check on the appropriate reward and indicated that the trainer must organise each teaching session so that the reward continues to be wanted throughout. Ensuring that rewards can be given easily and that they disappear immediately can, however cause difficulties which stretch the ingenuity of the teacher.

Rewards which are *cumbersome* to hand out can cause a number of problems, the most important being delay between the occurrence of the behaviour and the receipt of the reward; this topic is discussed in detail later in the chapter. Cumbersome rewards also use up training time and reduce the trainee's opportunity to learn. For example, if the reward for a particular child is fifteen seconds' play with an electric train set after each correct response, and this is achieved by the child moving from his teaching table to the train set and back after each correct trial, a great deal of time will be wasted. If the child is known to be equally fond of chocolate drops, a quarter of one of these could be popped into his mouth after each correct response and five or six times as many trials could be fitted into a training session.

Staff do not like cumbersome reinforcers, particularly if time has to be spent preparing them. At one time we had a boy who had a passion for hot, jam-filled pancakes – it would have been possible to make these before each session, chop them up and keep them warm on a heated food tray, and this approach was given serious consideration. It was clear, however, that each train- ing session would have to be preceded by cooking and followed by washing up. Fortunately, because the boy in question understood tokens, we were able to use these to reinforce him during training itself, and he purchased jam-filled pancakes at supper time. Such an alternative strategy cannot be used with all children, but it is an example of one way to get round the problem.

Another disadvantage of cumbersome rewards is that their very presence can distract the child from the learning task. This is particularly true of toy rewards which a child may keep looking at or reaching for. In an ideal teaching situation, until a new skill is reasonably well established, there should be as few distractions as possible to interfere with efficient learning.

The ideal reward should disappear as soon as it has been given; if it does not, the recipient will be likely to prefer playing with it and may be very reluctant to give it back when requested. This is understandable: it was chosen by the trainer *because* of its desirability. I once worked with a boy whose only interest seemed to be to play with toy cars. He would even do this in preference to eating or drinking. In the training sessions, the idea was that as soon as he did what I wanted he would be given his car to play with for ten seconds. He was then supposed to return it to me. The returning part of the procedure caused all manner of struggles between us, with me demanding the car and the boy hanging on for dear life. When I finally managed to retrieve it he would be upset for minutes on end, and it took a very long time to complete as few as ten trials. The eventual solution was to cut a car-sized hole in the table and to screw a model garage over it. Once the boy had played with the car for ten seconds he was told it had to go to the garage for petrol. He would push it in, I would catch it under the table and the next trial would follow smoothly. A solution had been found, but it was still somewhat cumbersome and most definitely not to the liking of the caretaker!

Ideal reinforcers which disappear, more or less, on being received include small items of food, sips of drink, tactile rewards, music, tokens which are popped into a bank and, most convenient of all, praise. Not all these rewards are suitable for all children because some have problems with their chewing and swallowing, while others do not hear, and so on. Once again it is clear that each person to be trained should be treated individually. Nevertheless, rewards which disappear on having been received generally create fewest difficulties for the teacher.

Stimulus Events and Perception
Staff who work in Beech Tree House come to grips with a small number of technical terms used by behaviour modifiers, enabling them to communicate very clearly with each other when discussing training programmes, and also helping when consulting the more

technical books and journals. While it is true that many of the
technical terms used are perfectly clear to the lay person, it may be
helpful to point out possible areas of confusion. In the first place 'a
behaviour' is something that a person does, not to be confused
with good or bad behaviour. The term 'Stimulus Event' is another
example.

The reader is referred to Diagram 20 which we use in staff training to clarify what is meant by a Stimulus Event. Here the little
man is seen surrounded with words which refer to types of
sensation that he might notice – that is to say, things he can be
aware of. These include those detected by the five senses and
internal states – hunger, pain, and so on. It is assumed that if the
little man is awake and in perfect health he will detect and be
aware of sounds, smells, jabs from needles or the position of his
limbs: this is known as 'Sensory Perception'. Some people,
because they have damage to a sense modality, do not perceive in
that particular modality; for example, totally blind people do not
perceive visual stimulus events. It would therefore be a very fool-
ish behaviour modifer who chose to reward such a person with a
smile.

Potential Stimulus Events

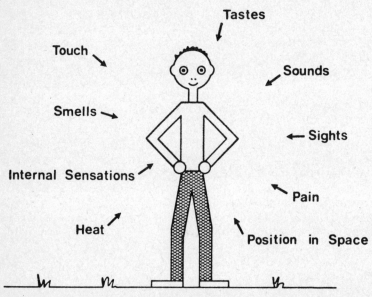

Diagram 20.   Potential stimulus events – the full range of
sensory perceptions that may stimulate behaviour.

Some people, particularly those who have suffered brain damage before, during and shortly after birth, (the cerebral palsied – often referred to as Spastics) have what are known as perceptual problems. Lay people often find these very difficult to understand because the sense organs are intact and it is only when signals from these reach the brain itself that difficulties arise. For example, we have worked with many children who obviously hear sounds but can make no sense of them. One can only assume that for them the spoken word is as meaningless as a totally unknown language is for us. It is clear that verbal praise will have little significance for such children; for all practical purposes they should be regarded as having little chance of *perceiving* it.

Over the years we have been amazed at the many professionals who have described children with problems of this type as stubborn, playing dumb or deliberately defiant. These terms have been used to 'explain' the children's inability to communicate in preference to recognising the underlying condition and exploring alternative methods of communication. The recommended strategy would be to select an alternative sense channel in which stimuli are more easily perceived – for example vision – and use a signed or symbol communication system.

The act of perception is *selective;* possibly one of the most remarkable feats of the brain is its ability to suppress the plethora of information which is fed to it at any moment. For example, the reader is able to focus his mind at will on the sensation of his bottom on his chair, his shoes on his feet, noises outside the room or the feel of this book in his hands, yet all of these sensations were probably suppressed until this paragraph refocused the reader's attention. It is useful to surmise that some children, but not all, often labelled inattentive or hyperactive, have a problem in focusing their perception – every sound, sight or smell bombards their brain and is possibly perceived with equal weight. If this is something like the case, it is little wonder they flit from task to task.

We have found it important to emphasise the problems of perception because it is difficult for staff, particularly those who have had little experience of working with multiply handicapped people, to understand that Beech Tree House children may live in a world which appears very different from the one with which they are familiar. Many areas of perception that we take for granted will be distorted or entirely missing. For example, we have even had children in the unit who appeared not to perceive pain or heat. Their lack of response to hot stimuli and their injurious effects mean that staff can not rely on the normal reflexes to protect such children from burns when ironing or making toast, so when they participate in skill training sessions of this type an entirely different dimension is added to supervision. If such children were ever to be exposed to a training regime which relied upon physical punishment to control behaviour they would be unlikely to learn much and would be at great risk, particularly if their failure to cry provoked further chastisement.

Discriminative Stimuli

Certain stimulus events tell us when to behave in a particular way. For example, a car driver approaching traffic lights will apply his brakes if the lights are red or continue on his journey if they are green. A simple change in the stimulus from one coloured light to another induces him to behave in a completely different manner.

There are a great many situations in life where it is important to know what signals to look for and how to respond to them; any confusion over the appropriate reaction can bring problems. It is quite possible for one man to be arrested for the same behaviour which another man does with impunity only metres away. The following example contrasts the unhappy fate of a man who mistakenly went into a women's toilet and passed urine against the wall, with that of a second man who used the adjoining men's toilet in a similar manner. The first man was mentally handicapped and unable to read. Fortunately there was no action taken once it became clear that an honest mistake had been made, but the mentally handicapped man suffered considerable humiliation through confusing the ladies and gentlemen signs.

The stimuli which indicates when to produce certain behaviours are termed 'Discriminative Stimuli' – they help us select the time and place for doing things, as illustrated in the preceding paragraph; for most of us the two toilet signs are very useful and unambiguous discriminative stimuli. However, many discriminative stimuli are very subtle, particularly those which control our social behaviour; even the way we laugh is determined by the setting in which we feel amused. For example, contrast the very gentle chuckle we might emit in a place of worship with the uninhibited laughter we can produce when among friends. Most children use similar discriminative stimuli in the classroom. For example, on the occasional mornings when a normally jovial teacher arrives looking washed out, with bloodshot eyes and bad breath, most of the class notice this immediately and spend the day working diligently and without fuss. Unfortunately the class buffoon, who is normally well tolerated by the teacher, fails to detect the tell-tale signs of a hangover and carries on in his usual way – to his inevitable downfall.

Many mentally handicapped people have difficulty in learning and interpreting discriminative stimuli, particularly social ones, and consequently their ready laughter, tears and open friendship can prove very discomforting to reserved non-handicapped people. Part of our work in Beech Tree House is to teach our handicapped children to recognise and respond correctly to discriminative stimuli. Some of the training is very basic indeed: children learn that sitting on a toilet pedestal is the only acceptable discriminative stimulus for bowel opening behaviour; at a more sophisticated level, we teach that there are differences in the way they should greet friends and strangers. A great deal of behaviour modification concerns teaching people the way to react to the discriminative stimuli that surround them.

The Jones Box may be used to give a clear example of how someone might learn to discriminate when to press a button. For this experiment the box is equipped with a small light, a button and a speaker. If the button is pressed when the light is on, music, which the little man is known to like very much, is played for thirty seconds and the light comes on again ten seconds after it finishes. If the button is pressed when the light is off, no music is played and the light remains off for another five minutes. The little man learns to press the button only when the light is on. The light can be said to be the discriminative stimulus for button pressing behaviour in this particular Jones Box situation. The task could have been made more complex and more in line with teaching social skills if the light had been replaced by a screen on which photographs of smiling and unsmiling faces were projected. The music could have been available when the button was pushed while a smiling face was displayed. Such an experiment would probably have resulted in the little man discriminating between smiling and non smiling faces and pushing the button accordingly.

Attending to Task
Among the most important signals that we teach children who come to Beech Tree House are those which train them to attend to task; that is to say, to get on with whatever work or play activity they are given to do. The signals used to stimulate the required behaviour may differ from one child to another but the goal is the same. A child who understands simple spoken language will hear his name, followed by 'Look, do this,' or 'Look, what is this?' according to the nature of the task. Children without understanding of the spoken word will receive similar instructions in sign or symbol form. In addition to the 'command' or 'instruction' which acts as a discriminative stimulus for the children to produce attend-

ing to task behaviour, they will also learn that certain environmental cues signal that attending behaviour is likely to be rewarded. Sitting at a table in a classroom with a teacher should eventually become a pretty potent signal that cooperative behaviours will be rewarded and uncooperative ones will, at best, be ignored.

Sadly, many people who work with mentally handicapped children do not appreciate that attending behaviour itself, and the occasions when it should be displayed, may have to be taught. Approximately one third of the children we have educated required programmes to teach them attending to task skills. In each case it was obviously unhelpful to avoid the teaching implications of their problem by describing the children as hyperactive, inattentive, or not yet ready for formal learning experiences; practical steps could, and should, have been taken. The truth of this statement is shown by the progress they made in Beech Tree House. The distraction low room has, of course, been a great help in teaching some of the children.

Operant Behaviour
On page 154 the little man in the Jones box was described as 'operating on his environment' when he pushed the buttons. This may have struck the reader as an odd way of describing his behaviour. However, it served to introduce the idea that certain types of behaviour can be thought of as operations by a person upon his surroundings. Behaviour modifers often refer to *operant behaviour* – those types of behaviour which can be modified (increased or decreased) by the stimulus events which follow them. In many ways operant behaviour can be regarded as the behaviour which people choose to emit – it is sometimes referred to as voluntary behaviour.

There is another class of behaviour which may be contrasted with operant behaviour (see Figure 21). This is termed *respondent* behaviour and occurs as a response to stimulus events; for example, blinking at a loud noise, sneezing after sniffing pepper, or an increase in heart rate on coming close to danger. In each case the behaviour has been precipitated by a particular stimulus and the ensuing behaviour is strikingly similar in different people. Such behaviour can also be termed *involuntary* behaviour – it is to a large extent outside the individual's control.

The distinction between the two broad categories of behaviour is not as clear-cut as the preceding paragraphs might suggest, for in practice there is often a blurring of the two types. Perhaps the most important aspect of the distinction is that operant behaviour

Respondent and Operant Behaviour

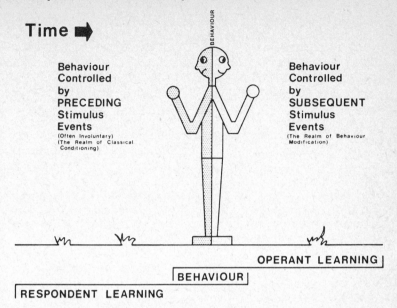

Figure 21.   Respondent and operant behaviour.

is controlled by what follows it and is therefore open to modification in ways outlined earlier, while respondent behaviour is not.

Rewards, Positive Reinforcement and Punishment

Lay people and many behaviour modifiers use the words 'reward' and 'reinforcement' as if they were synonymous. This is not the case. A 'reinforcer' is technically defined as 'a stimulus event which follows an operant behaviour and which changes the frequency with which the operant is emitted'. The definition does not indicate whether the frequency of the behaviour goes up or down; it merely states that it changes. If it increased after a particular reinforcer was used then the reinforcer could be regarded as a reward. However, if the stimulus event following a behaviour were unpleasant it would no doubt lower the frequency with which the behaviour occurred. In this second example the definition has once again been complied with but the reinforcer has not had a rewarding effect: it is, in fact, a punishment. Thus the term reinforcer is neutral – it indicates that a stimulus event changes behaviour, but gives no idea of the direction of change. Whenever it is used in a report of a training programme it should be suitably qualified so the reader is aware what type of reinforcement was used.

A *positive* reinforcer is equivalent to the layman's 'reward'. The technical definition is 'a stimulus event which follows an operant which increases the frequency with which the operant is emitted.' The definition is somewhat circular – something is only a positive reinforcer if the behaviour it follows increases. It has to be stated in this way because each individual has his own preferred stimulus events (rewards). As I have mentioned earlier, certain handicaps exclude some people from sharing whole ranges of stimulus events, and even if the same stimulus events are shared it does not follow that they are liked equally by all those who can share them. For example, I have described some children who perceived Smarties as punishment and shied away from them. (One very good reason for collecting data is to be sure that what is assumed by a teacher to be a positive reinforcer is regarded in the same way by her pupil. If there is evidence that the desired behaviour is increasing there are reasonable grounds to believe that this is the case).

The definition of punishment should cause no surprises: 'a stimulus event which follows an operant which decreases the frequency with which the operant is emitted'. The problem with the term is that people do not like to admit that they use punishment as a teaching technique, particularly with handicapped children.

The fact that punishment is used can be concealed in all manner of ways, perhaps the least acceptable being a tacit understanding by staff that physical punishment may be used so long as no injuries show and the practice remains undetected. I have worked in establishments where terms such as 'Thump Therapy' were in common parlance because a significant number of staff resorted to the practice. A second method of concealment is that of handling difficult residents roughly but not actually striking them. While no blows are given, the residents can have a very unpleasant time as they 'fall down steps'. 'bump into doors' and so on.

It seems likely that as the large institutions which care for mentally handicapped people become better staffed and more open to inspection such bad practices will die out. Nevertheless, there is cause for concern in the strength of professional organisations and unions to protect their members against the often confused testimony of handicapped residents who allege brutality and ill-treatment. Another worrying area is the growth of private establishments to cater for mentally handicapped adults. By and large the charities do the work well, but there is a growing tendency for business people to open units as money-making ventures, and while undoubtedly many of these will be well conducted, adequate legislation and an effective inspectorate are urgently needed to enforce good practice.

A more subtle approach to concealment is to call it Negative Reinforcement. This, as I shall explain later, is a complete misuse of the term, but it is one resorted to by staff attempting to avoid the censure that is often directed at those who use punishment as part of their training technique.

It seems to us vital that staff should be absolutely clear about how they may behave towards the children and adults with whom they work. The moment that any covert practices spring up, the avowed training procedures can be undermined. Even more serious are the dangers that the pupils or residents are exposed to. In the past ten years, despite improvements in staffing, there has been a steady stream of reports of violent and inhumane treatment in institutions for mentally and physically handicapped people.

One way of reducing the occurrence of such practices is to back up the guidelines on handling children by having senior staff periodically work alongside junior colleagues; this is what happens in our unit. The moment that senior staff divorce themselves from the clients for whom they are responsible they become dependent upon other people to pass them accurate information about shop floor practice. They appear to overlook the fact that there will almost inevitably be a filtering of the information they receive. The glossing over of disagreeable facts occurs because it is usually in the interest of intermediate management to paint as rosy a picture as possible of the areas for which they are responsible. In Beech Tree House we have avoided the filter effect and further enhanced the flow of information and good practice by our scheduled individual and group meetings between senior and junior staff, at which children, programmes and handling techniques are discussed.

Negative Reinforcement

Negative reinforcement should never be confused with punishment, and it is always useful to ask a person using the term to give an example of what they mean by it. We have found this a particularly important thing to do when we accompany parents on visits to schools and units to which their children may transfer from Beech Tree House. Our suspicions are roused from time to time when staff showing us round use the term 'negative reinforcement' in complete isolation from any other behaviour modification terminology. If they do use punishment techniques we feel that parents should know what *type* they employ; there is a world of difference between withdrawing tokens or attention and severe physical punishment or withdrawal of food for minor misdemeanours.

Punishment-based training strategies can have a place in educating mentally handicapped children, particularly in initially reducing the occurrence of disruptive behaviour and thereby giving an alternative appropriate behaviour a chance to be trained in. Whenever we feel that such a strategy might help a child in Beech Tree House we discuss the matter with the child's parents. If it is agreed to use the procedure, careful data is collected and reviewed on a weekly basis; if there is no evidence to suggest that the approach is working it will be abandoned and an alternative strategy will be tried.

Punishment *follows* a behaviour. It is something that is not liked by a child and has the effect of *decreasing* the behaviour. Negative reinforcement precedes and is stopped by the behaviour; the stopping is liked and has the effect of *increasing* the behaviour. It is clear that the two are very different indeed.

Perhaps part of the confusion comes about because in both cases there is a stimulus event which the child does not like. However, in one case it happens *after* the child has done something; in the other the child *escapes* from it by doing something. Perhaps a Jones Box example will help (see Diagram 21).

The box is fitted with a powerful extractor fan which the little man can turn on for one minute by pushing a button. There is also a large aerosol containing a nauseating smell which the experimenter can squirt by remote control. On the first occasion the smell is released the little man holds his breath and his nose while he looks round to see what he can do to ease his predicament. He pushes the button and the extractor fan rapidly removes the smell. The smell is released once more and the button is pressed immediately. The little man has been negatively reinforced for pushing the button. His operant behaviour has enabled him to escape from a very unpleasant stimulus event.

Negatively reinforced behaviour is very common. Often it involves voting with one's feet, that is, simply leaving a disliked situation; for example, a henpecked husband may escape to the pub. In other types the unpleasant stimulus event may be internal – as in the case of an anxious student who reduces her anxiety by studying; or of a chattering pupil who stops the teacher's frown

Negative Reinforcing Jones Box

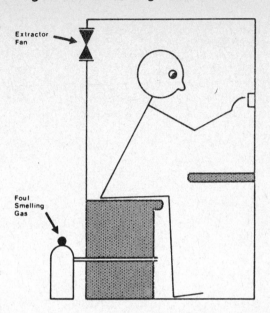

Extractor
Fan

Foul
Smelling
Gas

Diagram 21. Negative reinforcing Jones Box showing how behaviour can be discouraged by encouraging alternative behaviour.

and the fear it provokes by getting on with his work. For example, one boy would not eat his lunch, whatever was offered. We tried many approaches but had no success until we sat him at a table facing the wall until he cleared his plate. The negative reinforcement in this case was the boredom he suffered – this was enhanced by leaving the door open so that he could hear the fun that other children were having. If he ate his meal he was free to leave the disliked situation. There is nothing revolutionary in this strategy: it is what my mother did with me many years ago.

The Need for Parents to Understand the Principles of Effective Teaching

I have talked with a great many parents of mentally handicapped children about the methods that they use to train their children. Most have worked incredibly hard to teach them new skills but very few have received helpful professional guidance before their child started at Beech Tree House. It could be argued that parents of normally developing children do not receive tuition in child training techniques, although routine health guidance is generally offered to prospective mothers. Apart from child rearing books and articles in women's magazines, there is little or no preparation for parenthood. Nevertheless, most children make good progress and learn quickly and easily, probably because the skills that their parents need are passed on by grandparents, other relatives, friends and neighbours. Unfortunately mentally handicapped children are not comparable: few pick up appropriate new behaviour easily and the special understanding which is so vital for their parents is not shared by their acquaintances. It would therefore make a great deal of sense if the parents of such children could be trained in the rudiments of good teaching.

Although it strains both our credulity and patience, we still occasionally meet parents of young handicapped children who have been told that their children will not achieve anything and that the best they can do is put them away and start again. Such advice is no doubt well intentioned but it can only be based upon ignorance; there is extensive evidence to suggest that even very severely mentally handicapped people have a potential which was formerly unrecognised. To realise this potential, however, the handicapped children must receive good training from the moment they are born. The gloomy 'realists', as they would no doubt like to be called, do nothing to encourage this.

Nina Story, the acting Head of Beech Tree House, has worked in pre-school intervention programmes in America. The encouraging results of this work convinced her of the great value of early training for handicapped children and more importantly their parents. We hope that in our new community-based unit she will have an opportunity to explore a new service in which we will offer parent training for families who are experiencing problems managing their young handicapped children.

When Positively to Reinforce Behaviour
The first thing we teach parents whose children come to us is the importance of giving positive reinforcement the very moment a desired behaviour occurs. Unless this happens learning is very difficult, particularly for mentally handicapped children. This can be demonstrated by returning to the Jones Box. This time you, the reader, are asked to pretend that you have changed places with the little man and that you are in the original box with the three buttons. The conditions appear to be the same and a drink that you particularly like is available behind the small door. There is one slight change, however: Ken Ketteridge has devised an

electronic gadget which imposes a delay of thirty seconds between the pushing of a button and the operating of a device.

It is assumed that you are unaware of the fate of the little man, so you would probably size up the situation, push a button, wait a second or so then push another one, and so on. If nothing happened you might try pushing two or three buttons at once. Thirty seconds after you had touched the first button you would be subjected to a barrage of drinks and jabs interspersed by gaps where you had pressed the white button or sat thinking. As a result of repeated jabs and the appearance of numerous drinks, you would probably go into a state of shock and not touch any of the buttons for a considerable time. Your confusion would have been created by the delay between touching buttons and the stimulus event associated with each touch. If you can be so easily confused by a slight delay, consider the difficulty that mentally handicapped children must have if their behaviour is not immediately followed by a clear outcome of one sort or another.

Very few parents realise the importance of rewarding good behaviour the moment it happens so that the child can associate the behaviour with a pleasant consequence. The same can be said for many staff who may be acquainted with the theory but cannot be said to understand it at an operational level, since they hardly ever seem to put it into practice. Time and again we have visited units where staff believe that they are running programmes, for example toilet training, along behaviour modification lines, and cannot understand why they are getting poor results. The usual mistake is that staff are not positively reinforcing behaviour as it occurs. What tends to happen is that a child is placed upon a pot, often among a group of children who are similarly treated, and he is lifted and the pot checked every five minutes or so. If the pot is found to contain urine or faeces the member of staff will, with luck, sound very pleased as she gives praise and a sweet. Unfortunately it is rare that the child is lifted just as he is performing; that probably happened some minutes earlier. By her ill-timed positive reinforcement the member of staff may well have rewarded the behaviour that was going on when she picked the child off the pot – perhaps hand flapping or teeth grinding!

We avoid such problems in Beech Tree House by using the Pedestal Urine Detector. This signals the moment the bladder or rectum starts to empty and so we are able to reward this behaviour rather than something irrelevant which might happen later.

In a way positive reinforcement may be regarded as a form of *feedback* which reassures trainees that they are doing the right thing. Such encouraging 'knowledge of results' is of course particularly valuable to children who are unable to understand language.

Punishment should be used in exactly the same way as positive reinforcement – immediately after the behaviour which is not wanted. It is quite useless to tell a child who has difficulty with language and little or not concept of time that, because he has been a naughty boy all morning, his daddy will hear of it and will punish him when he gets in from work. He is most unlikely to understand the threat at the time it is given and will have no idea why his father is angry with him when he arrives home. This strategy is obviously as unlikely to change current behaviour as a promise of an ice-cream next time the child goes to town. The only ice-cream likely to affect behaviour in the here-and-now is one given in small pieces after each correct behaviour.

Not only are positive reinforcers and punishments given in the here-and-now effective in changing behaviour; nothing following a behaviour can have a significant impact as well – particularly if nothing happens regularly enough. This is probably the second most important fact about learning to teach to parents of mentally handicapped children.

Extinction

A great many people put money into fruit machines; most of them know that they are unlikely to win in the long run – the owners of the machines have to make a living after all – but each one hopes that he might be the person to strike lucky and hit the jackpot this particular time round. The machines periodically pay out varying small amounts of money and so the putting in of coins is positively reinforced. If a very greedy and very stupid fruit machine owner tampered with the mechanism of his machines so that they never stopped on a winning line, the public would very rapidly lose interest in putting money into them. Similarly the little man in the Jones Box would stop pressing the button to turn on music if it was disconnected from the tape recorder.

The process of gradually ceasing to produce a behaviour which is not rewarded is known as *extinction*. It is a phenomenon which can be used to advantage by behaviour modifers. It is true to say that, in many cases, if you ignore a behaviour it will go away, and in our experience the many odd or annoying behaviour patterns produced by Beech Tree House children at home are sustained by the attention that they attract from the parents. The 'Don't do that,' and the 'Oh, look what he's doing now!' reactions are sure-fire ways of getting children to pull down the curtains or thrust their fingers up their noses, particularly if quiet, acceptable play behaviour was previously being ignored. It is possibly wrong to call such behaviour *attention seeking*; a more accurate term might be *attention gaining*. I suggest this distinction because I am not convinced that severely mentally handicapped children deliberately set out to gain attention; whereas I am quite certain that many people, particularly loving parents, are all too inclined to give attention to unusual and disruptive behaviour.

There is only one secret ingredient for success if this method of dealing with unwanted behaviour is used and that is that the ignoring must be done consistently. For example, it is useless for parents to ignore a behaviour if grandparents react to it when they visit. Quite the opposite is true – research indicates that behaviour which is rewarded only intermittently is the most resistant to extinction!

Extinction procedures may be appropriate for mild problems but should be considered very carefully before they are used to treat dangerous behaviour, particularly self destructive behaviour. The reason for this is that when a behaviour which was formally positively reinforced is no longer rewarded it tends to increase in frequency and sometimes in ferocity. The dangers of such a possible development are obvious.

Competing Behaviour Strategies
Extinction procedures are usually most effective when they are combined in a programme in which appropriate behaviour, which is incompatible with the unwanted one, is positively reinforced – for example, when a child's hand flapping behaviour is ignored while any appropriate manipulation of toys is rewarded. If such a programme were successful it would give data of the sort shown in Figure 22. It is clear from the graph that as appropriate manipulation of toys increases, so hand flapping decreases. The two are in competition, so any increase in one must cause a decrease in the other. This training approach, appropriately called a Competing Behaviour Design, is a strategy often used in Beech Tree House. For example, Trevor was taught to fetch and use his rug making kit when he was not engaged in other activities; he was fined tokens if he damaged his clothes.

How Often to Reward?
When a child starts to learn a new skill, learning takes place most rapidly if every correct reponse is rewarded, but as the child's mastery increases it is good practice to *fade* out the rewards. To start with the teacher might positively reinforce every second correct response, then every third correct response, and so on.

Competing Behaviour Graph

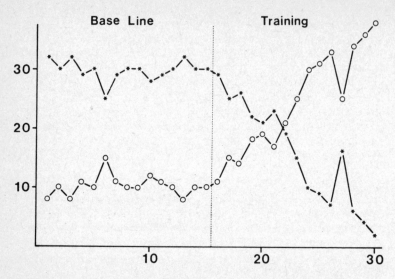

Figure 22.   Competing behaviour graph, showing the result of combining extinction procedures with positive reinforcement of alternative behaviour.

The most potent *reinforcement schedule* (the technical term for the chosen distribution of rewards to correct responses) is one in which the child cannot predict when the next reward will be given. This reinforcement schedule is considered to be the most potent not because it enhances learning, but because once a child has transferred to it the skill in question becomes very resistant to extinction.

Just as there are horses for courses so there are different reinforcement schedules for different stages in teaching and consolidating skills. W.T. Gardener (1971) has some particularly helpful sections in his book *Behaviour Modification in Mental Retardation*.

Behaviour Modification in Beech Tree House
We are sometimes disappointed to encounter people who appear to think that Beech Tree House and behaviour modification are in some way synonymous. We always stress that our methods are eclectic and that we are prepared to use virtually any technique which demonstrably works and is acceptable to the children's

parents and ourselves. Perhaps the behavioural label has become so firmly attached because we endeavour to evaluate everything we do by collecting data. This is only one aspect of the behavioural approach, but it is something of a hall mark. While rigorous evaluation of progress by means of data analysis is not exclusive to the behavioural approach, there is a tendency for the practitioners of a number of other techniques to be less hard-nosed in the way they assess the effectiveness of the procedures they use.

In our experience, the more a group of practitioners is committed to a particular technique, the less are they able to stand back from it and critically review what is really going on. It is almost as if their commitment to the method admits of no criticism. (This can be contrasted with the behavioural approach which uses data of progress, or the lack of it, to determine whether programmes will continue. Methods that do not work are modified or abandoned.) They become virtual disciples of the chosen approach and their critical judgement may be seriously affected. We have visited a number of residential schools where this process appeared to be at work and the staff were not prepared to discuss in any detail the training methods they used; they confined their conversation to examples of children who made progress and appeared to discount any possibility of failure. At one particular school we were told that the training manual was their 'bible' and that only staff were allowed access to it! Try a I might I was unable to discover how the children were taught or what sort of results were obtained. Needless to say I was unable to recommend the school either to the parents or the local authority who would be responsible for the fees.

Some schools, regrettably, do not have an explicit theory of learning underpinning their approach to teaching. This condition is nearly as worrying as the one described in the previous paragraph, since teachers in such schools work without the support of a shared teaching philosophy and do their own thing in their classroom castle. They are often unaware that many of the children's learning difficulties could be resolved if common teaching principles were adopted. If they ever got round to discussing what they were trying to do as teachers, rather than chattering about the imposition of playground duty or the unfairness of the latest allocation of ancillary staff, they would probably find that they did not share a common language to describe how children behave nor, without establishing a basis, would they be able to reach a consensus on how they should be taught.

At the present time a great deal of energy is being spent in special schools developing curricula for handicapped children.

This is obviously important, but in my opinion less important than developing a shared understanding by all staff of the processes believed to underly different types of learning. Without such a shared understanding quite unforgivable conflicts can crop up between the teaching styles of colleagues within the same school. Disastrous consequences for pupils can follow as they move from one class to another.

One such conflict occurred when a boy, who had been successfully trained to work alone by being given warm praise when he attended to task, moved to a class in which the teacher believed that children should work for the reward of completing the task itself. On his arrival she stated that he had been spoiled by his previous teacher and that she would not be going in for all that praising. The sad outcome was that within three weeks the boy reverted to his earlier stereotyped behaviour, a tragedy which I vowed would not happen in Beech Tree House, even when children moved between staff of different disciplines. I was convinced the problem could be solved by offering thorough staff training to everyone involved with the children.

Whether or not they recognise the fact, all teachers, qualified or untrained, work according to some guiding principle. Kathleen Devereux's book *Understanding Learning Difficulties* (1982) is particularly valuable in that it clearly defines the major theories behind different teaching practices and so helps staff to relate to each other's style.

An apparently trite example should clarify the above point and the problems that can arise when even traditional commonsense ideas are involved. A teacher who follows the practice advocated by the proverb 'Spare the rod and spoil the child' is working within a sort of teaching philosophy; she will tend to react in a firm manner to behaviour she judges to be bad, and it is likely that she would come into conflict with anyone who followed the contradictory philosophy, 'Beat out one devil and beat in ten more.' The dilemma posed by these conflicting views could probably be resolved by examining in the presence of both protagonists the conditions under which each approach might be effective, and by showing that neither approach has all the answers – that is, that the best possible approach would draw something from both propositions.

Because of our large annual turnover, the idea that *all* staff should be aware of the whole range of learning theories is impractical in Beech Tree House (it is of course a great advantage to have all core staff sharing the breadth of knowledge described above). Our conclusion has been that the next best solution is to train all staff to understand and practise *one* method in the first instance and then to extend their knowledge as the need arises. We teach the essentials of the behavioural approach at the staff training course and supplement this at Team Meetings throughout the year with information about other strategies.

We have chosen the behavioural approach because its techniques are particularly suited to the needs of the severely and moderately mentally handicapped children with specific and disabling habits who comprise the majority of our pupils. As I have stated earlier, we are convinced that most of the behaviour problems they display on arrival are learned strategies for dealing with an environment which they are unable to control by more orthodox means. We see our task with such children as teaching them more appropriate strategies, while eliminating those that are unacceptable. A behaviour modification approach is ideal for such training. It would be a rash person who advocated a counselling approach for a severely mentally handicapped child with extensive self destructive behaviour; on the other hand counselling would probably be a very suitable aspect of treatment for older children of average intelligence whose difficult behaviour appeared to have an emotional basis.

It should be noted that where we have chosen to use counselling techniques we have continued to collect data on the children's behaviour and, where appropriate, we have augmented the counselling with token contracts for good behaviour, straightforward skill training and so on.

Ethical Problems
Behaviour modification does not tell anyone *what* they should teach. It is a method, not a curriculum. If a behaviourist is teaching the wrong thing it has nothing to do with Behaviourism – the practitioner has simply chosen the wrong goal and is open to criticism like everyone else. Having said this, I must concede that the behavioural approach is a great deal more suited to training basic skills, simple discriminations and appropriate behaviour than it is for teaching complex skills, cognitive ability or moral concepts. To this extent the behaviour modifier's curriculum is fairly tightly circumscribed. In Beech Tree House we tend to duck the issue of what we should teach by dealing initially with the obvious educational blocks and then consulting with the parents and the staff at the units to which the children will probably transfer.

The *how* of behaviour modification is a more vexed question. There are rarely any problems over the principle of encouragement by positive reinforcement, but some people do question the use of sweets and other consumables through concern for diet and teeth. This can become fatuous when possible damage to teeth (which are cleaned very regularly in the unit) is argued to be more important than self inflicted damage which is clearly ongoing and yet can be improved by the judicious use of consumable rewards for the absence of such behaviour.

Another accusation is that of bribery, our positive reinforcers being construed as inducements to behave correctly; this pre-supposes the existence of moral absolutes and the theory that these need only be revealed to our children for the problems to be resolved. Children should learn to urinate on the toilet because that is the right thing to do – not because they have associated this act with a pleasing consequence. Those of us who actively use rewards are seen as being culpable of spoiling the children. What is overlooked is that a bribe is something offered before a behaviour and is intended to get the recipient to act out of character in a way which is to the advantage of the giver. A positive reinforcement differs in a number of aspects. It is given after a correct behaviour to encourage its repetition and the behaviour is primarily to the advantage of the receiver.

The use of punishment and time out strategies cause the greatest ethical problems. Here we feel unable to speak for any other practitioners. The position we take is that we will only use such techniques when we have failed to discover reward strategies which work. Moreover, we only do this with the full consent of parents or parent substitutes. Even so, we never employ tech-niques that we would shrink from using in front of a properly briefed member of the public. This latter point is probably the acid test as far as we are concerned in determining what teaching strategies we will consider.

Behaviour Modification in its Place

When used correctly, behaviour modification is a powerful and humane teaching technique. However, I have already indicated that it is not a panacea – it is more appropriate for teaching some skills than others. It has one other great drawback – the time and care that has to be taken in carrying out each programme. To succeed in a reasonable time these must be followed to the letter, and consequently only a relatively small number of programmes can be run at a time: staff cannot cope with more. In Beech Tree House it is rare for any child to be involved with more than three unit-wide programmes at a time, but even when kept to this number, staff are still involved in twenty-seven programmes with whose details they must be entirely familiar and which they must apply round the clock.

Because so few programmes can be run at any one time, the staff and parents have to make decisions about priorities and agree which are the most important problems or skills to tackle with each child. Having agreed the priorities, what happens to the many other potential areas of learning? We do not simply abandon them. Many skills are worked upon intensively during 'School' and are well followed up at other times, although not with the same intensity as the unit-wide programmes.

Another less formal means of instruction is employed by the staff: they *model* good patterns of behaviour, being courteous, well mannered and kind. Such behaviour contrasts very favourably with the practice we have witnessed in some units where there was unhappiness, tension and scant respect between staff. This was manifest in the way they spoke to each other and went about their work. Disparaging comments about senior colleagues and conditions of service were even exchanged in the presence of children. It is true that the pupils might well have missed the full significance of what they overheard, but many would have detected the staff's dissatisfaction and irritation by their tone of voice. We are certain that such models of behaviour are harmful to children who can grow to believe that they are acceptable and start to copy them.

Although we appreciate that the practice of staff modelling good behaviour is not a particularly rapid way of changing children's behaviour, we nevertheless keep our standards high at all times. We are often agreeably surprised at the changes parents report in their children in areas where we know there has been no direct teaching – we can only assume that modelling or maturation has caused the change. Since we cannot identify which is responsible and have no control over maturation anyway, we intend to go right on modelling good behaviour in the anticipation that there will continue to be a spin-off for the children.

A final point, occasionally confused with the practice of providing good models, needs to be considered when putting behaviour modification in its place. This concerns the emotional atmosphere in which children and staff live and work. A writer once used a sentence along the following lines when describing a behaviour modification unit: 'The corridors rang with insincere cries of "Good! Well done!" as staff doled out the mandatory social reinforcement.' The writer had obviously detected a distancing or alienation between the staff and the children. I realise that this can happen, particularly when staff begin to play a set role in a mechanical manner. I have actually heard people who use behaviour modification refer to themselves as 'behaviour change agents'. We doubt if this will happen in Beech Tree House because we have taken the precaution of sharing the lives of our children and their families and consequently begin to share their problems and triumphs, too. While the atmosphere in our unit is not always calm and suffused with warmth and love, it is never cold or regimented.

We are convinced that the organisation and atmosphere that we have created to live and work in demonstrate that we have put behaviour modification in its place – it is simply a very effective technique that we have at our disposal. We use it to help children who have problems which typically respond to a behavioural approach, and we have become known as advocates simply because the majority of our pupils fall into this category.

8   COLLECTING USEFUL AND RELIABLE DATA

Data in Mainstream Teaching
Most teachers in mainstream education work effectively without collecting data other than the marks their pupils earn for doing tests, examinations and regular work assignments. Periodically such teachers prepare reports on their pupils' progress and the parents, who receive the reports, praise their children or exhort them to greater effort depending upon the results their sons and daughters obtained.

Who is Responsible for Poor Pupil Attainment?
Mainstream children are usually regarded as being personally responsible for the quality of their work; if things are not going well it is the child who is expected to do something about it. From time to time, when an entire class is noticed to have done badly, a teacher may be regarded as being at fault, but this conclusion is rarely reached and there is a strong tendency to disregard the child who says, 'I can't learn it. Teacher doesn't tell us clearly enough how to do it,' on the grounds that such explanations are usually no more than an excuse for the child's inattention or laziness.

It is not only parents who fall into the trap of regarding teachers as virtually infallible and children as the weak link in the learning process. Teachers themselves are generally of the same opinion! Too few of them are prepared to examine statements of the type, 'John can't seem to learn to read,' and to reword them as follows: 'I can't seem to teach reading to John.' In the latter version the responsibility for getting John to understand the printed word clearly lies with the teacher who must try and establish what John's problems are and what steps to take to remediate them. From this perspective, John's lack of success can be thought of as reflecting the ineffectiveness of the teaching strategies used and not his culpability in refusing to learn.

This principle, that staff are responsible for finding an effective teaching strategy for each pupil – not that pupils must adapt their learning to the staff's teaching style – is very important in guiding the efforts of staff in Beech Tree House and much of our work is concerned with collecting data which will indicate precisely the nature of the problems interfering with the learning of our children.

Once the mainstream teacher in our example has identified the problems which are preventing her teaching John effectively, she may well conclude that she can do little or nothing to remediate them herself. Nevertheless, she will, at least, have avoided projecting the blame for not learning onto John, and in many instances she may be able to obtain help from other agencies. John's work may have been affected by an undetected visual difficulty which could be helped by an optician; he may have been seriously disturbed by a crisis at home which could be resolved by professional counselling; or he may have had a perceptual problem which made reading a very difficult skill for him to acquire – in this last case the teacher might be able to obtain specialist advice on appropriate teaching strategies.

In Beech Tree House it is difficult for staff to suggest that the failure of teaching programmes is the responsibility of the children since, in most cases, the children are physically, mentally or socially handicapped and there is little or nothing that they can do to overcome such problems themselves. If a particular programme fails it is quite pointless to abandon the *goal* on the grounds that the child appears poorly motivated to achieve it; the sensible thing to do is to abandon the failed teaching *strategy* and introduce another which might enable the child to achieve the desired goal.

Homogeneity of Pupils' Skills Affects Teaching Style
The teaching style of staff in Beech Tree House differs from that practised by teachers working in mainstream schools, largely because unit staff have to take account of children's physical and/or mental disabilities in addition to their often unenviable educational histories. It is reasonable for mainstream teachers to assume that children grouped into classes have certain skills and knowledge in common, and an English teacher confronted with a class of fourteen year-olds of average ability will have a fair idea at what level to pitch the lesson. A teacher confronted by a similar number of fourteen year-old multiply handicapped children would not be able to make the same, if any, assumptions; in fact, it would probably be true that no two children in such a group could follow the same teaching programme. It is therefore especially difficult to devise a satisfactory curriculum for the schools in which they are educated.

Most children who arrive in Beech Tree House readily display the reasons why they have been referred by running through their full range of acting out behaviour during the first few weeks in the unit; there is rarely any need to collect data to establish *what* the problems are. We do, however, usually establish a *base line* of the extent of each problem behaviour before training is commenced and data is also collected to identify any *patterns* to the behaviour and reveal what tends to *trigger* and *maintain* it.

Few mainstream teachers are involved in team teaching – most tend to work in 'classroom castles' in which they teach their class in isolation from the outside world. Teachers and children get to know each other's idiosyncrasies and, more often that not, good working relationships are established. Such a cosy approach is not possible when children require a form of education which continues right round the clock, day after day, throughout the year – this can only be offered by a team of people who work in a very similar manner. One effective way of achieving the required similarity of approach is to specify in writing all the teaching operations involved in each programme and train each member of staff to follow them to the letter. Having achieved this, all the staff must be kept up to date concerning each child's progress and be aware of any variations in the training method.

Data Collecting in Beech Tree House
Since the unit opened we have tried out many data recording techniques and have abandoned more than we have retained. In the early days we fell into the trap of developing a new technique virtually every time data were required; staff had to keep learning new methods and, as these increased in number, so did the possibility for confusion. The only real advantage we can claim for this approach is that long-serving staff became familiar with a wide range of techniques and the pitfalls involved in many of them.

After about three years of frenetically developing novel data collecting techniques, we rationalised our approach and settled on a small number of straightforward strategies that we realised would give the most reliable data. It seems that, as the number of people who are involved in collecting data increases, so the complexity of the technique should decrease; if this rule is not followed all manner of mistakes creep in. We are convinced that any possible loss of detail is more than outweighed by the accuracy with which we collect our data.

Slick Data Collecting
There are a number of general points about data collecting which can make the difference between a rather hit and miss affair and an efficient exercise. First and foremost, staff should be properly

trained for the task and there should be a regular opportunity for them to compare notes and resolve any problems. In Beech Tree House training and discussion takes place at the Team Meeting where there are facilities to project slides of any data schedule that may be causing concern.

Although it may seem obvious, it needs to be stressed that data schedules should remain clean, intact and readily accessible when needed. It is not good practice to have to scrabble under piles of paper on the Head's desk to find a child's toilet training data sheet, and finally locate it stained with coffee rings because it has been mistaken for scrap and folded up to protect the desk from a hot mug! It would be interesting to know how much valuable data has met a similar fate. The solution we have adopted is to provide each data schedule with a good-quality clipboard, clearly labelled and with a pen securely attached. If staff have to search for a pen, another incident may intervene and the data go unrecorded. It is also essential, for the same reason, to locate the clipboards in a known and convenient place.

Designated members of staff should be responsible for given sets of data; unless this happens data can be collected and then disappear into limbo instead of being used to refine the teaching strategy or positively reinforce the staff because progress is being made. For example, until the Playroom Group Teacher was made responsible for toilet training data, this information often ended up in the children's files without progress being reported to any-one; it might be left in the Toilet Training Area to gather dust or worse; be put on one side in the Office; or it might end up in the toilet trainer's personal file. Whichever fate it met, it was not being used to guide the following week's toilet trainer or being presented in summary form at a subsequent Team Meeting.

The nominated member of staff should also ensure that data are being collected in accordance with the agreed method. Unless someone checks for uniformity of approach there is always a tendency for inaccuracies to creep in. New staff find the nominated data person extremely valuable during their early days in the unit.

It is equally important for one person to be responsible for the simple equipment used to collect data: the Tally Counters, the Fixed Interval Timers, the Kitchen Timers, the Wee-Ds, and so on. All these items should be returned to a designated place where their working order can be checked and if appropriate their batteries recharged. In Beech Tree House we have a labelled rack which enables the person responsible for the devices to be able to see at a glance if any of them is missing.

Schedule A: Identifying What Precipitates Behaviour and What Maintains It

Introduction
People who use behaviour modification techniques to change behaviour may be said to be concerned with identifying and manipulating the functional relationships that exist between observable stimulus events and the specified behaviour of given individuals; or in plain English, they try to work out what makes a person behave in a particular way and, having done this, they use the information systematically to improve the behaviour.

For example, one of our non-communicating children worried his parents because he slapped his own face and screamed. They interpreted these outbursts as the 'outward signs of periods of deep inner depression and distress'. An experienced observer, however, would have noticed that this behaviour almost always occurred when the parents played with the boy's sister, attempted to do housework or watched television. The observer would probably have summarised his observations as follows: 'Whenever John slaps his face and screams, his parents rush to calm him or distract him from this behaviour. They offer him sweets, toys and rough-and-tumble games. John invariably ceases his screaming and slapping when dealt with in this way. The screaming and face slapping tend to occur when John is left to his own devices.'

The observer has therefore done more than simply report the occurrence of a certain distressing behaviour. Unlike the parents who inferred from John's behaviour that he was 'depressed and distressed', the experienced observer has detected a pattern in which one set of events set the behaviour going and the responses to that behaviour calmed it down. He has identified *antecedents* which appear to precipitate *behaviour* and *consequences* which probably reward and thereby sustain it.

This method of analysis has been called the 'ABC of Behaviour' – where A, B and C stand for Antecedents, Behaviour and Consequences. Data collected using this approach enables those responsible for helping people with problem behaviour to identify the events which trigger and sustain it. Such information can provide a solid foundation upon which to build behaviour change programmes.

The Layout of the Schedule
The Schedule is shown in Figure 23. The child's name is written in the box at the top right hand corner.

The following brief instructions appear above the three

A

A.B.C. OBSERVATIONS

ANTECEDENTS, BEHAVIOUR, CONSEQUENCES

SPECIFIED BEHAVIOUR

Please write in the Antecedents column exactly what was happening prior to the specified behaviour. Please write in the Behaviour column the exact nature of the behaviour observed, the date and time it occurred. Please write in the Consequences column exactly what happened for the child after the behaviour. Please initial your notes and draw a line across the page to separate your completed observations from subsequent ones.

ANTECEDENTS	BEHAVIOUR	Date and Time	CONSEQUENCES

Figure 23.   ABC Observation Schedule.

columns: 'Please write in the Antecedents column exactly what was happening prior to the Specified Behaviour. Please write in the Behaviour column the exact nature of the behaviour observed and the date and time that it occurred. Please write in the Consequences column exactly what happened for the child after the behaviour. Please initial your notes and draw a line across the page to separate your completed observation from subsequent ones.'

Above these instructions is a space labelled 'Specified Behaviour.' The behaviour which is to be the subject of A B C analysis is written here and serves to remind observers what they are looking for. It also distinguishes between schedules when two or more specified behaviours are being observed for one child.

The remainder of the schedule is devoted to three columns labelled 'ANTECEDENTS, BEHAVIOUR (Date and Time) and CONSEQUENCES'. Both sides of the schedule are used.

Completing the Schedule

Parents and staff who are involved in collecting ABC data are urged to write down observable behaviour and events rather than what they *think* is happening.

The need to do this is illustrated by the problems of Morris's parents who were convinced that he suffered from what they called 'brain pressure.' This ten year-old severely mentally handicapped boy, who had no spoken or signed communication, would periodically flop to the ground and squirm, flap his hands energetically and go 'La-la-la' in a high-pitched tone. His alarmed parents, who were convinced that sudden increases in the pressure inside his head caused him to flop, reported after a particularly difficult holiday that he had averaged more than five 'brain pressure episodes' a day. They made an appointment with their paediatrician who found no clinical condition to account for the behaviour – there was certainly no sign of 'brain pressure'.

An observant member of staff had noted earlier that, while Morris nearly always flopped when walking past the village post office and the general store, he never flopped outside the wool shop. She had also noted that the wool shop did not sell sweets and that, in general, the flopping behaviour rapidly tailed off as each term progressed. This evidence suggested that the behaviour was manipulative and so a training programme was agreed for use within the unit whereby Morris's flopping to the ground was consistently ignored by staff, once they were sure that he was uninjured.

The training was successful and flopping ceased to occur while

Morris was with staff. However, whenever his parents visited, it would dramatically reappear, and on one occasion, as his mother came through the door of the unit he flopped on the stairs at the sound of her voice. The behaviour also continued at its former rate when Morris went home.

Staff were initially unable to convince the parents that their son's flopping was a rudimentary, if unusual, form of communication; that, in fact, he was 'demanding' attention and goodies in a very effective fashion and that they were complying with these 'requests' by their great concern as each flop occurred. It was equally difficult to convince them that their attempts to coax him from his 'post-flopping distress' with sweets, biscuits and so on, was rewarding the very behaviour which upset them.

Despite their very understandable reservation about our interpretation, the parents agreed to keep an ABC record of flopping during an ensuing holiday. Within a week or so of going home a letter arrived at the unit enclosing the ABC schedule. After about twenty entries a note couched in the following manner concluded the parent's observations: 'No need to do any more of this. We can see what is going on. We shall try to ignore him like you do.'

It was this recognition of the real sequence of events which heralded the start of a successful extinction programme. All subsequent flops were ignored by both parents and staff and the behaviour eventually ceased.

Only Record Observable Data
The preceding example demonstrates the insight that can be obtained by simply recording *observable* behaviour. If, however, the parents had used the ABC schedule to record their *interpretations* of the flopping behaviour, no such insight would have been possible. A schedule completed in an incorrect fashion would probably have included notes of the following type:

Antecedents: Onset of brain pressure occurred. *Behaviour:* Morris fell to the floor. He waved his arms and said 'La-la-la' to indicate that he felt unwell. *Consequences:* After a few minutes lying down and being reassured that he was all right, the brain pressure subsided and he was able to stand and eat his sweets.

If the parents had continued in this fashion they would no doubt have consolidated their explanation of the problem and continued to seek medical help. It is vital therefore to convince users of ABC schedules that they should stick to recording observable data and not interpret what they see.

While accurate information is required, longwinded descriptions are unnecessary; if data collecting becomes a chore it will rarely be done well. In the case of Morris, notes of the type shown in Figure 24 would have been quite sufficient to record a flop occurring outside the village post office.

Agreeing What Should be Recorded

Before an ABC data collecting exercise is undertaken it is vital that all staff and parents understand the procedure to be followed and know exactly what the 'Specified Behaviour' is. In Beech Tree House all the necessary training and discussion takes place at the Team Meeting, or at meetings with parents, and a summary is placed in the child's file and on the ABC clipboard.

Any member of staff or a parent may alert the team that a child

A

A.B.C. OBSERVATIONS

Morris

ANTECEDENTS, BEHAVIOUR, CONSEQUENCES

SPECIFIED BEHAVIOUR Falling to the ground, accompanied by 'la-la' & hand flapping

Please write in the Antecedents column exactly what was happening prior to the specified behaviour. Please write in the Behaviour column the exact nature of the behaviour observed, the date and time it occurred. Please write in the Consequences column exactly what happens for two to three minutes after the behaviour. Please initial your note, and draw a line across the page to separate your completed observation from subsequent ones.

ANTECEDENTS	BEHAVIOUR DATE & TIME	CONSEQUENCES
Walking with Peter and Emma to park, along main street. Incident happened as we approached village store (Staff – Jane & myself)	Sagged at knees, hands to ground, lay on back and flapped hands. Looked at us intently. He got up and caught us up after we had walked on. J.S. 10.42 Sat 12 May	We all walked past him. I had to tell Emma to be quiet because she wanted to go to him. We walked a little more slowly once we had all gone past. Morris received no apparent attention

Figure 24.   Partially completed ABC Schedule showing how observations are recorded.

has a significant problem which might be better understood by doing a series of ABC observations and because other data collecting commitments must be taken into account, the team decides what priority to assign the request.

How to Collect the Data

A number of the data collecting techniques used in Beech Tree House require staff to use timing devices, tally counters and the like. From this point of view ABC data collecting is simplicity itself: all the observer does is remain alert for the occurrence of the Specified Behaviour and note down the relevant information once the behaviour has diminished or has been contained. Basically the observer has to do no more than look, listen and record accurately.

Concluding Comments

The ABC approach is investigative. It is rarely prescriptive. It does not change behaviour.

Good ABC data should give an idea of what precipitates a specified behaviour and what maintains it. This information is important if successful programmes to change behaviour are to be developed.

Schedule 'B': Counting How Often Things Happen

Introduction

Behaviour modifiers are interested in how *often* people do things. In therapeutic settings they are particularly interested in unusual and disruptive behaviour. For example, at Beech Tree House one child might scream frequently, another might throw equipment while a third might attack weaker children. Since these are probably some of the behaviour problems which brought the children to the unit, the staff will be very interested in obtaining a detailed picture of them.

It is our job to 'treat' such behaviours; that is, we have to eliminate them and give the children alternative, acceptable ways of dealing with their environment.

When behaviour modifiers tackle such problems they are keen to know whether or not the programmes they used have been effective. One way of ascertaining this is to contrast the frequency of occurrence of specified behaviours before and after the programme of treatment. For example, if it can be shown that a child screamed on average 342 times per day during the two weeks preceding a programme, and that this dropped to an average of 31 screams per day during the two weeks following the programme, it would seem reasonable to conclude that the work has been relatively successful.

Behaviour modifiers rarely confine their frequency counting to the periods before and after a programme. They are usually very keen to obtain a clear idea of how a child is progressing while a programme is in operation and so continue their frequency counting throughout the training. This 'on going' data indicates whether any progress is being made and if it is, at what *rate*. The efficacy of programmes evaluated in this way is therefore monitored on a continuous basis.

Frequency counting is a very straightforward technique so long as it used to collect the right sort of data. It is an ideal method where salient, discrete (that is, separate or individually distinct) behaviour is the focus of interest. It is inappropriate for collecting information about inconspicuous or continuous behaviour (see Table 4).

The examples given here should make it clear that this approach to data collecting is best used with types of behaviour which have a clear start and finish, only last a short period of time and by their very nature readily attract the attention of staff.

The Layout of the Schedule
The child's name is written in the box at the top right hand corner of the schedule.

The 'Specified Behaviour', the one to be counted, is written at

For Observation Purposes There Are Two Broad Categories of Behaviour

Salient, Discrete Behaviour	Inconspicuous, Continuous Behaviour
Screaming Leaving seat Throwing equipment Attacking someone	Daydreaming Working quietly Unpicking jumper Wetting self without a Wee-D

Table 4. The two main types of behaviour. Frequency counting is used for recording salient, discrete behaviour.

HALF-HOURLY FREQUENCY COUNTING

SPECIFIED BEHAVIOUR _____

B

_____ WEEK _____

	Monday	Tuesday	Wednesday	Thursday	Friday	Saturday	Sunday
12							
1							
2							
3							
4							
5							
6							
7							
8							
9							
10							
11							
12							
1							
2							
3							
4							
5							
6							
7							
8							
9							
10							
11							
12							

Figure 25.   Frequency Counting Schedule.

the top of the schedule together with the dates during which the data was collected.

There are seven columns, each headed by the appropriate day of the week, the first column being labelled Monday. See Figure 25. There are twenty-four rows, each labelled to indicate the appropriate hours of the day and night and divided by a dotted line into two half-hour blocks. This arrangement enables data to be recorded by the half-hour, day and night, throughout the week.

Completing the Schedule

The schedule is exceptionally easy to fill in. For example, the member of staff who has recorded how often a child screamed between one and one-thirty on a Monday simply writes the figure in the one to one-thirty row of the Monday column.

Agreeing What Should be Recorded

As with all data collecting that takes place in Beech Tree House, *what* data is to be collected is agreed at the Team Meeting.

All staff must know precisely on what behaviour they are going to focus; unless everyone shares the same criteria for the occurrence of the Specified Behaviour, two people observing the same half-hour period may end up with different scores, and if this happens the data will reflect, not how often the child produced the one agreed Specified Behaviour, but rather how often he produced a number of different behaviours specified by the different observers.

If a child's 'pinching' is to be counted, the Specified Behaviour might be defined as 'Any time Janet reaches out and grasps a person's skin between her fingers.' This definition does not include the times when she tries to pinch someone and the person avoids her hand or restrains it, nor does it include times when she pinches clothing rather than skin. It is true that these acts are themselves very interesting and might be the subject of a separate frequency count, but they are not included in the description of 'pinching' as originally defined. The quality of the pinch – whether it causes pain, breaks the skin, causes reddening, etc. – is also excluded from the definition.

It would be entirely in order to start with a definition of the Specified Behaviour as 'Pinching and attempts to pinch'. In this case, each time Janet tried to pinch would be included in the frequency count in addition to successful attempts. Both Specified Behaviours are equally workable – but they cannot be used simultaneously without giving misleading results.

How to Collect the Data

Although it is quite easy to make a small mark on a sheet of paper each time a Specified Behaviour occurs, we have found it simpler to use plastic tally counters. These small, lightweight devices which can be pinned to staff's clothing have a display similar to a car odometer. Each time the button on the top of the tally counter is depressed the number displayed increases by one, and at the end of an observation period the number is transferred to the data collecting schedule, the tally counter being reset to zero by turning a small knob.

It is always a useful precaution to stick a self adhesive label to each tally counter and note which behaviour it is being used to record. This avoids confusion when more than one behaviour is being observed.

Data collecting must be done by the clock, but working with our children is so engrossing that watching the clock or one's watch is an unsatisfactory way of noting the completion of the half-hour session. It is far better to use a Kitchen Timer or a Fixed Interval Timer. The Kitchen Timer is set for half an hour at the start of each session, and as soon as it rings the data is transferred to the schedule and the tally counter reset. The Fixed Interval Timer, which is described in detail on pages 71–72, serves the same purpose.

Concluding Comments

Frequency counting initially helps staff make a precise statement about how *often* a problem behaviour occurs; it does not by itself define what *impact* that behaviour has.

The difference, if any, between a frequency count taken at the start of a programme and one taken after its completion, can be helpful in determining how *effective* the programme has been.

Changes in the frequency with which a behaviour occurs during a programme can be a useful indication of whether the programme is moving towards its stated goals.

Schedule 'C': Keeping a Daily 'Diary'

Introduction

When behaviour modifiers are planning or conducting certain types of programme to change behaviour, it is often very useful to have a record of when, and for how long, certain events occur during the course of each day. In toilet training, for example, it is particularly useful to know whether children have a pattern to their urinating and defecating. Do they tend to go after meals? Do they wet themselves approximately every half hour throughout the day? Do they only wet themselves before lessons or when asked to do a task? We have experienced these three patterns and know that a different approach to toilet training is required for each of them.

One very straightforward way of collecting this type of data is to use a diary in which can be jotted down the time and nature of the behaviour, plus brief notes about the prevailing conditions.

Data recorded in this manner can, however, become confused and it can be difficult to identify trends or pick out key aspects of information, so rather than use a traditional diary approach, we have chosen to monitor a fifteen-hour period (seven o'clock until ten o'clock) by means of a series of lines which are divided into hours, quarter hours and five minute periods.

Not only does this type of schedule facilitate the recording of data concerning daily events, but the nature of the layout enables staff to detect the presence of any pattern which might be used to advantage in training a child readily and accurately.

In addition to recording *what* events occurred and *when* they took place, their *duration* can also be shown by drawing a line to show how long the behaviour lasted.

Further information concerning each recorded incident is easily noted by putting a reference number against the vertical line which marks the start of a given behaviour, and by making an appropriately numbered note in the Comments section of the schedule.

The Layout of the Schedule
The schedule has two distinct components: the fifteen hour 'Diary' and the Comments section (see Figure 26). The fifteen-hour period has been chosen to make the schedule convenient for collecting 'awake' data, but when necessary it can also be used to record night time behaviour.

In Beech Tree House the children usually start getting up at seven-thirty and go to bed between eight and eight-thirty at night, but older, 'privileged', children occasionally stay up until ten o'clock – hence the fifteen-hour period. When the schedule is used to chart night time behaviour, the observer simply starts at the time the child in question goes to bed and ceases recording when he gets up.

Completing the Schedule
The recording procedure is described below. In the example, a girl undergoing toilet training, the observer is reporting on both

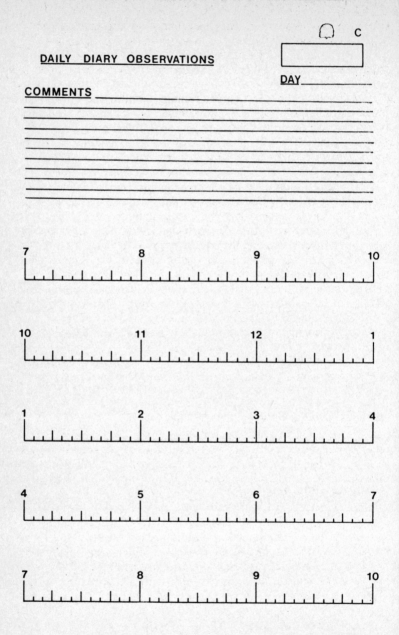

Figure 26.   Daily Diary Observation Schedule.

correct and incorrect 'performances' and on the behaviour of the child at the times she performs.

From Figure 27, which shows the first three hours of the day, it will be seen that Dorothy sat on the toilet for the first time at approximately eight twenty-two – this is indicated by the vertical line numbered (1) – and that she remained sitting there for three minutes (indicated by the solid horizontal line drawn from the base of the vertical line numbered (1)). The cryptic notes, 'Dry. P.U. no O.B. Co-op', indicate that she was dry on arrival at the toilet, that she passed urine but did not open her bowels and that she was co-operative.

In the Comments section of the schedule the following notes appear: '(1) Second day of period. Pad in place on arriving at toilet. Wearing elasticated skirt and towelling pants. (MCJ).'

Dorothy wet herself at approximately nine-thirteen, while having a tantrum, and details of how the two events were related are given in the Comments section. She did not sit on the toilet until nine twenty-one, and when she did she was neither co-operative nor did she perform during the five minutes she was seated.

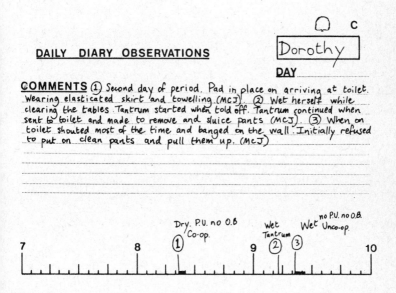

Figure 27. Daily Diary showing three hours of observation designed to detect any pattern in behaviour.

In the Comments section the following notes appear: '(2) Wet herself while clearing the table. Tantrum started when told off. Tantrum continued when sent to toilet and made to remove and sluice pants. (MCJ). (3) When on toilet shouted most of the time and banged on the wall. Initially refused to put on clean pants and pull them up. (MCJ).'

Notes on the Diary and in the Comments section continue in this manner throughout the day. Anyone who makes notes on the schedule initials them; this is vital if further information is required at a later date about a particular incident.

Agreeing What Should Be Recorded
Exactly the same procedures are followed as have been outlined for Schedules A and B.

How to Collect the Data
The procedure is particularly straightforward because the time is only noted when an event happens and does not otherwise require attention. It is the *occurrence* of an event which cues staff to consult the clock

Some programmes may be a little more complicated if a device is used to indicate the occurrence of a certain event. For example, a Wee-D might be worn by a child during the initial phase of a toilet training programme, so that staff know the moment that wetting has occurred, or in a night time training programme the Bed-Bug system would be invaluable to indicate whether or not the child in question was in bed. More often than not, however, no devices are used in conjunction with the Diary approach and staff rely on noticing when Specified Behaviour occurs.

Using the Schedule for Training
Schedule C differs from A and B in that it is often used to collect data while a programme is in progress – indeed, it is so frequently used in Beech Tree House to record toilet training progress that it is often incorrectly referred to as the 'Toilet Training Schedule'! When used within a programme it is likely that timing devices like the Potting Primer and the Fixed Interval Timer will be incorporated to cue staff to do something with a child, for example, to take her to the toilet or to reward her for having worked appropriately for a set period of time.

Concluding Comments
The Diary approach can be both investigative and also a means of collecting training data.

The data can reveal patterns which recur on a daily basis and training programmes can be planned to take advantage of these. The Comments section on the schedule allows considerable flexibility in the amount of data collected. Additional sheets of plain paper may be attached to the schedule if lengthy accounts of behaviour are required.

Schedule D: Collecting Data as Training is Carried Out

Introduction
We have devised and discarded many data collecting techniques for recording children's responses during training sessions. The schedule that we have finally agreed on is a general-purpose one with which all staff are familiar and which has the advantage of being adaptable to most training procedures.

The schedule is used in conjunction with the Training Programmes written for each child. These explain within a standard format exactly how each skill should be taught and if there are any minor variations in data recording procedures they are detailed here.

The Layout of the Schedule
The heading follows the standad format described earlier, with the title at the top and the box for the child's name to the right of this (See Figure 28).

The remainder of the page is divided into ten sections for recording data concerning individual training sessions. To the left of each section are two spaces, one to record the initials of the person who did the training and the other to note the duration of the session; to the right are three spaces to record the date of the session, the time it started and the name of the Training Programme taught.

All other information concerning the session is recorded in the central section headed 'Data and Notes'. Because each Training Programme details exactly how, where, with what, for how long, with which rewards and to what end each training session is directed, there is usually little to record other than the child's responses and any unusual events. By means of this strategy we have again achieved an economy in data collecting which helps prevent it becoming a chore.

Completing the Schedule
Children's responses are usually coded into four categories:
 1 No response.

				D
TEACHING SESSIONS RECORD				
DATES				

Initial / Duration	Data and Notes	Date / Time	Programme Number or Name

Figure 28.   Classroom Teaching Schedule.

2   Incorrect response.
3   Prompted response.
4   Correct response.

These responses are indicated in the following manner:

1   No response, with a short horizontal line.
2   Incorrect response, with a cross.
3   Prompted response, with a 'P'.
4   Correct response, with a tick.

Notes are also made, and details of these are given below.

Agreeing What Should be Recorded

The nature of a correct response, when and what to prompt, and what constitutes an incorrect response are detailed in the Training Programme which is drafted, after discussion with colleagues, by the teacher responsible for each child. This is rather different from the approach adopted for the other three schedules, where the Specified Behaviour is agreed at the Team Meeting after general discussion. The advantage of writing detailed Training Programmes, with equally detailed definitions of the types of behaviour that fall into the different recording categories, is that it affords a flexibility essential if programmes are to be tailored to meet the unique needs of each child.

Many users of behavioural techniques record whether or not pupils attend to the instruction or model given by the teacher at the start of each trial. We have avoided adding this detail to the burden of data recording simply by working on the principle that a trial has not started until a child's attention has been unequivocally given to the instruction. This strategy will not appeal to purists, but it is one way of reducing the time staff spend making notes. These moments can be exceedingly difficult with some new children who take every opportunity to disrupt teaching sessions.

Because some children have such pronounced difficulties in attending to the briefest instruction or demonstration, we sometimes teach attending behaviour as a specific skill. When such Training Programmes are run, attention itself is scored on the four-point scale in exactly the same manner as described for other skills.

If ten trials are given within a training session, the member of staff usually writes the responses, one after another, across the page. Such a procedure is appropriate for recording a task where each element takes quite a long time to complete, for example drying a plate; if, on the other hand, the programme requires thirty trials to be given within a training session, it makes good sense to teach and record these in three blocks of ten. Such a procedure is suitable for recording a task where each element can be completed relatively quickly, for example, by the child pointing to the correct Rebus symbol on hearing a word. (The Peabody Rebus Reading System of symbols has been adapted in Beech Tree House for simple communication. See the Introduction and Photograph 31.)

In addition to the ticks, crosses and lines described above, staff make notes to record unusual responses, suggestions for alternative teaching strategies and any other points which might improve the impact of the programme. If they wish to write more than can be squeezed into the section provided there are no penalties for over-flowing into another section. The point of collecting data and notes is to ensure that the children progress, so any information which is of value in ensuring this should be written down and shared with colleagues.

What Happens to the Data?

Many professionals, particularly psychologists, will know how often data, once collected, disappear into limbo. This is not the case with training data collected in Beech Tree House. The teacher responsible for each child summarises the data regularly and the results are used in the following ways:

1   To determine –
    a)   whether a programme will continue to run because a child is making steady progress, or
    b)   whether it will be terminated because a child has achieved the level of performance required and should therefore graduate to a new programme, or
    c)   whether is needs to be redesigned to help a child over-come difficulties which are impeding progress.
2   To up-date staff continuously on each child's progress. Staff are usually only too willing to redouble their teaching efforts if they receive positive reinforcment in the form of data which indicate that children are improving. Information of this sort is passed on at the Team Meeting.
3   To assist the teachers when they are preparing Half Term Reports. These summaries of progress are accurate because they are based on data rather than on impressions.
4   To enable the teachers to illustrate with data the progress made by children when they write the extensive Case Conference and Annual Reports.
5   To produce illustrative material for lectures used in staff training and for courses organised by the unit.

How to Collect the Data

Information is collected on scrap paper as each teaching session progresses and transferred to Schedule D, together with any notes, immediately afterwards. Use of scrap paper is advised because one can never be entirely certain that a sheet of paper will survive a teaching session. It is far better to lose the data of one ten-minute period than the data of all the sessions taught in a week. It is also to the child's advantage if the teacher is only momentarily diverted between trials to scribble down information; staff tend to be neater and take longer when they commit data to the schedule itself.

Children are taught by residential therapists who follow the training procedures drafted by the teachers. Although these are very detailed and the notes on how data should be recorded are comprehensive, occasions do arise when further clarification is needed; this can usually be given by the teachers because they are available for the major part of the time that programmes are being run. Before the training is started, residential therapists also discuss the programmes thoroughly with the teacher concerned and then carry them out initially in her presence. This high level of cooperation ensures that the data collected in the unit are particularly reliable.

Concluding Comments

Some visitors, commenting on the five minutes or so that staff spend filling in Schedule D after the teaching session, have felt that this time could be better employed teaching another skill. No doubt they have a point, but we remain convinced that the data we collect are vital, ensuring that our teaching is efficient, and we intend to continue the practice. In response to our critics, it is worth noting that very little time is ever lost in our unit by children repeating programmes unnecessarily (because they have mastered the skill) or unprofitably (because of a mismatch of some sort). One has only to recall the children one has seen endlessly completing form boards, or sitting rocking in front of an impossible task, to know how valuable our practice is.

It is a sad fact that, despite the good staff training courses that exist, many teachers are still content to let good intentions, tempered by their past successes, guide their present teaching strategies, rather than consult the data waiting in abundance to be collected. Without doubt they are missing one of the great satisfactions of teaching, because it is academically very exiting to search like a detective for the key to teaching a child with severe learning problems, and very rewarding to discover the key.

To Sum Up

The data collecting methods discussed in this chapter are those we have found to be the most productive, both in the sense that the data are useful for precise teaching and that staff are able to collect them reliably in sufficient quantity. Often there has to be a trade-off between the amount and detail of data collected and the practicalities of acquiring complex information. The compromise that we have reached is represented by the techniques reported here.

There are still occasions when we have to produce a special schedule or a special technique, but these are few and far between. We can usually find a way of using the schedules and methods already available.

If any rules can be formulated for effective data collecting where a cross-section of staff is involved, they should include the following:

1 Keep the techniques simple.
2 Continually inform the data collectors of the results of their efforts.
3 Have on hand experts who can resolve any problems when they arise.
4 Have nominated members of the team responsible for co-ordinating the collection of specified types of data.
5 Arrange training so that staff can work through examples together.
6 Keep schedules, pens, timing devices and all other equipment readily available in working order.
7 Ensure that all data entries are initialled.

9 EMMA – A CHILD WITH SEVERE NIGHT TIME BEHAVIOUR PROBLEMS

An Outline of Emma's Problems

When Emma came to Beech Tree House she had a range of behaviour problems and other difficulties, the most worrying being the way she behaved at night. This problem had started when she was about eighteen months old and had become progressively worse during the ensuing eight years. She would not go to bed before her parents and older sister, and once everyone was settled she would start a type of musical beds which continued throughout the night. Not only did Emma change places: by means of grunts and gestures she directed her family on a nocturnal merry-go-round. Her parents said that each night they would lose track of which room they were in and who they were sleeping with. Emma tended to settle for only ten or fifteen minutes between moves.

From time to time during the day Emma would appear drowsy, and occasionally she would manage to take a nap. Because she was very demanding of attention and her parents were usually so exhausted, they let this happen – it gave them a brief respite. Unfortunately in this way Emma caught up on her sleep and was consequently full of energy for her next night's exploits.

Emma's parents and sister were quite obviously exhausted when they first visited the unit to see if it would be suitable for her education. They were all very unhappy that Emma was probably going to leave home, but it was clear to them that, without help, both her behaviour and the condition of the family would be likely to deteriorate further. Emma had already been away for a number of brief 'respite' breaks, but the family had not seen these as particularly helpful to her. They explained that little more than care had been offered because the staff at the hospital concerned only had her for a few days at a time.

The family had sought help from many sources but nothing prior to Beech Tree House had been particularly effective. Both Valium and Mogadon had been prescribed to improve her night time behaviour, but neither had any lasting effect and the parents were not prepared to keep their daughter permanently sedated. As they pointed out, she was already sleepy during the day and this no doubt affected her ability to learn. They did not want to compound the problem.

Emma's mother had heard of Beech Tree House and our work with difficult children when she attended a lecture that I had given in her locality. She was particularly interested in finding out more about us because I had described how we use the Paget-Gorman Signing System to help a number of our children communicate. This seemed a particularly attractive bonus to her because she had just started to use this system to help Emma. Until her mother introduced Paget at home Emma had got by with her grunts and gestures.

A Co-operative Approach is Agreed

Emma's parents were supported in their approach to Beech Tree House by their education department whose officers also visited the unit and discussed with us in detail the nature of the programmes we would be likely to use with Emma. A very positive joint approach developed from the outset, with unit staff agreeing outline goals with both the family and the senior staff of the sponsoring Local Authority. In brief, we would attempt to eliminate the night time problems and her vomiting and manipulative urinating and defecating. At the same time we agreed to teach her to use the Paget-Gorman Signing System. The Authority, on their side, also undertook to fulfil certain obligations: primarily, to find a suitable school in Emma's locality, to which she could be transferred at the end of her stay in Beech Tree House. This entailed a willingness on the part of the receiving school to inform Beech Tree House of the skills Emma would need to ease her transfer, and the close collaboration of their staff, especially as her leaving date approached. The Authority were also prepared to make weekday residential care available if that should be necessary. Meanwhile, Emma's parents agreed to spend time in the unit and have staff live at home to help Emma transfer any new skills that she learned in the unit.

Emma Visits the Unit

When Emma visited us she looked very well – a contrast to her tired parents. She was very small for her age with beautiful auburn hair and a mischievous smile and infectious chuckle. All staff took an immediate liking to her, despite the reputation that had gone before her. She had no meaningful speech and only three or four Paget-Gorman signs, but this did not prevent her from letting everyone know what she wanted: she would point, look appealing and make demanding noises. On her first visit these were sufficient to galvanise staff into action because they wanted Emma to feel that she was welcome.

Details of Emma's Manipulative Behaviour

While Emma was meeting the other children and staff, her parents explained to us in detail what she did if she did not get her own way. She would begin to vocalise progressively more loudly, and this would turn into a series of enormous, angry screams. If she still failed to get what she wanted, she would thrust her head forward and make a disgusting gagging noise at the back of her throat; this was her way of warning everyone that if things did not go her way she would vomit. Sure enough, if they did not, she would be sick. This behaviour was entirely under her voluntary control.

Her parents might have been able to cope if Emma's behaviour had been limited to noise and vomiting; the problem was that she had more tricks up her skirt. If the vomiting failed she would adopt a semi-squatting position, concentrate hard and urinate. This devastated most opposition and she would win the day. On the few occasions when this dramatic ploy failed, Emma would play her trump card. Again she would squat, concentrate and go red of face, then would defecate into her pants or onto the floor if she was in her nightdress.

Now that readers know some of the tricks that this cute little girl could play, they will understand better why it was she was such a tyrant at night. I have no doubt some readers are thinking that *they* would not have let a little mentally handicapped child rule their lives in the way the parents described. If Beech Tree House staff had not known the full facts they would, no doubt, have felt the same. As it was, we knew the score and awaited her arrival with some trepidation.

Distress at Parting

Two or three days after term had started and the other children had settled, Emma arrived with her parents. Although she had already visited the unit, she still displayed that combination of apprehension and inquisitiveness which young children often show in unfamiliar situations. Her parents helped her arrange her things in her room and, after two or three hours of settling her in and chatting to staff, they prepared to leave. Emma became increasingly agitated and screamed and struggled as her parents walked to their car. We know that for many children and families this is the most heartrending aspect of placing a child in Beech Tree House. Parents have told us that they only managed to drive a short distance before having to stop to cope with tears and deep emotional distress. Emma's parents reacted similarly.

Can Residential Schools for Handicapped Children be Justified:
If such unhappiness is experienced by parents and children it calls
into question the entire practice of residential schools for children
– particularly for those who are handicapped and doubtless need
even greater emotional support than their non-handicapped peers.
An obvious solution is for each education authority to provide
suitable facilities for children near their homes and it is encouraging to report that there are growing improvements along these
lines. One sign of this is that in recent years the Spastics Society
has closed two of its large residential schools because there has
been insufficient demand for places; charities providing residential
facilities for children with other handicaps are reporting a similar
trend.

Photograph 32 shows Emma a year or so after joining the unit,
still upset as her parents drive away. How can we justify a
residential approach at Beech Tree House if it causes such
distress?

Vindication is particularly hard for us because we are convinced
that, if families were offered expert help when behaviour problems
first appeared, few, if any, would ever need full residential treatment for their children. I must qualify this statement by saying that
the help of *any* expert will not do. There is no reason why a
general practitioner, health visitor, social worker, school teacher
or educational psychologist should have the necessary experience
or expertise to help families train such children. Our survey suggests that many muddle-headed suggestions have been made by
just such experts who were clearly out of their depth in this
difficult field. Nevertheless, any of these professionals could
obtain the necessary skills to become the resource person for
families within a given area. Such a service would need an unusual
degree of cooperation between professionals in referring children,
but such an arrangement ought not to be beyond the bounds of possibility and would go a long way towards making units like Beech
Tree House a thing of the past.

Unfortunately, since few such services exist, Beech Tree House
is very much a development of the present catering for families
with exceptional needs not being met elsewhere. Our waiting list
suggests that we are likely to continue in business for a while
longer.

For older children with established behaviour problems Beech
Tree House is likely to retain its *residential* form, for, despite our
reservations, we believe for the following reasons that the
residential component is critical to our success:

   1 By the time their child is offered residential training at Beech

Tree House, families like Emma's are usually physically and emotionally exhausted. It follows that they need a period in which to recoup their energies in readiness for their child's return.

2 Over the years patterns develop within families which sustain the very behaviour causing the distress. In Emma's case her messing behaviour could not be ignored by her parents and as a consequence it was usually rewarded by her getting her own way. The only escape from such a closed loop is to break it at some point. Both the child and the family must make a new start, with a definite watershed between their former practises and the new strategy. This is usually exceptionally difficult in the home because years of incorrect treatment will have consolidated both the behaviour of parents and the expectations of children.

3 When the first attempts are made to change the unwanted behaviour children usually respond by giving full rein to their behaviour, in some cases possibly out of sheer fury that their formerly very effective strategies are no longer rewarded. Emma certainly responded in this manner when we started to ignore her night time tantrums; she upped the stakes so much it is difficult to imagine how neighbours would have coped, let alone her family.

4 Because behaviour can be extreme in the early stages it is often necessary to have special facilities available to contain them, such as our Safe Bedroom which is designed for easy cleaning. This was essential for Emma because when her hand was finally called the faeces certainly started to fly. In an ordinary bedroom the consequences would have been virtually impossible to contain or clean up satisfactorily.

5 Equipment and opportunities to reward correct behaviour, always available in our residential unit, are also vital. In Emma's case she was particularly fond of receiving tokens to spend in the Music Dispenser and the Sweet Dispenser. Eventually these were made available for her at home – but not until they were known to be effective.

6 At the start of any programme designed to eliminate problem behaviour, the strain on those working with the children concerned is extreme. The great advantage of a training environment in which staff are employed, as opposed to being 'family', is that everyone gets time off. Our forty-odd hour weeks are trivial compared to a mother's one hundred and sixty-eight hour marathon and for this reason alone it would have been completely unrealistic to have handed

Emma's mother a detailed programme of the type we followed and expected her to get on with it. She would hardly have had time to do the cleaning and washing involved, let alone train her daughter!

7   However fond staff become of individual children, they, are rarely as emotionally involved as the parents. It is therefore easier for them to be firm and not unduly distressed by the sort of filthy state into which Emma got herself and her room in the early stages of her programme. Within a close knit and supportive staff like that at Beech Tree House, any adverse emotional reactions can be helped by sympathetic colleagues. Such support is rarely on hand for parents.

8   To be treated successfully major behaviour problems need to be worked on round the clock. This is less important when new skills are being developed – these can be established by working on them for short periods so long as the training is given regularly – but severe behaviour problems usually resist all but the most intensive and continuous programmes. Almost by definition, they cannot be dealt with successfully on a part-time basis, and this, no doubt, accounts for the problems experienced by many day schools where, although good work is done, the children return home or go back to hostels or wards. Even co-operation of the highest level between school and parents or parent substitutes is no alternative to the same staff following the same continuous programme in the same environment. In Emma's case there were often relapses when she went home in the early days of the training.

Where children with severe behaviour problems are to be helped, the advantages of a residential unit therefore outweigh the disadvantages – indeed they are as *essential* as hospitals are for the gravely ill. We would nevertheless urge that such units be distributed widely round the country so that parents can keep in close contact with their children.

Emma's First Few Weeks
Like any new child, Emma spent her first night in the safe bedroom. It was well that she did. Virtually throughout the entire night she shouted, screamed, pounded on the walls and door and managed to spread vomit, urine and faeces around the room. Clearly her parents had not exaggerated the problems in any way.

During the first night, and for the next four or five, we tried to diminish Emma's distress and limit the mess by periodically going into her bedroom to attempt to calm her and to clean things up. Although by doing this we were behaving in much the same way as her parents at home – namely we were in danger of rewarding the unwanted behaviour – we nevertheless felt that we should start in this way in order to reassure Emma that there were adults about who were concerned for her. We believe that there will always be occasions where behavioural principles must take a back seat in order to meet children's emotional needs. It is worth noting, however, that our excursions into Emma's bedroom coincided with lulls in her bad behaviour. By choosing these times we felt we were less likely to reinforce the extreme elements.

After six days all staff discussed Emma's behaviour at the Team Meeting and a series of graduated training strategies were proposed. These would start with attempts to reason with Emma about her behaviour and would become progressively more directive as weeks went by. Each strategy would be tried for two weeks and the data would be evaluated at the subsequent Team Meeting where a decision would be taken whether to continue in the same vein or change the strategy. Emma's parents were contacted and agreed to the proposals.

During the first two weeks we used the agreed strategy of kindness and gentle persuasion. We explained to Emma that if she went to bed at the same time as the other children, settled down quickly and slept peacefully, she would not feel so tired the following day. This was done very carefully in simple terms, with staff acting Emma going to sleep and getting up to enjoy the following day. We were convinced that Emma understood exactly what we meant. While we were not confident that this method would work, it was in line with our philosophy of always starting training with the least restrictive/directive approach.

The only positive outcome of this initial strategy was that by the second week we had purchased a vacuum cleaner capable of sucking up disinfectant, water and the byproducts of Emma's night time behaviour. It was agreed at the Team Meeting and by telephone with Emma's parents that a firmer approach should be tried.

Strategy two followed. Staff would no longer go into the bedroom to attempt to calm Emma or to cajole her into going to sleep; once they had cuddled her and tucked her into bed, perhaps settling her with a brief story, all their subsequent forays into the bedroom would be conducted in a disinterested manner. They would simply enter and tell Emma to get back into bed, physically guiding her if this was necessary. If she attempted to leave her room the member of staff stationed outside the door would simply tell her to go back. Sometimes Emma had to be physically guided back.

This second procedure was no more effective than the first. It was agreed that the third strategy would involve closing the bedroom door in such a way that Emma would not be able to get out on to the landing – the handle was simply repositioned at a height she could not reach. Emma was told that she would be put to bed as before, but that as soon as she got out of bed and started to misbehave her bedroom door would be closed. When this happened, a few minutes after the member of staff left the bedroom, it was clear the she remembered what would happen because she pointed to the door and vigorously signed and said her 'no' word. When the door was shut her protests were possibly even more vigorous than we had witnessed before. Staff continued to enter the bedroom periodically to order her back to bed.

Within two weeks it was clear that, as her parents had predicted, firmness and closing the door were not having any impact upon her behaviour. It was agreed that once Emma returned from the half term holiday we would try a mild punishment strategy: whenever she got out of bed and started to make an unacceptable amount of noise or started to dirty the floor, the member of staff on duty would go in, reprimand her very firmly, then unceremoniously dump her back into bed and march out. Two weeks of this strategy proved as ineffective as everything else that we had tried.

Clearly Emma had the upper hand. She continued to maintain it for nearly two more terms as we ran through different permutations of the strategies outlined so far and staff became more exhausted and disillusioned. It was clear that we must devise a way of monitoring Emma's behaviour without obliging staff to spend much of each night outside her room, and to meet this need the Bed-Bug system, the Safe Bed and a forerunner of SAM were invented and installed. (See Chapter 3.) Although this equipment did not help Emma directly, it did ease the burden on staff who felt prepared to try yet again.

Additional impetus was given to the new programme by Frances Gardner, a psychology student on an experience placement in the unit towards the beginning of Emma's fourth term. She became particularly interested in Emma's problems and was responsible for collating the data presented in this chapter. Frances is typical of the majority of students who undertake placements in the unit; They come with a freshness which enables them to ask challenging questions and an energy which we can easily tap to provide an even greater training input for a particular child. They usually produce a written project, and quotations from the one prepared by Frances will help to illustrate the remarkable progress made by Emma once an effective programme was introduced.

She set the scene as follows: 'At home, if the parents wished to have more than just a few minutes of quiet in which to sleep, they found it necessary to comply with all Emma's wishes. Thus they had to allow her to sleep in the company of various family members, in succession, throughout the night, playing a kind of "musical chairs" and often changing beds every twenty minutes. The alternative, the parents found, was to ignore her for short times, wake up the whole neighbourhood and be threatened with messes all over the carpet, usually carried out. At Beech Tree House, it is much easier to cope with threats of this kind, with a completely waterproofed room, some soundproofing, a high door handle and an unbreakable window. However, both at home and at Beech Tree it seems likely that the tantrum behaviour is being reinforced by the attention and adult compliance it produces. Many times each night staff enter her room and attempt to make her be quiet, but this usually produces only a few moments' peace during which other children are somewhat less disturbed; then the screaming and banging typically recommence, staff enter the room again, and attempt angrily (part of the present policy) to persuade her to go to bed. Being severely told off and placed quickly in the bed may not seem at all like pleasant experience, but Emma does succeed in gaining the assurance that adults are present and are prepared to pay attention to her (even punishing attention) and that she will rarely be alone for more than fifteen minutes at a time. Moreover, if she vomits or defecates on the floor, she succeeds in getting an adult to come into her room for five minutes or more, to turn on the lights and to clean up the mess, which is probably very positively reinforcing.'

The final two sentences of this extract accurately reflect the conclusion that had been reached by the staff. If they were correct, two training strategies were indicated: firstly, to find a punishment which was so strong it would outweigh the reward Emma got from adult attention; secondly, to use an extinction procedure in which all the problem behaviours would be ignored. We considered that extreme forms of punishment were out of the question, and the extinction procedure was particularly attractive now that the Bed-Bug system and SAM One were installed, since we could monitor Emma's behaviour very accurately without entering the room.

I have previously expressed reservations about using extinction procedures by themselves and have suggested that they are usually most effective when used in conjunction with positive reinforcement for an alternative appropriate behaviour. As always there

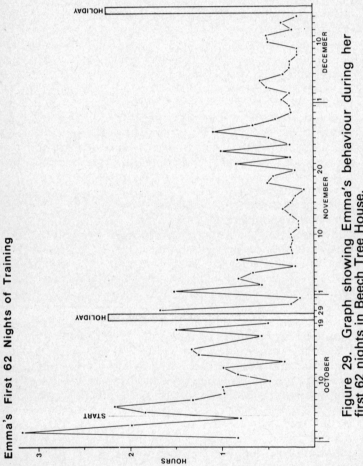

Figure 29. Graph showing Emma's behaviour during her first 62 nights in Beech Tree House.

are exceptions to rules and Emma provided one. The alternative behaviour we should have liked to reward was settling to sleep, but unfortunately we were quite unable to think of a positive reinforcement which would not *disturb* sleeping behaviour. Emma loved music, but would have woken to clap or sing if it had been played; she liked sweets, but would have had to reach out and take them, even if we had dispensed them by remote control; she liked adult company most of all, but would have woken to enjoy it and become distressed as it was withdrawn. A straightforward extinction procedure, in which we ignored all unwanted behaviour, seemed to be the best course of action.

The programme was directed specifically at out-of-bed and noisy behaviour which was regarded as a separate problem from the dirtying behaviour. The latter left tangible evidence which could be 'discussed' with Emma in the morning when action could be taken; the noisy behaviour disappeared as soon as she settled and was consequently only available for later 'discussion' if Emma could recall it. It is notoriously difficult to treat recalled behaviour effectively, particularly if the person doing the recalling has very limited communication skills.

The treatment programme, a two-pronged attack upon the night time problems, took account of this distinction. The noise and out-of-bed behaviour was extinguished by being ignored; the dirtying behaviour was punished by token fines; clean behaviour was positively reinforced by token rewards. Although the programmes ran simultaneously, for the sake of clarity I shall describe them separately.

Treatment of the Disruptive Behaviour

The noisy and out-of-bed behaviour was worse some nights than others, probably because after a particularly bad night Emma needed to catch up on her sleep. Figure 29 shows that the graph of time out of bed went up and down like the teeth of a saw. It was typical that a relatively good night, during which she was only out for fifty minutes, was followed by one in which she was out for three hours and ten minutes. The reader should bear in mind that she was not out for a fifty-minute period at the start of any evening and then asleep; the fifty minutes would be made up of a great many noisy but short out-of-bed episodes throughout the night. A typical night prior to the successful training is shown in Figure 30, which is an accurate transcript of an actual night.

Reference to Figure 29 will show the dramatic change that took place in Emma's behaviour during the first three months of the

A Typical Night's Data

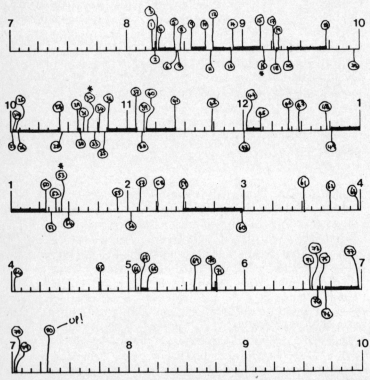

Figure 30. Daily Diary recording Emma's pre-training behaviour throughout one night.

programme. Data were recorded in exactly the same way until she left.

The extinction programme started on the fifth of October and was the treatment policy from that time on. Emma was put to bed with the usual cuddles and warmth. She was reminded that her door would remain open unless she got out of bed, and that if she did get out it would be closed. She was offered the chance to go to the toilet at both ten o'clock at night and six o'clock in the morning. Staff only went into her room to ask if she wanted the toilet if she was quiet, and it might well be ten thirty before she was quiet for long enough for the member of staff to make the offer. For the remainder of the night Emma remained in her room and she could scream, bang, shout, dirty the floor or what she would, without staff paying any apparent attention. They did of course monitor her behaviour very carefully by means of the Bed-Bug, the SAM and the observation window in her door.

The data from the start of the programme until the Christmas holiday are shown in Figure 29. Initially there was no evidence of change, the saw-toothed pattern continuing for the first twenty-four days with no apparent difference between Emma's behaviour prior to and after the October half term holiday.

A remarkable change occured on the seventh of November and continued for eleven days, during which time she was never out of bed for more than twenty minutes. It was almost as if Emma realised that no matter what she did, she would get no attention, and that if this was the case she might just as well be warm and comfortable in bed as rampaging around her bedroom, cold, dirty and distressed. A relapse occurred for no apparent reason between the eighteenth and the twenty-eighth, then things settled nicely until the Christmas holiday.

At that time we were by no means confident that we had found the solution; we felt that the marked improvement might have been a coincidence and nothing to do with our training programme. Consequently we did not ask Emma's parents to make any changes in the way they had been coping with her night time behaviour.

We assumed correctly that, rather as Trevor had reverted to his earlier pattern of behaviour when placed in a setting which rewarded these rather than his new skills, so Emma would probably slip back into her earlier disruptive night time strategies once she returned home. We also predicted rightly that she would display her bad behaviour on returning to Beech Tree House. We hoped, if our extinction procedure was effective, that she would then rapidly return to the improved night time behaviour she had

Emma's Post Christmas Improvement

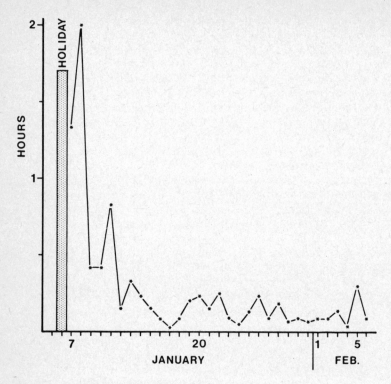

Figure 31. Graph showing Emma's improved behaviour after the Christmas holiday.

shown prior to the Christmas break and Figure 31 clearly indicates that this occurred remarkably quickly.

Armed with convincing data like this, we felt much more confident about asking Emma's parents to make certain alterations to her bedroom, so that a similar programme could be run at home.

Tokens to Improve Dirtying Behaviour

The token programme used with Emma had many similarities with the one used with Trevor. Emma was trained to value tokens initially by using them in the Sweet Dispenser and then in the Music Dispenser, before they were used to modify her dirtying behaviour, the Music Dispenser being preferred both by Emma's parents and ourselves because she had a weight problem. Once she was hooked on the tokens the programme to resolve dirtying behaviour commenced. This was very straightforward: Emma received five tokens if her room was clean in the morning; if it was dirty she did not get the tokens.

There was one major problem with this programme – how was Emma to understand that she was losing the *right* to have something (her tokens) because of the way she had behaved earlier? It requires quite a degree of sophistication to understand that one is losing something one has not already got. We felt that Emma would not grasp this idea, so we resolved to give her her five tokens on going into her room in the morning, let her hold them and only then discuss whether or not she had dirtied her room. If she had offended in this way the tokens were taken away again. It is of course a great deal easier to understand that you have lost something if it is taken out of your hand.

As with all unit-wide programmes a detailed schedule of how staff should behave was drawn up. This was as follows:

BEECH TREE HOUSE INDIVIDUAL TRAINING SCHEDULE ACTION TO BE TAKEN TO REDUCE EMMA'S MESSING BEHAVIOUR

1   Emma will be rewarded with five tokens if she has refrained from defecating, vomiting and urinating in her room throughout the night.

2   These tokens will be exchangeable only for music played on the token-operated cassette.

3   She will not be allowed to exchange her tokens until she has tidied her room, replaced her duvet cover and pillow case and so on.

4   Emma is to be taken to the toilet every night at 22.00 – whether or not she says she wants to go. She is to be taken to the toilet as soon as she wakes after 6.00, but then taken back to her room.

5   The token giving should be done as follows:
   a)   Enter room – preferably when Emma is quiet. Have the tokens with you as you go in. Say 'Hello' in a friendly manner.
   b)   Note whether she has messed her floor or bed, but give no apparent attention to this.
   c)   Sit on bed (if clean) and give Emma her five tokens. Then ask, 'Have you been sick?' 'Have you done a wee?' 'Have you done a poo?' Ask these so that the

question referring to the offending act (if any) comes last.

d) If the floor/bed is clean, praise Emma and let her keep the tokens. Remind her that she can spend them on music as soon as her room is tidy.

e) If the floor/bed is dirty, the tokens should be taken from Emma and she should be 'told off' very firmly.

f) Emma must clean up her own mess. This should not be allowed to become fun or a social activity between her and the member of staff.

g) Once the floor is clean, Emma should be showered in a socially non-committal manner.

h) Once Emma is dressed, she should tidy her room. No tangible rewards to be given.

i) Once her room is tidy, Emma should be treated as if nothing has happened. It is suggested that no discussion about her behaviour should be conducted in front of her.

6   The token-operated cassette should be used in the battery-powered mode. Emma should listen to it in her room.

7   Please note whether tokens are given, what actions are taken and Emma's responses to them.

Within six weeks of introducing the token programme Emma's dirtying behaviour improved from at least one incident virtually every night to no more than one incident per week. Happy, rewarding scenes like that in Photograph 8 in which Emma is receiving her tokens, became the rule. Within two terms the only dirty floors occurred the night before she went home and the night before she came back. It was almost as if Emma was reminding everyone that she was still capable of bad behaviour, but it is more likely that she was simply reacting adversely to the moves between home and school.

Long before dirtying behaviour had been eliminated at night, Emma stopped using it as a manipulative strategy during the day. We had dealt with it by refusing to be intimidated by the bad behaviour or the threat of it and by making Emma clean up any resulting mess. We attempted to press on with whatever task Emma was protesting about in the manner of a relentless robot that neither noticed nor cared about the mess she might produce. The absence of an 'upset', emotional response from the staff, coupled with having to do whatever it was that she had been told and then clean up the mess, soon made daytime dirtying unattractive to Emma.

It must also be remembered that Emma was living in a happy, busy, structured family group in which she was learning many new appropriate skills. Perhaps the most significant change was in her communication skills. She rapidly learned to use Paget-Gorman signs in three and four word sentences – and then started to speak! Emma has a guttural voice and new acquaintances find some difficulty in understanding her, but she now talks in well formed, if short, sentences. Before she left Beech Tree House she had started to read and write, too, and these skills have continued to improve at her new school. Shortly before writing this chapter we received a letter from Emma in which she told us that she had been to see the film *ET*.

Part of Emma's preparation for her new school involved attending a local infants' reception class where she learned to cope with all the hurleyburley of a large group of children. Photograph 33 shows her involved in a small group teaching session with some of the infants and their teacher. After a term of weekly morning visits the teacher reported that, 'At no time has Emma disturbed the class or taken more of my attention than any of the other "normal" children . . . in my opinion Emma would be able to cope in an infant class with the help of a classroom assistant.'

Transferring Emma's Improved Night Time Behaviour to Her Home

The first step was to present the data to Emma's parents in order to convince them that the programme was worth trying, for without their enthusiastic commitment it was unlikely that the programme would run long enough for it to be successful. Moreover, changes would have to be made to Emma's bedroom which would involve the family in spending time and money. I visited Emma's home and presented our proposals to her parents who readily agreed to try the programme. We subsequently spent an hour or so deciding what changes would have to be made to the bedroom to make the undertaking possible.

Certain changes were considered essential. The windows, which were made of leaded triangles of glass and were very susceptible to damage, needed to be protected. This was done with 4mm perspex screwed to the window frame by means of inexpensive, do-it-yourself double glazing strips. The floor was covered with vinyl finish which Emma could not pull up at the edges. Locks were fitted to her cupboards so that she would not get out her clothes and toys to damage or dirty. A new door with a perspex observation window was fitted – this was essential because

Emma's mother said that if Emma was ever quiet she was even more worried than when she was noisy. Emma had suffered from epilepsy in her early childhood and her mother wanted to be certain that silence did not indicate that she had had a fit. The bed was screwed to the floor so that Emma could not push it around the room and thereby gain access to the door handle at the top of the door.

Non-essential yet important items were a baby alarm which allowed Emma's parents to listen to her from various parts of the house, and a Bed-Bug which enabled them to monitor and record the amount of time that she spent out of bed. The latter item was made in a modified form so that Emma could not get at the wires and damage them.

I accompanied Emma home and spent the first four nights with the family. On the first three I put Emma to bed, took her to the toilet at ten and six and gave her her tokens in the morning. Apart from a little grizzling on first going to bed, everything went perfectly and the floor remained clean. Each evening Emma's parents and I sat and watched television or chatted – but it has to be admitted that most of our attention was on the sounds from the baby alarm, any of which might have presaged an outburst of difficult behaviour.

On the fourth night Emma's parents put her to bed while I hovered in the background. Emma possibly grizzled for a little longer but settled without much fuss; apart from waking briefly once or twice, all went well and the floor was clean. Her mother was able to give her lavish praise and her tokens.

The fifth night Emma's parents were left to run the programme themselves and I received a telephone call early the next morning to say that things had not gone well. Emma had screamed, shouted and messed until approximately one thirty when there was a tremendous crash from her bedroom. Her parents rushed into her room to find that Emma had managed to rip her bed from the floor and tip it over into the mess. Photograph 34 shows that one leg remained fixed to the floor; it had been wrenched from its mounting point in the base of the bed. The fact that the photograph was taken at all is a testimony to the parents' commitment to the Beech Tree House work, even at this time of disappointment and crisis. Apparantly Emma's mother said, 'Malcolm will want a picture of this, won't he?' and rushed to get her camera. Needless to say, the slide does have great impact at lectures.

I returned to Emma's home and her father and I secured the bed more firmly to the floor. We decided that, despite this early set-back, it was worth continuing with the programme, since Emma had responded well when I was present and the data were encouraging.

The remainder of the first holiday was difficult, but the data revealed a hopeful trend. Subsequent holidays saw the night time behaviour steadily improve and eventually Emma's family were almost as successful in getting her to go to bed and to sleep as the Beech Tree House staff. The problems that arose were caused by events unknown in the unit; for example, impending visits by Father Christmas, holidays in caravans and hotels, knowledge that exciting visitors were coming, and baby sitters. The night before returning to Beech Tree House she was also unsettled.

Transfering Emma's Improved Behaviour to her New School and Weekday Hostel.

Emma remained in Beech Tree House for longer than two years because initially it was difficult to find somewhere which would meet all her needs. Eventually a vacancy occurred at a school near her home which had recently been amalgamated with a small adjoining hostel. The new head was responsible for both education and care and so could ensure that Emma continued to receive co-ordinated training. The transfer was carefully planned and the level of cooperation between the respective staffs and Emma's family was so high it can be regarded as a model.

The senior residential social worker from the hostel and Emma's future teacher visited Beech Tree House in order to meet Emma, get to know the staff responsible for her, and to familiarise themselves with the way Emma was educated and managed. A visit by Beech Tree House staff was made to her new school and hostel so that they would know exactly how Emma should be prepared.

The hostel visit was particularly important because it enabled Beech Tree House staff to help select a suitable bedroom and advise on how it might be adapted to accommodate Emma. A fixed bed with a built in Bed-Bug was subsequently provided, together with a washable floor and a fixed, lockable wardrobe; the window was reglazed with unbreakable material. A sound-monitoring system already existed.

A subsequent visit to the school was arranged at which Beech Tree House staff gave a talk, illustrated with slides, about the problems that Emma had had and the programmes that had been used to remedy them. There is usually very understandable concern in the minds of staff who are about to receive a child from a unit which specialises in educating children who have had severe behaviour problems. Unless the transfer can be sensitively managed all manner of preconceptions can affect the way the child is treated on arrival. The material presented at this talk and at other meetings was supported by the detailed reports about Emma that had been prepared during her education in the unit.

Great importance should be attached to the interest shown by the head of Emma's new school. She also visited and stayed at Beech Tree House so that she would see Emma in classroom and residential settings. A number of heads have acted in this manner and we always feel that interest and commitment of this sort bodes well for the children who transfer to their schools. Heads who know their pupils are much more likely to foster a teaching and residential climate that meets the needs of their children than heads whose role is little more than that of administrator.

Emma was prepared for the transfer very carefully. She met the staff who came to Beech Tree House and renewed this contact when she visited the school and hostel. The staff who were going to work closely with her supplied recent photographs of themselves and these were used to familiarise Emma with their names.

A 'Leaving Book' was prepared which started with pictures of other children who had left and whom Emma knew, enabling staff to talk about leaving Beech Tree House using examples of children with whom Emma was familiar. Subsequent pages showed pictures of the new school, the staff who would be there and so on. A game, rather like snakes and ladders, was prepared in which Emma's counter moved through the days towards the time when she would transfer. Pictures marked special days like her visit to the school, days when staff were coming from the school, the holiday which preceded transfer, her brief return to Beech Tree House before leaving, and so on. The words used throughout the book were taken from her Breakthrough to Literacy vocabulary so that she was able to read her book to other people.

When the actual day of transfer arrived Emma was accompanied to her new school by the senior teacher from Beech Tree House. Over a period of three days she helped her settle in the school and progressively withdrew from the situation. Likewise, in the hostel, she worked with Emma for the first two nights then moved more into the background. Because it was anticipated that difficulties were most likely to occur at night, Emma's key residential therapist replaced the teacher for the fourth and fifth nights. The first five days were extremely encouraging. Emma took a while to settle but once in bed slept throughout the night. She did not dirty her room at all.

Emma's parents were understandably very worried about her reaction to the transfer, so they were invited to visit the hostel after she had gone to bed, in case their anxiety affected her and encouraged her to misbehave. They sat in the room with the teacher from Beech Tree House and listened to the intercom. Emma móved around her room for a while and shouted a few times. She was quiet by approximately ten o'clock and behaved well when taken to the toilet. On returning from the toilet she settled quickly and even called out 'Good night!' Needless to say, everyone was delighted and very relieved.

The transfer to school was equally successful and Emma coped very well with the new class and all the routines of a very much bigger school. It is worth noting that before leaving Beech Tree House she was weaned off tokens and onto sticky stars as a reward for good behaviour, since this was the system at the new school. They proved to be equally effective in rewarding the clean floors which Emma maintained.

One Year Later
So that the information here may be as up to date as possible I made two telephone calls before writing these final paragraphs: to Emma's mother and to her head teacher. The latest information from home is that Emma's family are thrilled with the progress she has continued to make. Apparently the most exciting changes have been in her speaking. She is now spontaneously using complex sentences and her articulation has greatly improved. Emma's mother runs a small post office which is attached to their home and she gave a beautiful example both of Emma's ability to speak and of her increasing skills. During a recent weekend she came into the shop where her mother was starting to stock the sweet shelves. She said, 'Oh. More sweets,' and trotted off to the stock room. She went to and fro stocking all the shelves correctly, and when her father called her to go to him, she called back, 'No, I'm helping Mummy.' Emma has obviously come a very long way since she left the special care unit.

Her night time behaviour at home during weekends is disappointing. She is very good on the Friday night and fairly good on the Sunday night, but Saturday nights are difficult. Her mother thinks that she may be objecting to the fact that her elder sister is usually out on this particular evening – and one of her early patterns was to insist that every member of the family should go to bed when she did. If this is the case Emma has obviously got to learn that the world does not revolve around her, even when she comes home. It is easy to see how she might have got this impression because she has a very warm and loving family.

The report from school is outstanding. In the year or so she has been with them she has only been difficult at night on three occasions – only three dirty floors! In the school and hostel they have seen great progress, particularly in her ability to speak. The head actually went so far as to thank me for having sent them such a delightful and rewarding child.

APPENDIX

Between January 1977 and January 1982 nineteen children completed a period of education in Beech Tree House. A further nine joined the unit after January 1983 and are in residence at the time of writing.

We have started to analyse the progress made by these pupils; where they went on leaving; what their parents thought about the education they received in Beech Tree House and so on. Such an evaluation takes time, but a comprehensive report should be available by the end of 1983. To date, an initial examination of the data has been completed and, since certain aspects of this descriptive information may be of interest to readers, some simple tables have been prepared. Most of these are self explanatory, but short comments have been prepared.

Table A
Distribution of Boys and Girls 1977-81.

Boys	🧍🧍🧍🧍🧍🧍🧍🧍🧍🧍🧍🧍🧍	13
Girls	🧍🧍🧍🧍🧍🧍	6
	Total	19

As a general rule most handicapping conditions which are not sex linked affect more boys than girls. Often the ratio is as high as 2:1. Such a ratio was evident among the first nineteen children educated in Beech Tree House, but surprisingly this trend has not continued. (See Table 1 page 236) We are not absolutely certain why this should be the case; it could be chance, but a more probable explanation is that at a time of severe economic crisis girls with serious behaviour problems are more readily sponsored than boys because they are perceived as being more 'deserving' of help. We have detected a tendency among some staff responsible for making referrals to think in this way. If this is the case, we are uncertain what provision is being made for the boys who do not reach us.

Table B

The Number and Sex of Children in Each Age Category on Entry 1977-81

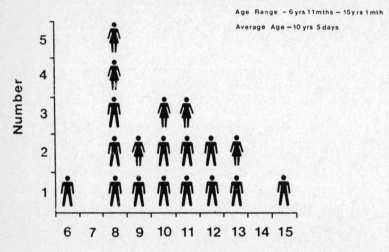

Age Range – 6 yrs 11 mths – 15 yrs 1 mth

Average Age – 10 yrs 5 days

Age in Years

Although the first nineteen children covered a wide age range, the majority came before puberty and were therefore still relatively small and manageable. They were referred because they were perceived as having special educational needs which could best be catered for at Beech Tree House. Reference to Table J (page 237) will show that there has been a marked increase since 1982 in the age at which children enter the unit. It appears that many local authorities expect their school staff and the children's parents to cope with children with severe behaviour problems until they have become quite beyond control. There is an obvious, short-term, economic advantage to such a policy, but the long term financial implications are less attractive.

It comes as no surprise to us that many older children are placed with us by authorities who officially have a total embargo on sponsored placements. Their hand is finally forced – but often at a time when the child has practised unacceptable patterns of behaviour for much longer than necessary or conducive to eventual improvement. Our experience suggests that the short-term financial gains of withholding special residential education until crisis is reached is very much to the children's disadvantage.

Table C

The Distances Children Lived from Beach
Tree House, 1977-81 Group

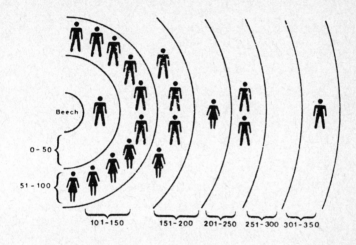

Distance in Miles

The clustering of children in the fifty to one hundred mile zone is
accounted for by the large number who came from London and its
suburbs. We believe that if we had been located in Birmingham
rather than Meldreth, these same children would have been
referred. Since demand does not appear to be generated by the
existence of a local facility but is absolute and will go wherever a
suitable resource is available, we consider that until Beech Tree
House-type units are provided as a matter of course by local
authorities near to children's homes, it will make sense to locate
new units catering for a national intake near large centres of
population on sites which are easily accessible by road and public
transport. The Spastics Society is doing exactly this with its
second unit which will be built just south of Preston.

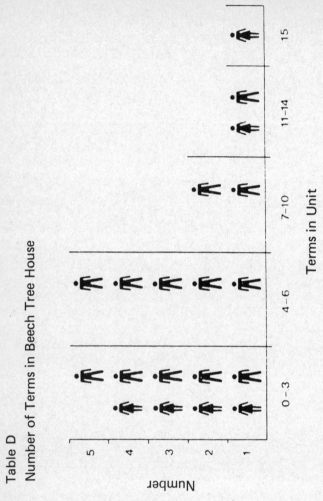

Table D
Number of Terms in Beech Tree House

This table shows that although the policy of the unit states that children should stay for a maximum of two years (six terms), a degree of flexibility exists and some stay considerably longer. However, nearly 74% of the children were able to leave within the two year period, 47% leaving within one year. Most of the children who remained in the unit for more than two years could have left earlier if suitable schools had been found to cater for their physical and mental handicaps.

Table E

Number of Children who Received Drugs
to Control Problem Behaviour and
Epilepsy Before Joining Unit

Key
* – drugs discontinued prior to entry.

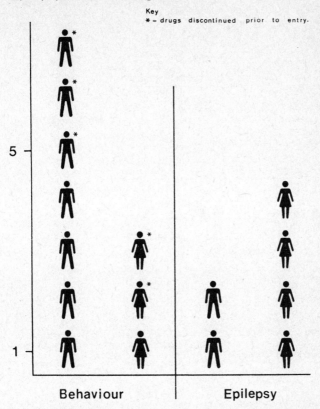

Drugs were in use to control the behaviour of 26% of the children when they arrived. In all cases these were phased out. An additional 26% of children had received drugs to control behaviour at some time prior to entering the unit. In most cases these had been discontinued at the insistence of the parents.

Drugs to control epilepsy were used in 31% of the cases. One child eventually ceased taking such medication while in the unit; unfortunately in the case of another child anti-convulsants had to be prescribed during her time in the unit when she started to suffer from epileptic episodes.

Table F

The Fate of Parent Relationships While Their Children Were in the Unit.

Relationship	Outcome	Count
👫	➤ Throughout	👤👤👤👤👤👤👤👤👤👤👤
👫	➤ Separated	0
👫	➤ New Partner	👤👤
👩	➤ Throughout	👤
👨	➤ Throughout	👤
👩	➤ Married	0
👨	➤ Married	0
No Involvement		👤👤
Minimal Involvement		👤👤

Children who display severe behaviour problems put their families under a great deal of stress – it is surprising how resilient most of our families appear to be. Nearly 58% of the children's families had come through the period prior to their child going to the unit without separating – and remained together until their child left. In two cases new partners were found by the parents who took on the main responsibility for the child when a separation occurred. It was almost as if, having found a suitable placement for their multiply handicapped child, the couples concerned were able to sort out their own difficulties.

Summary of Each Child's Progress.

Key

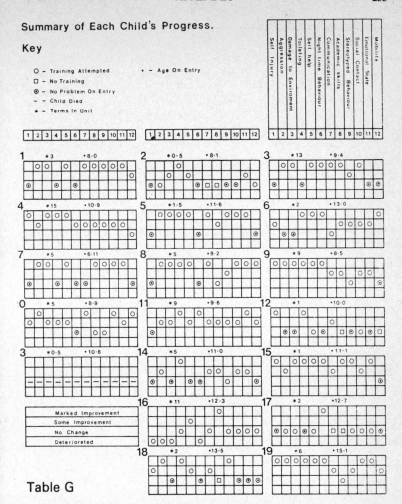

Table G

This rather complicated-looking table allows the reader to evaluate in some detail the progress made by individual children.

The categories Marked Improvement, Some Improvement, No Change and Deteriorated need explaining. Marked Improvement typically indicated that a problem was solved. For example a child with delayed continence became clean and dry; a self destructive child ceased self destructive behaviour; or a withdrawn child with few communication skills developed interpersonal skills and sought out the companionship of other children or adults. Some Improvement indicates that progress was made but that the problem that existed at entry was not entirely resolved. No Change and Deteriorated mean precisely what they say.

The decision about which category to score for each skill or attribute was made on the basis of parent interviews and information documented in reports.

We do not feel that a sufficiently large number of children have been educated in the unit to draw any general conclusions about which type of children respond best to which teaching methods. Perhaps in the future we shall be able to reach conclusions of this type.

Table H Analysis of Progress in the Twelve Areas of Potential Change for the First Nineteen Children.

	5	4	11	10	2	7	3	8	9	1	6	12
	Self help	Toileting	Emotional State	Social Contact	Aggression	Communication	Damage to Environment	Academic Skills	Stereotyped Behaviour	Self Injury	Night Time Behaviour	Mobility
Marked Improvment + Some Improvement	○											
	○											
	○	○	○	○	○	○						
	○	○	○	○	○	○	○					
	○	○	○	○	○	○	○	○				
	○	○	○	○	○	○	○	○				
	○	○	○	○	○	○	○	○				
	○	○	○	○	○	○	○	○	○	○		
	○	○	○	○	○	○	○	○	○	○		
	○	○	○	○	○	○	○	○	○	○	○	○
	○	○	○	○	○	○	○	○	○	○	○	○
	○	○	○	○	○	○	○	○	○	○	○	○
	○	○	○	○	○	○	○	○	○	○	○	○
	○	○	○	○	○	○	○	○	○	○	○	○
	○	○	○	○	○	○	○	○	○	○	○	○
No Problem on Entry										◉	◉	
										◉	◉	◉
										◉	◉	◉
										◉	◉	◉
										◉	◉	◉
	◉						◉			◉	◉	◉
	◉	◉					◉	○		◉	◉	◉
	◉	◉	◉	◉	◉	◉	◉	○	◉	◉	◉	◉
No Training Undertaken								□				
								□				
							□	□				
						□		□				
						□						□
No Change Despite Training									○			
									○			
				○					○			○
	○		○	○	○				○			○
	○	○	○	○	○	○	○		○			○
Deteriorated					○		○			○	○	
Child Died	–	–	–	–	–	–	–	–	–	–	–	–

This table at first glance appears to suggest that we are most successful at improving children's self-help skills – fifteen children show either Marked or Some Improvement. That we appear best in this area is the case simply because more children had problems in this area when they were admitted than in any other. If the number of children who improved in what appear to be two of our least successful areas, Self Injury and Night Time behaviour, are expressed as a percentage of the number of children who entered with these problems, then remarkably it becomes clear that virtually the same percentage improve in these two cases as for Self-help skills.

Self-help skills (15 out of 17)   88.2% improve
Self Injury (8 out of 9)   88.8% improve
Night Time behaviour (8 out of 9)88.8% improve

Certain children were referred to the unit for training in a limited number of specified areas. This training had to be completed by a specified date. In such cases no training was offered in other areas, although it was apparent to us that deficits existed. This point is exemplified by the four children who received no academic skill training. This·practice is justified on the grounds that once the problems which precipitated referral were ironed out the children were able to transfer to schools that could concentrate on the skills not tackled in Beech Tree House.

Table I
Distribution of Boys and Girls Admitted in 1982.

Boys	🚶🚶🚶🚶	4
Girls	🚶🚶🚶🚶🚶	5
	Total	9

This table shows the trend away from more boys than girls being admitted. Compare with the data in Table A.

Table J
The Number and Sex of Children in Each Age Category on Entry in 1982.

Age Range – 9yrs 2mths – 17 yrs 5mths

Average Age – 13yrs 3mths 20 days

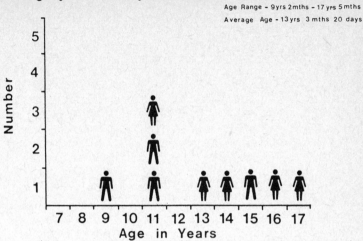

This table shows the increase in the age of children referred to Beech Tree House. The average age of 13 years 3 months for this table should be contrasted with 10 years in Table B.

The Distances Children Lived from Beech Tree House, 1982 Group.

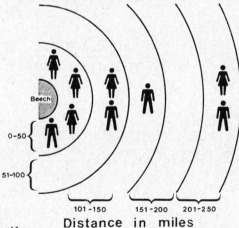

Distance in miles

Table K

There appears to be no significant change in the distances from which the children are sent to the unit. There is still a predominance of children from London and the Home Counties.

BIBLIOGRAPHY

GOFFMAN, E., *Asylums*, Anchor Books, 1961.

PARISH, P., *Medicines: A Guide for Everybody*, Penguin Books, 1976.

CARR, J., *Helping your Handicapped Child*, Penguin Books, 1980.

PERKINS ,E.A., TAYLOR, P.D., CAPIE A.C.M., *Helping the Retarded*, Institute of Mental Subnormality (now the British Institute of Mental Handicap), 1976.

SCHRAG, P., DIVOKY, D., *The Myth of the Hyperactive Child*, Penguin Books, 1975.

STONE, J., TAYLOR, F., *A Handbook for Parents with a Handicapped Child*, Arrow Books, 1977.

KIERNAN, C., JORDAN, R., SAUNDERS, C., *Starting Off*, Souvenir Press, 1978.

OSWIN, M., *The Empty Hours*, Penguin Books, 1971.

FOXX, R.M., AZRIN, N.H., *Toilet Training the Retarded*, Research Press, 1973.

McMULLIN, G.P., *Children who have Fits*, Gerald Duckworth & Co. Ltd., 1981.

DEVEREUX, K., *Understanding Learning Difficulties*, The Open University Press, 1982.

BOWLEY, A.H., GARDNER, L., *The Handicapped Child*, Churchill Livingstone, 1957.

GARDNER, W.I., *Behaviour Modification in Mental Retardation*, Aldine-Atherton, Inc., 1971.

BLECK, E.E., NAGEL, D.A., *Physically Handicapped Children: A Medical Atlas for Teachers*, Grune & Stratton, Inc., 1975.

BECKER, W.C., ENGELMANN, S., THOMAS, D.R., *Teaching 1: Classroom Management*, Science Research Associates, Inc., 1975.

INDEX